THE
AUTOHARP BOOK

by
Becky Blackley

i.a.d. Publications
Brisbane, California

Cover design based on the cover of *The Autoharp and How it Captured the Family* (second edition, 1895). The *New York Herald* (September 29, 1895) describes the drawing:

"Terpsichore, the fairest of Apollo's Nine, has stepped awhile from Thessaly to colder climes . . . Before her stands the sacred tripod, and on it—What? The Autoharp, of course.

The popularity of this instrument throughout the trade and buying public seems to be ample proof that the gods, yea, even the greater gods that be upon Olympus, have taken it under their especial patronage."

Published by i.a.d. Publications
P.O. Box 504
Brisbane, CA 94005

Edited by Henry Rasof.
Typesetting by Carol McCoy, San Francisco, California.
Book design and layout by Becky Blackley.
Printed by Service Litho, San Francisco, California.

The term Autoharp® is the registered trademark of Oscar Schmidt-International, Inc., Northbrook, Illinois.

The term "autoharpoholic" and the ⬛® logo are the trademarks of Becky Blackley.

Library of Congress Cataloging in Publication Data

Blackley, Becky.
  The autoharp book.

  Bibliography: p.
  Includes indexes.
  1. Autoharp. I. Title.
ML1015.A9B6 1983   787'.8   83-81145
ISBN 0-912827-01-7 (pbk.)

First printing 1983
Second printing 1983

To A. Doyle Moore and Mike Seeger.

A. Doyle Moore

Although the Autoharp is over one hundred years old, there has been to date only one acknowledged definitive account of the history of the Autoharp. A. Doyle Moore's article "The Autoharp: Its Origin and Development from a Popular to a Folk Instrument," originally printed in the December 1963 issue of the *New York Folklore Quarterly,* has for the past twenty years been the source of virtually all historical information on the Autoharp.

A man of many talents ranging from music to the visual arts, Moore is a graphic arts professor at the University of Illinois. His research into the history of the Autoharp came from his personal interest in the instrument, and his fine playing can be heard on the 1962 recording of the *Philo Glee and Mandoline Society.*

As a historian Moore had to search through completely uncharted territory and collect, sort, and piece together the information that he found. In doing so he cleared the path down which others could follow. To this day Moore remains enthusiastic about sharing his knowledge, his resources, and his materials. His continuing contribution to the history of the Autoharp is gratefully acknowledged.

The history of the Autoharp would be of considerably less interesst if its music had been lost. Mike Seeger has probably done more to preserve and promote the Autoharp and its music than any other individual. As an accomplished player Seeger introduced many musicians to the Autoharp through both solo performances and concerts with the New Lost City Ramblers. His Autoharp playing can be heard on dozens of records.

As a musicologist Seeger traveled into remote areas of the United States to record the music of some of the finest traditional musicians of our time. Without his dedication and diligence, the unique styles of many players might never have been recorded. Most notable among Seeger's field recordings is the classic Folkways album *Mountain Music Played on the Autoharp,* which illustrates beautifully some of the ways the Autoharp can be used as a solo melody-playing instrument.

Seeger continues in this role today, playing the Autoharp (and numerous other stringed instruments) in concerts and writing articles on the traditional music of America. His efforts to preserve this part of our heritage will be appreciated for all the generations to come.

Mike Seeger

3

CONTENTS

PREFACE

In April 1980 *The Autoharpoholic* magazine published its first issue. As the fledgling publication grew, readers began to request information on the history of the Autoharp, an interest usually sparked by the discovery of an old Autoharp at a flea market or garage sale. The most commonly asked questions were, "How old is this harp?" and "What can you tell me about it?" As the editor of *The Autoharpoholic,* I began to try to find some answers, originally planning to print my findings as a feature article in the magazine. Starting with the information in A. Doyle Moore's article "The Autoharp: Its Origin and Development from a Popular to a Folk Instrument," I set out to locate the original sources cited in his footnotes. Soon I realized that there was far too much material to fit into a single article and decided that rather than covering the subject briefly in the magazine, I would gather as much information as I could and write a separate book.

In the past two and one-half years, I have collected the information presented here. Eventually, I was lucky enough to locate Mr. Moore himself, who shared all that he had found with me. The present owners of Oscar Schmidt-International, Inc., Fretted Industries, opened the company files and storage closets and let me explore, photocopy, and photograph anything I wished. Libraries, museums, and archives were all helpful and cooperative, but the most significant source of information proved to be the hundreds of readers of *The Autoharpoholic* who filled out questionnaires and survey forms on their Autoharps. They provided most of the information and many of the photographs included in the chapters on the Autoharp models. They inspired the project with their questions and helped finish it with their answers. Without them this book would not have been possible.

Every attempt has been made to make the information as complete as possible. However, information for the bibliography sometimes came from photocopies and clippings that lacked full publication data. Complete discography information also was not always available. Omissions undoubtedly exist. Even with the Autoharp models themselves, there are certainly variations, harps that won't fit the exact descriptions given here. Prototypes and one-of-a-kind models that find their way into the hands of collectors will remain unexplained oddities. However, I do believe that all the basic production models are included, either by photographs or catalog drawings.

I feel as if I have completed a huge jigsaw puzzle with thousands of pieces. After putting all the pieces together, I ended up with a definite picture, but I also had the perhaps inevitable frustration and disappointment of having some unfilled gaps left and a couple of pieces that didn't seem to fit anywhere. With any subject that covers more than one hundred years, the Autoharp story will continue as those missing pieces are found; but after almost three years of research, I had to accept that some questions may never be answered. If you have any answers, comments, corrections, additions, or further questions, please write to me c/o i.a.d. publications, P.O. Box 504, Brisbane, CA 94005, or phone me in my office at *The Autoharpoholic* magazine, (415) 467-1700, between 1 p.m. and 5 p.m. "Talking Autoharp" is one of my favorite activities, and I look forward to doing that with many of you.

Harpin' on . . .

Becky Blackley

ACKNOWLEDGEMENTS

A harper's heap of thanks to

Gordon Blackley for assisting, encouraging, and loving me through it all.
Yvonne Dickerson for making the impossible seem easy.
The John Edwards Memorial Foundation for preserving what otherwise might have been lost.
Richard and Lynn Johnstone for opening the company files and the Johnstone home.
A. Doyle Moore for paving the way.
Woody Padgett for being a good listener and objective critic.
Gary Putnam for photo processing above and beyond the call of friendship.
Henry Rasof for questioning, suggesting, and turning the words 'round right.
Rudolf Schlacher for letting me into the "morgue."
Mike Seeger for answering a million questions.
Ivan Stiles for going into graveyards . . . alone.
Merle and Rosie Zimmerman for always making me feel that someone was interested.
Charles F. Zimmermann for inventing the Autoharp.

I would like to express my deepest gratitude for the valuable assistance given me by the following:

Chris Abernathy
City of Alhambra, Cal.
Amherst College
Archive of Folk Culture
Tina Louise Barr
Stevie Beck
Jane Bennett
Bob Bergin
Bluegrass Unlimited
Evo Bluestein
City of Boston, Mass.
Boston Public Library
Vonah Boudro
Bryan Bowers
Bryan Bradfield
Darlene Brady
Onetamae Britton
Helen Brown
Brenda Bury
Karen and Richard Butera
California Historical Society
Mary Ann Carmichael
Janette Carter
The Carter Family
Loyce Chaffin
Lisa Chandler
William Childs
Bill Clifton
Mary Lou Colgin
Tom Colonese
Columbia University
Patrick Couton
Country Music Hall of Fame and Museum
Beverly Cox
Reverend Ronald Dahlheimer
Mark Dixon
Dolgeville Public Library
Carl Dudash
Terry Eriksmoen
John Evans
Barbara Finney
Mrs. Harold G. Finney
Tennessee Ernie Ford
Nathalie Forrest
Tim Forsythe and the Forsythe Family
William Foshag
Sherry Fox
The Franklin Institute
Eleanor Franz
David Fullerton
G. Willikers
Florence Galloway
Gryphon Stringed Instruments
Ezio Guaitamacchi
Margot Gunzenhausen

Lindsay Haisley
Marilyn Hartzog
Richard Hensolt
Joe Hickerson
Historical Society of Pennsylvania
Michael Hobbs
Michael Holmes
Mabel Honeycutt
Mike Horner
House of Cash Museum
David Illar
Jeri Jacobson
Joyce Kennedy Jenkins
City of Jersey City, N.J.
T. L. Johnson
Garrison Keillor
Paul Keller
Frances Kimball
James Kimball
Michael King
Meryle Korn
Esther Kreek
Bill Kurth
Robert Larson
Ardath Lehmer
Rita Libby
Library of Congress
Jim Loakes
Pat Lucas
Bill and Dorothy MacKenzie
Peggy Marsheck
David Martin
Mike McClellan
Carol McCoy
John McCutcheon
David Moliis
Montgomery Ward Co., Inc.
Tom and Mary Morgan
Suzanne Mrozak
Karen Mueller
Bill Murney
The Musical Museum
Ed Nelson
Neptune Rising
New Jersey Department of Health
New York Public Library
Kathryn Nichols
James Nikl
Cecil Null
Oscar Schmidt-International, Inc.
Ozark Folk Center
Linda Painter
Patent Information Clearing House, Sunnyvale, Cal.
Sally Paul

Ron Penix
University of Pennsylvania
Glen Peterson, Jr.
Meg Peterson
City of Philadelphia
Philadelphia Free Library
Philadelphia Historical Commission
Bonnie Phipps
Audrey Podl
Princeton University
Ruth Reneau
Rhythm Band Inc.
Ronald Rich
Jean Ritchie
Karen Rodgers
Terry and Janet Rodgers
San Francisco Public Library
Arthur Sanders
Janice Schaeffer
Lory Schluenz
Sears, Roebuck Company, Inc.
Secretary of State, California
Secretary of State, Maine
Secretary of State, Massachussetts
Secretary of State, New Jersey
Secretary of State, New York
Peggy Seeger
Charlie Seemann
Sally Senior
Barbara Sesnewicz
Roger Siminoff
Willard Smith
The Smithsonian Catalog
The Smithsonian Institution
Carol Stober
Michael Stokes
Patsy Stoneman
The Stoneman Family
Dawn Such
Lenore Swoiskin
City of Toronto, Canada, Department of the City Clerk
Traditional Arts Services
Ron Wall
Walnut Valley Association
Washington State Historical Society
Joe Weed
Mary Weed
Bob Welland
Rick Whitaker
Charles Whitmer, Jr.
Margaret Worrell
Kyle Wyatt
Keith Young
Phyllis Zimmermann

In addition to the above, hundreds of Autoharp enthusiasts filled out survey forms and questionnaires from which much of the information for this book was gathered. Although I'm unable to name them all individually, I thank each of them.

Charles F. Zimmermann

Alfred Dolge

William Copeland

Oscar Schmidt

AUTOHARP CHRONOLOGY

1881   Invented.

1882   Patented.

1885-1892 Manufactured by *Charles F. Zimmermann,* Philadelphia, Penn.

1893-1899 Manufactured by *C. F. Zimmermann Company,* Dolgeville, N.Y. (Alfred Dolge and Rudolf Dolge).

1900-1910 No Autoharps manufactured.

1910-1926 Manufactured by the *Phonoharp Company,* Boston, Mass. (William Copeland)

1926-1931 Manufactured by *International Musical Corporation,* Hoboken, N.J. (William Copeland, Oscar Schmidt, Walter Schmidt, and Harold Finney).

1932-1936 Manufactured by *Oscar Schmidt-International Corporation,* Jersey City, N.J. (under Harold Finney).

1936-1963 Manufactured by *Oscar Schmidt-International, Inc.,* Jersey City, N.J. (under Harold Finney).

1963-1966 Same as above (Glen Peterson, Jr.).

1966-1978 Same as above, Union, N.J.

1978—   Same as above (Fretted Industries: Rudolf Schlacher and Richard Johnstone).

H. G. Finney

Glen Peterson

R. W. Johnstone

Rudolf Schlacher

INTRODUCTION

The Autoharp is one of the few musical instruments that can claim to be truly American in origin. From its birthplace in Philadelphia to its present home in Union, New Jersey, the Autoharp has always been manufactured in the United States, justifying its nineteenth century slogan, "an American instrument of American invention."

Invented in 1881 and patented in 1882, the Autoharp has had a remarkable hundred-year history. After being proclaimed "the nation's favorite musical instrument" and then nearly fading into obscurity, the Autoharp has taken its manufacturers from rags to riches to rags to riches, time and again. As a nineteenth-century parlor room favorite, it was finally replaced in popularity by the phonograph. But the Autoharp didn't die. It just retreated to the mountains where it underwent a metamorphosis from a parlor instrument to a folk instrument. From there it came out into our schools to become a standard classroom feature, and finally has emerged as a popular instrument for the serious musician.

As it enters it second century of manufacture, the Autoharp is gaining a popularity that may rival its nineteenth century level. The recent renewed interest in the Autoharp was the impetus for this centennial project. The research presented here is a detailed account of the Autoharp and the people who have affected its development. The text is divided into six periods of production. Each gives the history of the company, followed by a detailed description of the Autoharps made during that time.

Several other sections are included on subjects of related interest: notation systems, unusual or exceptional models, the Autoharp factory today, professional Autoharp performers, and other types of chorded zithers, old and new. Three appendices include Autoharp accessories, patents and trademarks, bibliography, discography, and sources of Autoharp information and activities. In addition to the usual subject index, there is an Autoharp index to help the reader locate a particular model of interest. This should be especially helpful to instrument collectors trying to determine the age of an Autoharp.

Whether you are an Autoharp player, a student of American folklore, or a collector of antique musical instruments, you should find the first one hundred years of the Autoharp an interesting and unusual story.

Charles F. Zimmermann

3

## CHAPTER 1

C. F. ZIMMERMANN

I believe it is the best work which a human being so far has achieved on earth.

C. F. Zimmermann

When C. F. Zimmermann received the patent for the Autoharp in 1882, he was nearly sixty-five years old. His life had not been an easy one, and although the Autoharp would prove to be more successful than any of his previous ventures, it, too, would fail to bring him the recognition he deserved. Most of what is known about Zimmermann's life and the development of the Autoharp comes from Zimmermann's unpublished autobiography.[1] Though the story it tells is incomplete and often puzzling, it at least gives us a glimpse of the life of an unusual man and at the musical instrument he invented for what he hoped was the good of mankind.

Carl Friedrich Zimmermann was born on September 4, 1817, in Morgenroethe, a city in Saxony, Germany. He was the first of six children born to a poor family. When he was still young, his mother managed to arrange music lessons for him, at first on the piano, later on the violin. Since his parents could afford only occasional lessons, much of Carl's musical knowledge came from playing music with his friends on Sundays. Music was a social event that made him happy and earned him many friends.

Carl's father was a traveling lace salesman and often gone from home. His mother died when he was only fifteen years old, leaving Carl to care for his five brothers and sisters.

Although he had less time to make music with his friends, life was tolerable. A year later, however, his father remarried, and Carl's intense dislike for his stepmother led him to leave home. He went to Chemnitz, where he became an iron-founder apprentice to his uncle.

The next three years were to be remembered by Zimmermann as the happiest in his life. While working as an apprentice, he found that he could earn extra money for clothes by playing music. But for reasons unknown, Carl gave up his life in Chemnitz and returned home, where he joined his brother as a traveling lace dealer. When the business floundered because his stepmother wouldn't supply the brothers with the goods they needed to sell, Carl, again dissatisfied with his life, once more turned to his music. When his accordion playing earned him praise in a Danzig publication, he decided to make music his career.

Carl's first step was to try to build a bigger and better accordion than the one he had. Although lack of funds compelled him to build a simple one-row accordion, he was learning the basics of instrument building, the craft that was to become his main occupation in life.

Over the next three or four years, Zimmermann finally managed to build three accordions to his satisfaction. He toured briefly with his brother and a friend, all of them playing concerts on the instruments. When the trio later broke up, Carl decided to continue with his instrument building.

Apparently he did well, for eventually he had a business that employed seventy-six workers. Yet despite his initial success, Zimmermann soon found that he couldn't keep pace with his competitors, who had more capital and produced a cheaper product.

Zimmermann briefly joined his brother-in-law in establishing a blown-glass factory, but once again something told him it was time for a change. In 1864, at the age of forty-seven, C. F. Zimmermann took his wife Sophie and six of their eight children to the United States, where his brother already had migrated, and took over his brother's music store in Philadelphia. With the Civil War still in progress, however, times were tough: only four months after Zimmermann's arrival, his brother returned to Germany.

Zimmermann, who was left trying to make a living repairing French accordions, decided to stay in the United States, and on September 8, 1864, he swore in the Philadelphia Court of Common Pleas his "intention to become a citizen of the United States, and to renounce forever all allegiance and fidelity to any foreign prince, potentate, state or sovereignty whatever, and particularly to the King of Saxony of whom he is now a subject." After the five-year residency requirement, he became a U.S. citizen on September 20, 1869. The document is signed by Carl Friedrich Zimmermann of 238 N. Second Street, Philadelphia, but the petition is in the name of Charles F. Zimmermann, the name he was to use for the rest of his life.

Zimmermann continued to work on accordions in his shop on Second Street, but his real interest lay in developing a new tone-numbering system that would enable anyone to learn to play music easily, without learning how to read standard music notation. Zimmermann traveled abroad to try to convince the music world to adopt his new system, but had no luck. Returning home, he worked day and night to revise the system. Finally, on January 3, 1871, Zimmermann was issued U.S. Patent #110,719 (see Appendix B for details).

The Better and More Natural System of Writing Music With Figures

Forest of notes, who planted thee?
The low bush, the gigantic tree;
Ten centuries have made thee old,
System of priests, thou has lost thine hold.

Falseness of tones in book and sound,
The Lord and mankind always found;
And we, who love the music mild,
Are right to fear such army wild,

The tones become like dog and cat,
In case of octave sharp and flat;
And still their character is bound
With signs for single basso's sound.

The tone in our creation is found
In all octaves of equal sound;
Seven tones and seven octaves ought
To be admired, as nature taught.

Five whole tones and only two halves,
Are nature's scale of sounding waves;
Divide in half-tones each whole one,
Then twelve tones chromatic will run.

The sketch I give the world below,
Will something far better show,
And every man will it easy call
To understand the music all.

We write with seven figures fine,
The twelve tones on the guiding line;
The octave, as it there is cast
Has this common with the rest.

Tone "I" commences each octave,
As corner "C" it leads the staff
Commanding, how in careful drill
The tones march up and down the hill.

Time, number, value of each sound,
With figures easily can be found;
The measure of the musical time,
By quarter spaces will upwards climb.

The scale is very precious,
When taught how nature gives it us;
When eyes and ear learn both at once,
How naturally from tone "I" it runs.

Mother with scales sing baby to sleep,
That the little mind impresses deep
The music, it will with powerful arm
Keep it noble, and proud, and warm.

Hail, Muse of Music! come and see
The palace I have built for thee.
Where the good seeds may richly grow:
Music for all — for high and low.

From Zimmermann's *Directory of Music in General*

Zimmermann's new tone-numbering system became his lifetime obsession. Convinced that he could revolutionize music notation, but recognizing that old, established methods are hard to change and that his system would be difficult to introduce, Zimmermann abandoned the accordion and set about designing a stringed instrument that would use his notation system exclusively. He envisioned a multistringed instrument that would use bars with dampers to create chords by suppressing the sound of all the strings not contained in each chord.

After two years of continuous experiments, the Autoharp was born, and Zimmermann proclaimed the instrument "the best work which a human being so far has achieved on earth." He applied for the patent on December 10, 1881, and was issued U.S. Patent #257,808 on May 9, 1882. However, both the design and method of operation of the original Autoharp differed greatly from the Autoharp finally put on the market. The patent shows an instrument with a totally different shape and chord bars that moved sideways rather than up and down. A special "flageolet" bar touched all the strings exactly at the midpoint, resulting in a harmonic tone one octave higher in pitch. A look at the patent in Appendix B shows many manufacturer's problems inherent in the design, and Zimmermann must have spent several years developing a workable product.

By 1884 Zimmermann had moved next door to 240 N. Second Street, where within about a year he began to manufacture "Miniature Autoharps," the earliest models.[2] An 1885 instruction book, *Collection of Popular Figure Music for C. F. Zimmermann's Miniatur* [sic] *Autoharp*, shows

238 N. Second St., Philadelphia, was the address of Zimmermann's music store. It was probably in this building that he perfected the design of the Autoharp. This photo, taken in 1982, shows a parking lot next door (left).

Zimmermann moved to 240 N. Second St. in 1884. Here he began to manufacture the Autoharp. The building was demolished in 1977 (right).

4

5

three models — #1, #2, and #2¾ — with the first page announcing the Autoharp as "The Greatest Novelty of the Age!" From September 15, 1885, to October 31, 1885, Zimmermann displayed his invention in the "Novelties" Exhibition in Philadelphia, where it was awarded an honorable mention by the Franklin Institute. The exhibition catalog describes the Autoharp as a "new musical instrument with steel music strings, similar to a piano and used like a zither, with bars running across the strings to act as a mute upon certain strings." The Autoharp proceeded to win numerous awards at various exhibitions. The novelty did not wear off quickly.

## 7

Instruction book, ca. mid-1885 (after May 1885 exhibition, but before October 1885 exhibition).

But Zimmermann wanted the instrument to be more than a novelty item: he wanted to enlighten the world with his new system of music notation. To help spread the word, he printed a detailed chart entitled "C. F. Zimmermann's Appeal to the musical people in the World for the New Notation of Music," which won a "first degree of merit" award at the 1885 "World's Industrial and Cotton Centennial Exposition" held in New Orleans. Next came a booklet, *C. F. Zimmermann's Simplified Harmony Teacher and Short-hand Writing of Chords* (ca. 1889), containing chapters on "The Entire Science of Harmony in Music in a Nut-Shell" and "A Very Excellent Self-Teacher of Harmony is the Autoharp. C. F. Zimmermann's Greatest

Triumph," the latter fully explaining the new Zimmermann notation system.

Neither Zimmermann's belief in himself and his system nor his publications were quite enough to change a system that had existed for centuries, however, since only his own music used the system of numbers. Nevertheless, the Autoharp itself was becoming increasingly popular. In the first three years of production, over fifty thousand harps were sold,[3] and by 1889 seven models were being made: #1, #2, #2¾, #3, #4, #5, and #6. In turn, advertising and media coverage reflected the instrument's success. An ad in the October 1889 *Philadelphia Musical Journal* shows the top-of-the-line #6 model and includes the same glowing testimonials printed in the *Simplified Harmony Teacher*. The *Boston Transcript* said that "words are inadequate to express the sweetness of its music," while one satisfied customer jubilantly proclaimed in the *New York Observer*: "If [my Autoharp] were the only instrument of its kind in existence, I would not part with it for five times the amount charged for it. If you want a delightful surprise, and an experience of perpetual musical pleasure, secure an Autoharp."

The Autoharps built were of consistently high quality, and it is not uncommon to find Philadelphia Autoharps in near-perfect structural condition; by contrast, harps from later years of mass production are often

Book cover, ca. 1889-1890.

8

splitting at the seams. Despite the high quality — a reflection of care — and sales in 1892 of a quarter of a million dollars,[4] something was wrong. Not only had no new models been developed for three years and a proposed model #7 apparently never put on the market,[5] but at the end of 1892, Zimmermann sold his company to Alfred Dolge, a successful manufacturer of piano parts.[6] Whether Zimmermann sold the company because he was getting old or for some other reason is unknown. Obviously he had not lost interest in the Autoharp, for he continued to work on its design and reflected his unwavering enthusiasm for his work in the last Philadelphia catalog, where the Autoharp is still called "the greatest musical wonder of the age!"

Alfred Dolge was trying to build up his small upstate New York town by bringing in foreign businesses. After two years of negotiations, Dolge had arranged the move of a German wool factory to Dolgeville. But the deal fell through when Cleveland won the 1892 presidential election and new, less favorable tariff legislation seemed likely.

Dolge then was forced to look toward domestic companies to build up the town. His piano supply businesses were suffering from an economic slump due to the lowering of restrictions on imports, and he needed to find a domestic product that could use the parts he already made in Dolgeville: felts, sounding boards, and piano wire. The Zimmermann Autoharp was a perfect choice.[7]

Dolge set out to bring the Zimmermann factory to Dolgeville, and the negotiations were closed on November 2, 1892. The good news was reported in Dolgeville that the C. F. Zimmermann Company, with paid-up capital of one hundred thousand dollars, would soon be moving to Dolgeville with between 100 and 150 employees. An estimated population increase of 400 to 500 was predicted for the town. Everyone was grateful to Alfred Dolge.

The transfer had its problems, however. Evidence indicates that Zimmermann regretted agreeing to the sale and tried to stop the move to Dolgeville. The dispute was

[Showing how the Autoharp is played.]

9

Illustration from the Harmony Teacher.

well publicized, and various accounts appeared in several publications, the first report coming on December 3, 1892, in the *New York Press* as a "special to the *Press*" from Philadelphia dated December 2, 1892:

C. F. Zimmermann, a manufacturer of musical instruments in this city, today began equity proceedings against Alfred Dolge, the noted philanthropist, to recover his business. He claims that Dolge bought the business for removal to Dolgeville, paying $63,502 and giving six hundred fifty shares of stock in the Little Falls and Dolgeville Railroad in payment.

Zimmermann now claims that this stock is worthless, and he wants the courts to prevent by injunction the transfer and compel the surrender of the business on tender of the stock.

According to the *Little Falls Journal and Courier* (December 6, 1892), "it appears . . . that Mr. Zimmermann is sick of this bargain and wants to be released from fulfilling his agreement . . . . The outcome will be watched with interest." The *Herkimer County News* (December 9, 1892) from Little Falls, New York, understandably defended Dolge, stating that the suit was initiated to prevent the move of the factory to Dolgeville:

All who were acquainted with Mr. Dolge knew that the statement was wrong in whole or in part, for he is not a man who would attempt to swindle anyone.

The truth appears to be that some of Mr. Zimmermann's children became frightened at the bargain made by their father and endeavored to pursuade him to back out. But when they made an investigation for themselves, they became so well satisfied, that they at once withdrew their objections, and the factory will be removed to Dolgeville at once.

On the stock referred to, Mr. Dolge has guaranteed the dividend for three years, and at the end of that time if the Zimmermanns are not satisfied, he will take it back.

A perhaps more objective account three years later in the *Music Trades* (December 21, 1895) seems to indicate that the Zimmermann relatives were not "so well satisfied,"

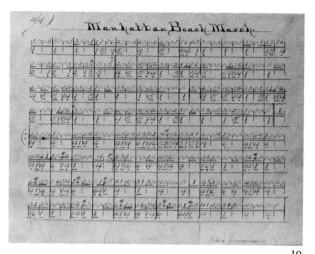

10

Handwritten music in Zimmermann figure notation signed by Clara Zimmermann, granddaughter of C. F. Zimmermann.

however. Despite Dolge's offer to guarantee the dividend on the questionable stock, apparently the disagreement was settled by more forceful methods:

In the early part of the year 1893, Mr. Alfred Dolge, with his wonderful insight into the possibilities of a good thing, purchased the autoharp business from the veteran Zimmerman [sic] of Philadelphia, who had run it for a number of years and had amassed a large fortune.

The price paid was $60,000. This sum Mr. Dolge liquidated with some cash and the balance with stock in the Dolgeville Railroad. The relatives of Mr. Zimmermann claimed that he had been improperly treated, on the ground that the stock of the Railroad had no value. They carried the case into court, on the ground that Mr. Zimmermann was of unsound mind.

They also caused injurious telegrams to be inserted in various leading papers, in which Mr. Dolge was plainly charged with deceit.

These telegrams appeared on a Saturday morning.

Bright and early on the Monday following, Mr. Dolge appeared in court in Philadelphia with a certified check for the whole amount, and so not only settled the case, but established his good faith.

It is doubtful that Zimmermann was of unsound mind. He was competent enough to register the Autoharp trademark on December 22, 1892. (U.S. Trademark registration #22,339, granted January 17, 1893, appears in Appendix B.) One day later, on December 23, 1892, the sale of the Autoharp company to Alfred Dolge was closed, and the move to Dolgeville was soon begun.[8] Why Zimmermann decided to register his trademark at this time is unclear. He had been using the name since he registered the patent in 1882, but had never seen the necessity of registering it as a trademark. Now that it was inevitable that the factory was to be moved to Dolgeville, he suddenly decided to register the Autoharp in his own name.

11

This family scene appears to be some type of memorial service with the black draped photograph on the wall. The Autoharp is an early Model #1 (ca. 1885-1887).

Another unexplained oddity is that Zimmermann printed a new catalog, dated January *1893*, showing the seven models made in Philadelphia and a full line of parts and accessories. On the first page Zimmermann declares that "I am the inventor and sole manufacturer of the Autoharp. Each and every instrument will bear my name and stamp U.S. Patent, May 9th, 1882. Any without my stamp are infringements, and all parties trading in such will be prosecuted according to law." But the company, already sold, was moving to New York (without Zimmermann). Why did he print this catalog?

Whatever the reasons for his actions, Zimmermann didn't hold the rights to the trademark for very long. On March 2, 1893, he transferred all rights "pertaining to said Autoharp and Trademark to Alfred Dolge of Dolgeville, New York . . . in consideration of the sum of One Dollar to me in hand paid by said Alfred Dolge." The trademark transfer was registered in the U.S. Patent office on March 9, 1893. Although the Autoharp patent was never officially transferred to Alfred Dolge,[9] the rights to manufacture the instrument were clearly given in the above trademark transfer. The Autoharp now belonged to Alfred Dolge.

Zimmermann remained behind in Philadelphia when manufacture of his beloved Autoharp was moved to Dolgeville, but he continued to work on improving its design. On May 25, 1897, Zimmermann received another patent (#583,162, filed September 13, 1895), which he assigned to the C. F. Zimmermann Company of Dolgeville, New York. It was the last patent issued to Zimmermann. On October 20, 1898, Charles F. Zimmermann was killed by a horse-drawn streetcar in Philadelphia. He was buried in Mt. Vernon Cemetery in Philadelphia, in the family plot he had purchased in 1876 for ninety-six dollars. His wife, Sophie, several of his children, and other relatives are buried there with him.[10]

12

Gravestone in Mt. Vernon Cemetery.

17

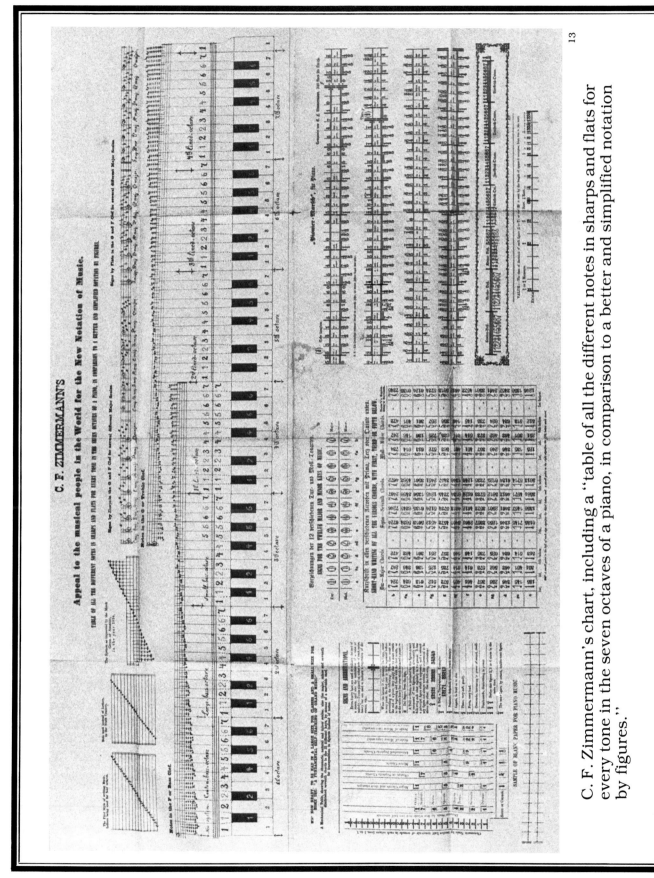

C. F. Zimmermann's chart, including a "table of all the different notes in sharps and flats for every tone in the seven octaves of a piano, in comparison to a better and simplified notation by figures."

## CHAPTER 2

C. F. ZIMMERMANN'S SYSTEM OF MUSICAL NOTATION

Charles Zimmermann gives a lengthy explanation of his tone-numbering system in his book *Zimmermann's Directory of Music in General* (ca. 1878). The book predates the invention of the Autoharp but predicts that "in the future musical instruments of different ranges of tune, still more fit for such numbered keys, will make their appearance." By 1881 he perfected the Autoharp and developed the notation system that would be used for it.

The system, of course, was modified and expanded over the years as it was used. The explanation given here covers the final system used for most of the Autoharp music printed around the turn of the century by Alfred Dolge & Son. In addition to the *Directory of Music in General*, the following sources were used: *C.F. Zimmermann's Simplified Harmony Teacher and Shorthand Writing of Chords (ca. 1889), C.F. Zimmermann's Popular Figure Music for the Autoharp (ca. 1891),* the *C.F. Zimmermann Company Catalog* (1896), and R. S. Tracy's *The Zimmermann Autoharp Instructor* (ca. 1925).

THE SCALE

The seven tones of the C-major (diatonic) scale (*c, d, e, f, g, a, b, c*) are represented by the figures 1, 2, 3, 4, 5, 6, and 7, while five chromatic notes (*c-sharp, d-sharp, f-sharp, g-sharp,* and *a-sharp*) are represented by dotted figures. The chromatic scale is shown in Figure 1.

To indicate the appropriate octave, the numbers are written above a dotted line, used either alone or combined with one or two heavy leger lines. The dotted line is called the staff. When the figures are directly over the dotted line, the tones are in the middle octave. When one leger is above the staff, the tones are in the higher octave. When two leger lines are above the staff, they are in the highest octave. Similarly, one leger line below the staff indicates the lower octave and two lines means the lowest or bass octave. The scale for the #2¾ harp (five chords, twenty-three strings) is shown in Figure 2.

TIME

Autoharp music is divided by heavy black lines into measures, which in turn are subdivided by lighter lines into divisions. Each division is equal to one count. Thus a measure in 4/4 time would be divided into four divisions. The player counts "one, two, three, four" and plays whatever note is in the corresponding division of the measure.

For eighth notes there are two notes in one division, and the player counts "one, and, two, and, three, and, four, and." A dot after a note increases its value by one half. The division is divided into half-counts, and the count for a dotted quarter note would be "one, and, two." A vacant division means that the preceding note is held over through that division (similar to a "tie"). The figure "0" is used to denote a rest (see Figure 3).

THE CHORDS

Major chords are indicated by a dot (.) placed under the figure. A cross (+) is placed under the figure for a minor chord. Seventh chords have a dash (-) under the figure, and diminished seventh chords have a small circle (∘) below the figure:

$\underset{.}{4}$ = F major $\underline{4}$ = F7

$\underset{+}{4}$ = F minor $\underset{\circ}{1}$ = C diminished seventh

While the melody notes are denoted by the figures above the dotted staff line, accompaniment chords are shown by the figures and signs below the dotted line.

PLAYING TECHNIQUES

There are three basic ways to sound the strings: making runs, picking, and making melody runs. A run is made by pressing a bar and allowing the thumbpick to carelessly sweep over the strings (below the chord bar assembly). Runs always begin at the very bottom of the scale and never extend beyond the middle of the scale or above the melody note.

Picking is done with the basic "pinch," which Tracy's book explains: "Use just the same movement you would use in picking some small object up from the table. Let the thumb strike wherever it will. But watch the finger and try to make the strings you strike with it sound clear and distinct, predominating above everything else."

Simple runs and picking are used together to play the scales. The proper bar to use for each note of the scale is explained and must be memorized. There are no choices with this system of notation. In the key of C, the C-major chord is always used for the *c, e,* and *g*. The G7 chord is used for the *d, f,* and *b* (but not for the *g*, which is played with the C chord). The F chord is used only for the *a*. Similarly, in the key of F, the chords are F (*f, a,* and *c*), C7 (*e, g,* and *b-flat*) and B-flat (*d*). The student must be careful not to confuse the two scales: the *f* is played with a G7 chord in the key of C, but with an F chord in the key of F!

It is thus assumed that the player knows the chord bar to use for each note of the scale in each key. Consequently the music shows only the chords for the rhythm accompaniment. The melody notes in the music are indicated just by the figure representing the proper note in the scale. The player must know which chord to press to get that note.

In a melody run the melody and the accompaniment are played at the same time. Melody runs differ from simple runs in that they end on a specific note. The run is played a little softer, so that the final melody string can be accented by playing it a little louder.

THE MUSIC

To use the Autoharp as an accompaniment to singing, everything written above the dotted line may be disregarded. Merely pressing the bars indicated by the figures below the line, and sweeping the strings with the pick, will give the desired accompaniment.

When a chord appears alone below the staff without a figure above it, a simple run is to be made. When the figure above the staff appears alone without a chord indicated below it, the regular picking movement, the "pinch," is used. When there are *both* a figure above the dotted line and a chord below the staff, the player makes a melody run, strumming the chord up to (and accenting) the melody note (see Figure 4).

Figure 1:
The Chromatic Scale

1	1	2	2	3	4	4	5	5	6	6	7	1
c	c#	d	d#	e	f	f#	g	g#	a	a#	b	c

SIGNS

∨   This sign means to make the run down the keyboard, from treble to bass, with the *fingerpick.*

∧∨   This sign means make the run first up the keyboard with the thumbpick, then down the keyboard with the fingerpick in one continuous motion.

▬   This "thumb dash" sign means to play the note with the thumb instead of the finger.

∿∿∿   This sign below the staff means to continue the pressure on the bar until all the figures of the melody corresponding in length with this sign have been played.

{   This sign means to play the different sounds of the chord with a slight accent, slower than usual. When the dot is at the bottom, the chord is played from bass to treble; if it's at the top, the chord is played downward from treble to bass.

EXCEPTIONS

As with any system, exceptions and variations are inevitable, particularly in the choice of chords to use for a given melody note. A small figure written just above a string means to play the string with a different chord than the one memorized. The little figure tells which bar to press.

Occasionally one must pick a note without depressing a chord bar. A "o" written above the string shows this exception. Care must be taken to pick only one string.

When a melody run is to be made on a chord lacking the melody note a "●o" is placed above the note. This tells the player to make the run with the bar down ("●") but release the bar when the melody note is reached ("o").

An example of music written in this notation system follows. Versions in standard musical notation and a modern tablature are also given. (The modern tablature system is explained in Chapter 14.)

Figure 2:
Model #2¾ Scale

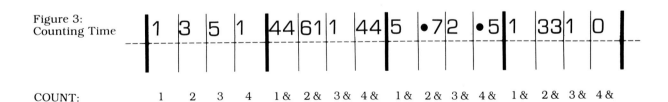

Figure 3:
Counting Time

COUNT: 1   2   3   4   1& 2& 3& 4&   1& 2& 3& 4&   1& 2& 3& 4&

Figure 4:
Playing Techniques
S = Simple Run
M = Melody Run
P = Picking

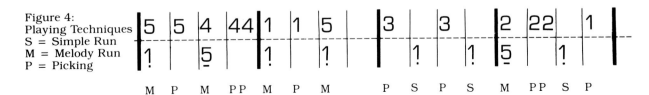

M P M PP M P M   P S P S M PP S P

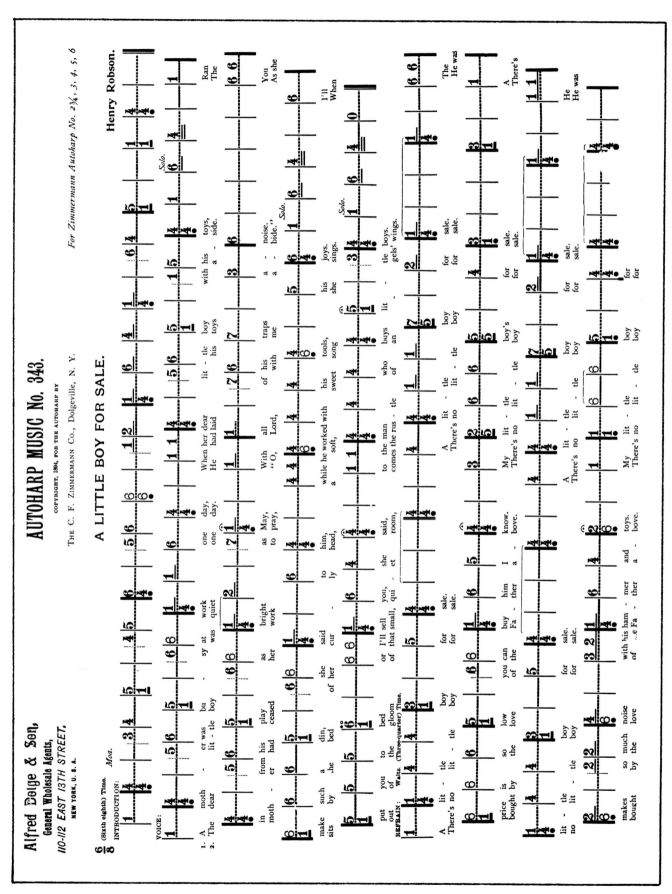

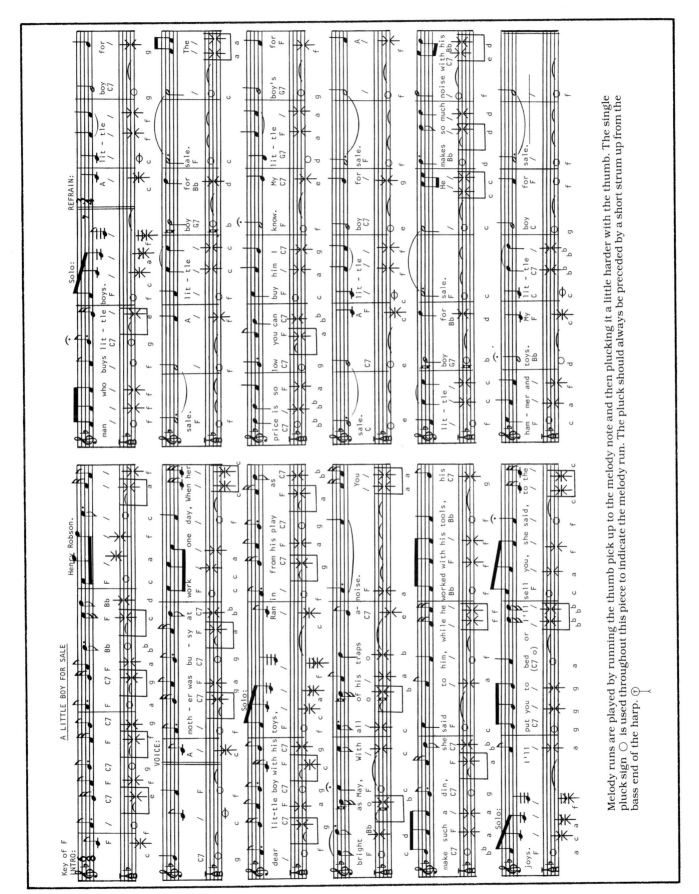

Melody runs are played by running the thumb pick up to the melody note and then plucking it a little harder with the thumb. The single pluck sign ○ is used throughout this piece to indicate the melody run. The pluck should always be preceded by a short strum up from the bass end of the harp. ⓣ

23

## CHAPTER 3

AUTOHARPS 1885 to 1892

Autoharps made by C. F. Zimmermann, Philadelphia, Pennsylvania.

MODELS

#1	#3	#6
#2	#4	Unknown model number
#2¾	#5	Proposed #7

FEATURES

Logo: Two types. Place of manufacture not given.
Label: Three types. Place of manufacture not given. Printed on pale blue-green paper.
Holders: Wood. Painted black. Glued to soundboard.
Bars: Wood. Painted black.
Buttons: Round, slightly concave, cream-colored celluloid.
Bar labels: Paper or celluloid. Zimmermann figures for chord names.
Music scale: Paper or celluloid. Zimmermann figures for string names.
End cover: None or slotted wooden strip.
Feet: Three brass nailheads.
Music stand holes: Two on slanted edge.
Bridges: Wood. Painted black. Single metal rod inset.
Tuning pins: Angled backward slightly.
Strings: Loop-end strings attach over hitch pins.
Soundboard, back and sides: Natural finish.
Decorations: Lines painted around edge and around soundhole.
Prices: 1893 company catalog.

#1

21 strings.
3 bars.
3 chords: C, F, G7.

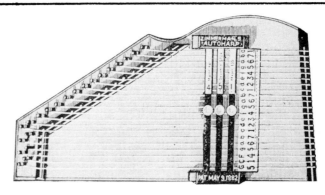

Catalog drawing shows pyrography on chord bar holders, probably for the convenience of the artist. Other drawings show pyrography along the bass side of the soundboard.

Logo: Burned into wood by pyrography.
Label: "Miniature Autoharp."
Felts: Red.
Bar labels: Pale blue-green paper.
Music scale: Pale blue-green paper. Glued to wood strip nailed to harp.
End cover: None.
Price: $4.00
Introduced: By 1885.

This early "Miniature Autoharp" #1 with first logo, first label, was damaged and restored. (Bar labels are on wrong side of buttons.)

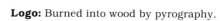

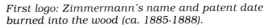

First logo: Zimmermann's name and patent date burned into the wood (ca. 1885-1888).

14

15

16

*First label: "Miniature Autoharp" in block letters
(ca. 1885 to 1888).*

17

*Second label: Block letters, "miniature" removed
(ca. 1888 to 1892).*

Logo: Celluloid plate.
Label: Block letters.

Bar labels: Celluloid, nailed to bar.
Music scale: Celluloid, nailed to harp.

Later model #1 with second logo, second label.

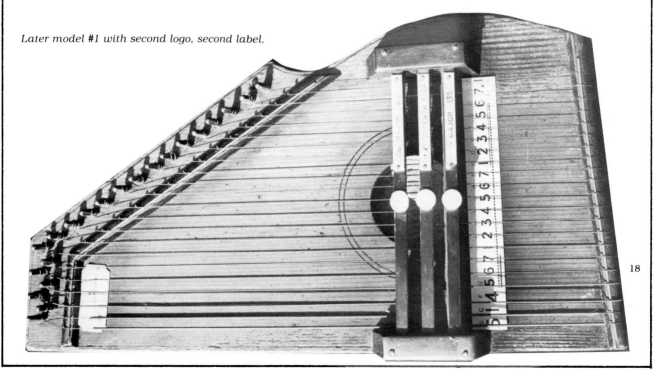

18

#2

23 strings.
4 bars.
4 chords: C, F, G7, C7.

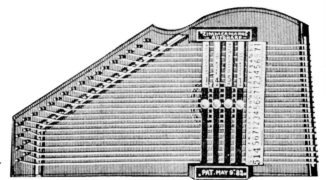

Catalog drawing.

Logo: Celluloid plate.
Label: Block letters.
Bar labels: Celluloid.
Music scale: Celluloid.
End cover: None.
Price: $5.00.
Introduced: By 1885.

Celluloid plates were made by Baldwin & Gleason Company using a process patented in 1886. Below Zimmermann's picture "Pat. 1886" is etched, but not inked, making it not visible in the photograph. Other plates plainly said, "Baldwin & Gleason Co., Ltd., N.Y. Pat. 1886."

20

Second logo: Celluloid plate (ca. 1887-1892).

19

Model #2 with second logo, second label.

#2¾

23 strings.
5 bars.
5 chords: C, F, B-flat, G7, C7.

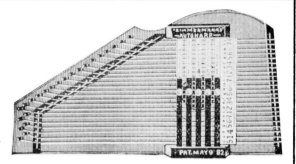

Catalog drawing.

Logo: Celluloid plate.
Label: Block letters.
Felts: Red.
Bar labels: Celluloid.
Music scale: Celluloid.
End cover: None.
Price: $5.50.
Introduced: By 1885.

Model #2¾ with second logo, second label (left).

Model #2¾ with cast iron tuning key, metal thumbpick, and brass spiral fingerpick (below).

22

21

23

Chord bars from a "miniature" Autoharp. Note paper labels.

24

Lower bridge on Philadelphia Autoharps had a single metal rod. "Grain" of wood is painted.

Logo: Pyrography.
Felts: Red.
Music scale: Paper.
Size: 17¾ inches by 9½ inches.

Label: "Miniature Autoharp."
Bar labels: Paper.
Back and Sides: Imitation rosewood with painted "grain."

"Miniature Autoharp" #2¾ (first logo, first label) with wire music stand in place. Pyrography is visible at upper edge.

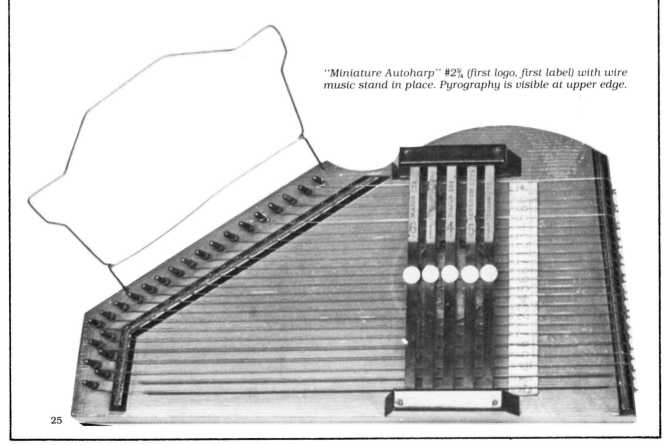

25

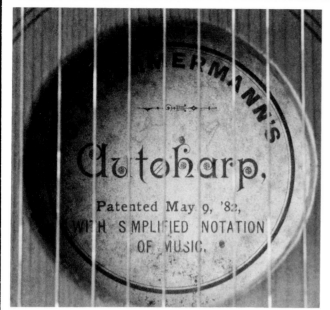

Third label: Script style letters (ca. 1892).

26

Logo: Celluloid plate.
Bar labels: Celluloid.

Label: Script style letters.
Music scale: Celluloid.

Late model #2¾ with second logo, third label.

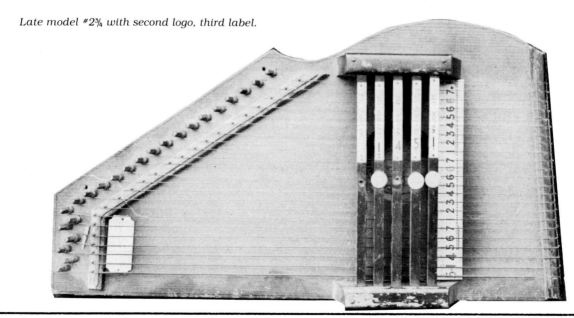

27

#3

28 strings.
4 bars, 5 shifters.
9 chords: C, F, B-flat, G, G7,
C7, D7, Am, Gm.

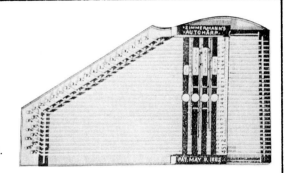

Catalog drawing.

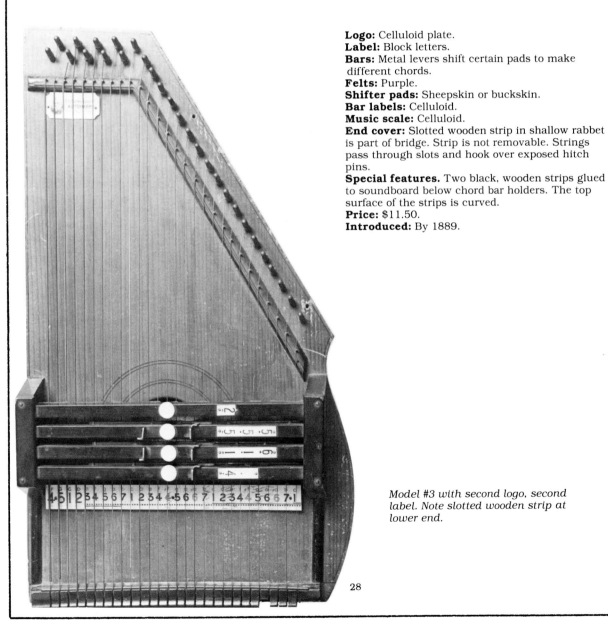

Logo: Celluloid plate.
Label: Block letters.
Bars: Metal levers shift certain pads to make different chords.
Felts: Purple.
Shifter pads: Sheepskin or buckskin.
Bar labels: Celluloid.
Music scale: Celluloid.
End cover: Slotted wooden strip in shallow rabbet is part of bridge. Strip is not removable. Strings pass through slots and hook over exposed hitch pins.
Special features. Two black, wooden strips glued to soundboard below chord bar holders. The top surface of the strips is curved.
Price: $11.50.
Introduced: By 1889.

Model #3 with second logo, second label. Note slotted wooden strip at lower end.

28

#4

28 strings.
5 bars, 6 shifters.
11 chords: C, F, B-flat, G, D, G7, C7, D7, Am, Gm, Dm.

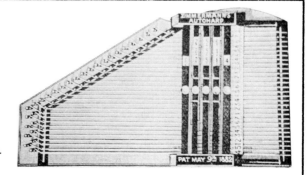

Catalog drawing.

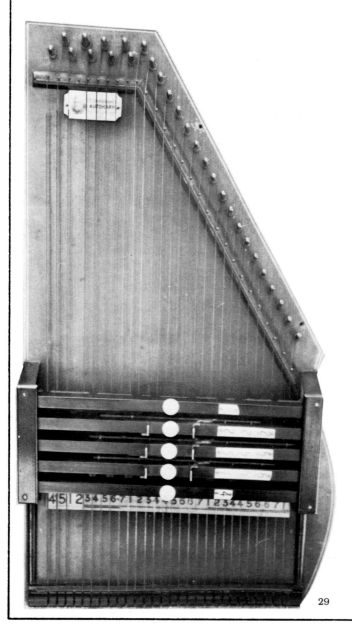

Logo: Both pyrography and celluloid plate.
Label: "Miniature Autoharp."
Bars: Shifters change chords.
Felts: Purple.
Shifter pads: Sheepskin or buckskin.
Bar labels: Celluloid.
Music scale: Celluloid.
End cover: Slotted wooden strip.
Back and sides: Imitation rosewood.
Binding: Inlaid wood.
Special features: Strips below holders.
Price: $15.00.
Introduced: By 1889.

Model #4 with first and second logos, first label. This harp has both the pyrography and the newer celluloid logo plate.

29

#5

28 strings.
5 bars, 8 shifters.
13 chords: C, F, B-flat, G, D, G7, C7, D7, Am, Gm, Dm, Em, Bm.

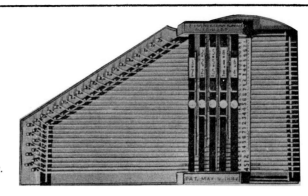

Catalog drawing.

Late model #5 with second logo, third label (below). Felts are green. The separate end pin cover, which is attached with screws, covers the hitch pins completely and must be removed to change strings.

30

Logo: Celluloid plate.
Label: Block letters.
Bars: Shifters change chords.
Felts: Purple.
Shifter pads.: Sheepskin or buckskin.
Bar labels: Celluloid.
Music scale: Celluloid.
End cover: Slotted wooden strip.
Soundboard: Birdseye maple (veneer).
Back: Rosewood (veneer).
Binding: Inlaid wood.
Special features: Strips below holders.
Price: $20.00.
Introduced: By 1889.

Model #5 with second logo, second label.

31

#6

32 strings.
6 bars, 10 shifters.
16 chords: C, F, B-flat, G, D, A, G7, C7, D7, A7, Am, Gm, Dm, Em, Bm, C-sharp diminished seventh.

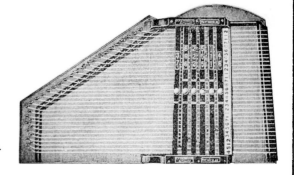

Catalog drawing.

Logo: Celluloid plate.
Label: Block letters.
Bars: Shifters change chords.
Felts: Blue.
Shifter pads: Sheepskin or buckskin.
Bar labels: Celluloid.
Music scale: Celluloid.
End cover: None.
Back and sides: Imitation rosewood.
Binding: Inlaid wood.
Price: $27.00.
Introduced: By 1889.

Model #6 with second logo, second label. Note curved lower bridge and flattened wood strips below holders.

32

Model number unknown

44 strings.
12 bars, 27 shifters.
1 "flageolet" bar.
60 chords: All major, minor, dominant seventh, minor seventh, and diminished seventh chords.

This harp is similar in appearance to the drawing in the original patent, and the harp has the patent number and date on it. However, its description is considerably different from that of the original patent. It more closely resembles the proposed model #7 (described below) and may have been a prototype for that model.

33

Bars: "Flageolet" bar raises the pitch of each string one octave. Bars are (from left to right) A-sharp, F, C, G, D, A, E, B, F-sharp, flageolet, C-sharp, G-sharp, D-sharp major.
Shifters: Change chords to minor, dominant seventh, minor seventh, and diminished seventh chords.

(Proposed model) #7 (Description from catalog, ca. 1889-90.)

3½ chromatic octave strings.
10 bars, 1 "flageolet" bar.
42 chords: F-sharp, B, E, A, D, G, C, F, B-flat, D-sharp major;
F-sharp, B, E, A, D, G, C, F, B-flat, D-sharp minor;
F-sharp, B, E, A, D, G, C, F, B-flat, D-sharp seventh:
and all twelve diminished seventh chords.

Summary: Autoharps 1885 to 1892

Autoharps made by C. F. Zimmermann, Philadelphia, Pennsylvania.

Models: #1, #2, #2¾, #3, #4, #5, #6, one unknown model number, proposed model #7.
Introduced: Models #1, #2, and #2¾ by 1885. Models #3, #4, #5, and #6 by 1889.
Logo: 1) Burned into wood (pyrography). 2) Celluloid plate. Some harps have both types. Both say "C. F. Zimmermann's Autoharp. Pat'd May 9th, 1882."
Label: 1) "Miniature Autoharp" in block letters. 2) Block letters, with "miniature" removed. 3) Script style letters. All say "C. F. Zimmermann's Autoharp Patented May 9, '82, with Simplified Notation of Music," printed on pale blue-green paper. No place of manufacture given.
Holders: Wood. Painted black. Glued to soundboard.
Bars: Wood. Painted black. Some have metal shifters to change chords.
Buttons: Round, slightly concave, cream-colored celluloid.
Felts: Red, purple, blue, or green.
Shifter pads: Sheepskin or buckskin.
Bar labels: 1) Paper. 2) Celluloid. All have Zimmermann figures for chord names.
Music scale: 1) Paper. 2) Celluloid. All have Zimmermann figures for string names.
End cover: Models #1, #2, and #2¾ have no covers. Models #3, #4, #5, and #6 have a slotted wooden strip as an extension of the bridge. The hitch pins are still exposed beneath the strip. A separate end cover, attached by two screws, was designed around 1892. It completely covers the hitch pins and has to be removed to change strings. It was probably used only on the top-of-the-line models (#4, #5, and #6).
Feet: Three brass nailheads on the back of the harp.
Music stand holes: Two holes on the slanted edge of the harp.
Bridges: Wood. Painted black. One metal rod inset.
Tuning pins: Angled backward slightly.
Strings: Loop-end strings wrap around lower end and attach over hitch pins.
Soundboard, back and sides: Natural finish. Some have "grain" painted on the sides and back.
Binding: Models #4, #5, and #6 have inlaid wood edges.
Decorations: Lines painted around edge and soundhole.
Special features: Some models have wooden strips glued to the soundboard below the holders.

First logo: Burned into wood by pyrography (ca. 1885 to 1888). 15

Second logo: Etched on celluloid plate (ca. 1887 to 1892). 20

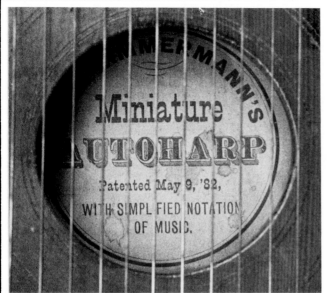

16

17

First label: *"Miniature Autoharp" in block letters (ca. 1885 to 1888).*

Second label: *Block letters, "miniature" removed (ca. 1888 to 1892).*

Third label: *Script style letters (ca. 1892).*

26

Alfred Dolge

Rudolf Dolge

## CHAPTER 4

THE C. F. ZIMMERMANN COMPANY

I leave my footprints here which cannot
be erased whatever may come . . . .
Alfred Dolge, *Dolgeville Herald*
(May 4, 1899)

His influence on the village of Dolgeville, New York, is undeniable. Alfred Dolge was loved by many. He was called a genius, a great man, and he was lauded for turning a small village into a major manufacturing center. But many others thought differently. He was accused of fraud, and blamed for bankruptcies and even suicides! No matter which view is held, Alfred Dolge was clearly a very important and controversial figure in this small upstate New York community.

Alfred Dolge was born in Chemnitz, a town in Saxony, Germany, on December 22, 1848. As young Alfred grew, he showed an early aptitude for business, starting several small enterprises. Although some of his endeavors got him into trouble both at home and school, the boy was definitely successful at what he did.[1]

When he reached his mid-teens, Alfred was forced to leave school by his father, August Dolge, who insisted that his son serve an apprenticeship in the factory of his piano-making firm, A. Dolge and Company. Meanwhile, his mother and uncle helped him get through the evening school run by the Masonic Lodge in Leipzig. Once he had finished his education, Alfred began to feel that Germany was too narrow-minded and restrictive, so he sailed to the United States in July 1866. He was only seventeen years old and spoke no English.

After a succession of jobs in the first few years, Alfred Dolge finally ended up employed in a piano factory, where he worked hard while studying at night to learn everything he could about piano making. He already had a dream of importing all the materials necessary to make pianos.

One of the most important parts of the piano is the hammer, which at that time was almost always covered with leather — domestic leather. Dolge knew that the German leather was far superior, and while still just an ordinary journeyman at the factory, he decided to import a small amount of German leather. The effort was not unsuccessful: he managed to sell his entire stock of leather in only two days! The profit from that sale bought more leather, which also sold quickly, and Dolge was firmly established in the import business. Next came piano wire.

By 1869 he had enough business to open a store in New York City. He had long hoped to import the felt necessary in a piano, but all the felt was made abroad and sold through manufacturers' representatives. They refused to sell to Dolge, so he decided that he would simply start making his own. He set up a small factory in a loft in Brooklyn and financed the endeavor with his profits from importing the other products. The business and his reputation for quality grew. In 1873 his felt won first prize at the Vienna World's Fair. As more orders for felt came in, he knew he had to find a better location for his factory.

In 1874 Dolge selected the site for his new factory: Brockett's Bridge, New York, population 300. There he bought an old tannery site for seven thousand dollars, to be paid in thousand-dollar installments. The location was ideal, with pure flowing water good for making the felt and generating energy. When Dolge made the move he brought along his wife, Anna, his son, Rudolf (born December 1, 1869), and ten employees from the Brooklyn factory. In the years that followed, the factory's business grew to include the making of piano soundboards, and even felt shoes and slippers. Dolge, who paid his workers well and equipped his factories with conveniences such as automatic sprinklers and electric lights, attracted workers from everywhere. In 1885 Dolge set up a workers' gymnasium and clubhouse for the Turnverein, a club for exercise and social gatherings.

The whole town prospered with the Dolge industries, so much so that on December 13, 1881, the residents changed the name of the town to Dolgeville to honor the man who had

36

Bryan Bowers playing a Dolgeville Harmonette at the Walnut Valley Festival, 1982.

done so much for them. By 1895 the population had grown to 3,000, with taxable property assessed at $1.2 million.

One account in *Freund's Musical Weekly* (October 30, 1895) reads:

> Under Mr. Dolge's excellent management, the town of Dolgeville has become one of the most prosperous and thrifty of the manufacturing towns in the state. It is well provided with schools, and has an excellent public library, parks, electric light and other modern conveniences, and seems to be a model home for workmen.
>
> This result is largely due to the judicious intelligence of Mr. Dolge in carrying out his plan of "earning-sharings," and in diversifying the industries of the town.

Dolge's "earnings-sharing" plan (set up in 1890) gained him national attention. Together with his employee pension plan (established in 1876) and his other insurance funds to cover accidents, illness, and death, the "earnings-sharing" program was quite radical for its day and given extensive coverage in the national newspapers. The *American Art Journal* (December 21, 1895) described the plans in detail, commenting on its success:

EASY TO SELL.

Bagsey—"Say, Ragsey, I'm going inter business."

Ragsey—"Ye beant thinkin' o' workin', are ye, Bagsey?"

Bagsey—"O' corse not, ye idjot; I'm goin to sell Autoharps."

35

From the American Art Journal, ca. 1895.

It has attracted wide attention among American economists . . . and the practical application of these broad principles has brought Alfred Dolge the most beneficient results. There are no thoughts of strikes about his great factories. Strikes spring from dissatisfaction, and not from content.

Not everyone saw the Dolgeville plans as a model Utopia, however. The *Music Trades* (February 9, 1895) described Dolge's system as "autocratic" and "paternalistic." It was later estimated in the *Herkimer County Commemorative Brochure* (1954) that the various plans for the workers' welfare ran Dolge's expenditures well over a quarter of a million dollars. Dolge detailed his plans in *Economic Theories as Practically Applied in the Factories of Alfred Dolge & Son at Dolgeville, N.Y.* (1896)

This, then, was Alfred Dolge, the man who purchased the Autoharp company from Charles Zimmermann in late 1892. It certainly offers a different perspective on the man who supposedly tried to swindle the elderly Mr. Zimmermann. In his own town at least, the man was considered a hero.

With the impending arrival of the Zimmermann Autoharp, Dolge brought his oldest son, Rudolf, into the business. In a full-page ad dated January 1, 1893, Alfred Dolge announced in the *Musical Courier*: "I take pleasure in informing you that I have admitted my son, Rudolf Dolge, as partner in my business. The firm name will from this date be Alfred Dolge & Son." On January 4, 1893, a certificate of incorporation was filed in Herkimer County for the "C. F. Zimmermann Company of Dolgeville, New York." Rudolf Dolge was put in charge of the new corporation and headed the wholesale office of Alfred Dolge & Son in New York City.

The twenty-fourth annual reunion of the employees of Alfred Dolge was held in Dolgeville on January 28, 1893. Rudolf Dolge arrived from New York City and brought with him a satirical publication called *The Autoharp* (January 28, 1893). The masthead featured a cartoon depicting many of the better-known employees gathered around a burning phonograph. Out of the flames the Autoharp rose like a phoenix. Underneath the cartoon were the words "Our Motto: Harmony. There are no discords between our bars." The *Musical Courier* (February 8, 1893) reported later that "the reading matter was of a local nature, crisp and bright, and created no end of merriment . . . . We will not attempt to interpret the full significance of the cartoon, as some of its features pertain wholly to incidents connected with the inner workings of the New York office, and would be appreciated only by those familiar with them."

Masthead from The Autoharp, January 28, 1893.

37

38

The Autoharp and How It Captured The Family (First edition, ca. 1893-1894).

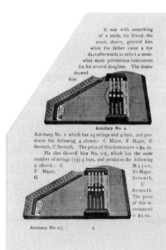

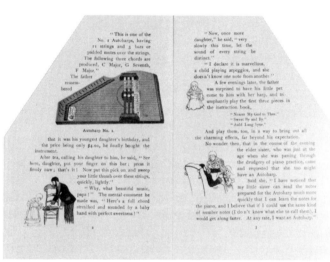

"He was a good while determining between this and Autoharp No. 4, which has sides and bottom of imitation rosewood, edges inlaid, and is very highly polished. This instrument has 28 strings and 5 bars, producing the following 11 chords: B♭ Major, F Major, C Major, G Major, D Major, C Seventh, G Seventh, D Seventh, A Minor, G Minor, D Minor. The price of this instrument is $15.00.

"He finally chose No. 4 because, he thought, it would give

the best results in the long run."

"Well, we're running wild in the direction of Autoharps, it seems to me, at our house."

"Oh no, you will find it has a refining influence on the boy; better encourage Tom in his musical whim; it will do him no harm."

So the indulgent father left the store well pleased with his purchase, and not altogether dissatisfied with the action of his boy, Tom, either.

Autoharp No. 4.

Not a great while after this, my lady, Tom's elder sister, a graduate of the conservatory, and hence a finished musician, made up her mind that the delicate harmonies evoked from Tom's Autoharp were just the thing as an accompaniment for her songs, so she made a journey to the store of the music dealer.

It was difficult for that gentleman to restrain the smile which crept round the corners of his mouth as she disclosed her mission. But she wanted a better instrument still.

So with all the gravity of the obliging salesman, he showed her Autoharps No. 5 and No. 6, explaining the points of difference, saying that No. 5 had edges inlaid, and was highly polished, and had 28 strings and 5 bars, producing the following 13 chords; D Major, G Major, C Major, F Major, B♭ Major, D Minor, E Minor, G Minor, A Minor, B Minor, C Seventh, G Seventh, D Seventh. Price $20.00.

Autoharp No. 5.

But he could specially recommend No. 6, which in appearance and finish is like No. 5, save that it has 32 strings and 6 bars, and produces 16 chords, A Major, G Major, C Major, F Major, B♭ Major, A Seventh, D Seventh, G Seventh, C Seventh, D Minor, E Minor, G Minor, A Minor, B Minor, C Diminished Seventh Price $25.00. He told her that this was the most complete instrument of its kind made, and it is needless to say, that she purchased it without much hesitation.

Autoharp No. 6.

It was a few weeks later when the two friends met again, and the father said : " Your Autoharp has certainly captured our family and no mistake. We have it now in four degrees, and if the children do not all play at once, when one is not practising, the other is. First, it is the youngster with her " Home, Sweet Home " on No. 1. Then comes my second little girl accompanying herself to some Sunday-school hymn. Then there is Tom, making life miserable for the rest with "Tara-ra-boom-de-ay," and finally my lady, either playing alone some operatic air or in duet with Tom (surprisingly well too, by the way), so that we have Autoharp music from sunrise to sunset. Still, I do not complain, for I have made up my mind that the Autoharp is a musical instrument and no mistake.

By the way, I have looked into this system of figure notation, and it seems to me that it is bound to revolutionize the musical world. This method of representing complex chords by a single figure is certainly most ingenious, and I am going to look into the matter still further, for I can see no reason why it should not be

applied successfully to the piano and all other instruments equally as well.

It is at once so simple and universally applicable, that one learns far more than he thinks he does, while becoming proficient on the Autoharp.

" Well, I told you so," said his friend, the dealer, "your experience is not new to me. I have heard it before from several people to whom I have recommended the Autoharp. It is indeed an auto-harp. It almost plays itself. Press whatsoever bar you please on any one of these instruments, and then pass your hand over the strings, and a complete chord is the result, soft and sweet, or strong and loud, as you may desire. It is simplicity itself. It almost seems to contradict the statement that "there is no royal road to learning", for even the most dull discover soon that it far more quickly yields satisfactory results than can be accomplished by the difficult way of piano practice.

Then too, the workmanship of the instrument is as near perfection as modern skill and machinery can attain. The scale of the instrument is perfect. It is well tuned, and, by the way, it is tuned to the "International Pitch of 435 A," which was recently adopted by the Piano Manufacturers' Association of the United States. The finish is excellent and in every way worthy of the high reputation which the instrument has acquired for itself in so short a time.

It is no wonder, therefore, that we dealers have recently been importuned to handle no end of imitations of the genuine Zimmermann Autoharp. It has been beseigingly imitated and some of the imitations are put on the market as being fully equal to the genuine, and in some cases they are even being palmed off as the Zimmermann harp, but the public, fortunately, will have no difficulty in finding out whether it be as represented, if they just remember this Trade-Mark.

found on every *genuine Zimmermann Autoharp.*

Dealers are growing less and less eager to attempt to push instruments which are flagrant imitations of original goods when the original can be obtained at a fair price.

" Well," said the father, "as I said before, the Autoharp has certainly captured our family, and I heartily admit that my first impressions in reference to the instrument were wrong, and I am glad to welcome it as an additional source of harmony at home."

An account of Rudolf Dolge's speech was then given:

> I am supposed to talk about the "Autoharp." Well, as to the "Autoharp," it speaks for itself. Everybody Auto have one. [Cries of "Oh! Oh!" and laughter.] I for one believe that it is [the] greatest thing that ever came from Dolgeville. I do believe that the Autoharp is the one thing that is bound to make our thriving village known the world over. It will show to the world what Dolgeville is, and can do, in every one of its details. [Applause.] Its very entirety is the keynote of our success—"harmony." [Applause]
>
> But the Autoharp represents another thing—it represents the young blood that is to infuse further life into Dolgeville, and you will therefore pardon me if I speak more personally. We "young blood" are willing to learn how to steer the ship and keep it on the course which it has sailed so successfully these twenty years and more, and with such able and kind assistance as we have to guide and discipline us we hope to grow up an able and useful crew. [Applause.] I will try to do my part, and I know you will do yours. [Cheers.]

The move of the Autoharp company from Philadelphia to Dolgeville had begun immediately after Dolge finally acquired the company. Seventy to eighty men left Philadelphia with the first load of machinery on January 3, 1893.[2] Among those to arrive in town were the various department heads: Aldis J. Gery (finishing department, i.e., the "tuning department"), Theodore H. Roth from the New York office (business department), Christian Heisch (varnish department), and George Bachman (case-making department).[3] Conspicuous in its absence is the name of Charles F. Zimmermann, who

The C.F. Zimmermann Company factory, ca. 1896.

39

remained in Philadelphia and was no longer a part of the Autoharp business.

The new industry was temporarily installed in the old clubhouse for the Turnverein Club, which was moving to a new building. The old building (originally the first home of the Dolgeville Academy) was undergoing massive changes to convert it to a factory. The *Dolgeville Herald* (December 28, 1892) described the renovation:

[The new factory is to consist of] a building eighty-eight by thirty-six feet and four stories high with a tower in the center, twenty-one feet high. Attached to this building on the west side a boiler house will be built thirty-two by fifty-three feet, and in the rear a large cistern will be built. In the boiler house (it will be two stories high) the pump and heater will be located. The first story or the basement will be ten feet six inches high, the second, thirteen feet eight inches high, the third, twelve feet six inches high, and the fourth, ten feet four inches. In the tower will be located the water tank, eight feet in diameter and six feet high, for furnishing the supply for the automatic sprinklers with which the building will be furnished.

The front entrance to the clubhouse as it now exists will be closed up. The entrance to the factory will be on the east side near Elm Street. On the right of the entrance will be one stairway going down to the basement and another to the third floor. The stairways will be so arranged that an operative can pass from his own department to the street without going through any of the other departments in the works. In the front of the building two commodious offices are provided: one for general office and the other a private office located in the west corner.

The upper floor which is now occupied by Phillip Lang, the janitor, and family will have to be vacated. This floor has been used for various purposes besides the living rooms of the janitor. One part was used as the village trustees room, and another room was used for the school society's meetings. The room they occupied was where the Dolgeville Academy first started, and where plans were first devised for the present splendid system of schools that the village of Dolgeville today enjoys.

The clubhouse was erected by Alfred Dolge for his workmen as a place of amusement, and he has spent many thousands of dollars to improve it for their benefit during the past years. The rapid advancement of the village now demands that the amusement hall must be given up for the manufacturing purposes. A carload of machinery for the new manufacturing industry has already arrived in this village. For the present, the firm will occupy part of the Brambach piano factory. The first and second floors of the clubhouse will be fitted up as rapidly as possible so they can be utilized. On the start about 150 men will be employed, and if the new industry proves to be what is anticipated of it, another large addition will be built by this factory next season.

No time was wasted in getting the men to work, and business began on January 13, 1893. The *Saturday Globe* (January 14, 1893) reported that "about 3,000 finished instruments were shipped from Philadelphia to this village. The instruments are all sold, and during the past week the men in the finishing department have been engaged retuning them." Roth, of the business department, announced that every completed instrument would be shipped from the factory by the end of the week.[4]

40

No sooner was the last of the inventory from the Philadelphia factory finished and sold, than orders for more harps began to pile up. Five more carloads of machinery arrived at the beginning of the next week, completing the move. The C. F. Zimmermann Company of Dolgeville, New York, was now in business, and great things were predicted for the future.[5]

In Philadelphia in 1892, annual Autoharp sales had amounted to a quarter-million dollars, with little effort put into promotion. Now the Dolges planned a massive marketing campaign, and anticipating an increased volume of production, they advertised for "about thirty men who have an ear for music, wanted at once to work in the finishing department."[6] In addition to those men needed to tune the completed Autoharps, more men were hired in other departments, creating a temporary housing shortage in town.[7]

The Dolges immediately started to promote and advertise their new product. They had two separate exhibits at the 1893 World's Columbian Exposition in Chicago, one for their piano supplies and another for the Autoharp. The official catalog from that exposition (published by W.B. Conkey Co.) has this listing: "The Autoharp is shaped like a zither, having bars or padded mutes, which in connection with the Zimmermann system of figure music enables anyone to play the most difficult airs and chords. Patented May 9, 1882. Alfred Dolge & Son, general wholesale agents, 110-112 E. 13th St., New York."

A special award was given to the Zimmermann system of figure music at the exposition. In an 1896 catalog the company proudly announces the honor: "The award reads: for originality and simplicity of system and educational value, especially in connection with the Autoharp." The Dolges used the award extensively in their advertising as "the only system that received an award . . . ." It may very well have been the only system to win an award, but it certainly wasn't the only award. A full list of the award winners lists the C. F. Zimmermann

The Dolge Building, 110-112 East 13th St., New York City, was the wholesale office of Alfred Dolge & Son.

Drawing of the Dolge Building from the 1896 company catalog (left).

The Dolge Building being converted to condominiums, March 17, 1982 (right).

41

42

STRINGS
TUNED TO TRADE

B.C.1894

A.D.1894

SEPT 1894

Cover from Strings, published by Alfred Dolge & Son. The caption reads, "Music, having thrown away her lyre and taken in its stead a Zimmermann Autoharp, is about to be crowned with the laurel wreath of public approval."

43

Company as a recipient of one of the thirty thousand prizes given at the Chicago exhibition! [8]

The prestige of the award did the Autoharp little good in 1893, however, for in April of that year an unexpectedly severe financial panic began to sweep the nation. When all hope for a strong protectionist tariff bill appeared gone, the uncertainty of many businesses resulted in a severe drop in orders for the rest of the year. During the winter of 1893-94 the Dolge factories actually had to close down for several months . . . the first time in twenty-five years! [9]

Alfred Dolge managed to get through the panic of '93, but in 1894 had to sell off some of his businesses.[10] The factories were then reopened, and the Dolges resumed business with renewed vigor. New products were developed, and by the end of the year the company held nine patents on the Autoharp. A New York Autoharp Club was formed under the direction of Herman Hermanson to promote the use of the Autoharp in ensemble playing. An ad in the *Youth's Companion* (October 25, 1894) states: "The New York Autoharp Club has done much to develop the Autoharp for concert use. For

At the Seashore
Two's a company, three's a crowd.
Strictly no visitors allowed.
He offers, as he pleads his suit,
Himself—and Autoharp "to boot."

The Summer Girl
Dainty fans and filmy laces
In her trunk the maiden places;
But, for snaring men this summer,
Her Autoharp is just a "hummer."

The Stay-at-Home Girl's Song
No need for me to go for rest
To ocean's side or mountain's crest;
At home here I, contented quite,
In Autoharp and song delight.

On the Mountain Lake
Keeping time with voice and oar,
Echoes sounding from the shore,—
Ah, this fair coquette was sharp
When she bought an Autoharp.

From the 1896 company catalog.

44

this we offer a Quartette Outfit complete. The Autoharps are arranged for their respective parts . . . . [The quartette] consists of one treble, one tenor, one baritone, and one bass Autoharp."

Strings, October 1894.

45

Advertising was begun again. The Autoharp appeared in the very first catalog published by the Sears-Roebuck Company in 1894, and from that time on catalog sales would be one of the Autoharp's major outlets. The advertising paid off, as is evidenced in this account from the *Indicator* (January 5, 1895):

> The careful manner in which the great supply house[s] have brought the Autoharp to the attention of the people has been shown by the holiday advertising of the instrument in the leading periodicals of the nation. A great deal of money has been expended for the purpose. But the money has been wisely spent and the results have been of a fruitful character. It is said that more than 10,000 Autoharps were sold by Alfred Dolge & Son as Christmas presents. And certainly that large sale ought to justify the expense incurred in bringing the harp before the people. Benefits from the judicious advertising are not always

immediate. Like the seed that falls upon fruitful ground, as we read in the parable, it yields its product in the future. And there is no doubt that the public, now thoroughly appreciating the possibilities of the Autoharp, will return to it with more real pleasure than ever.

The twenty-sixth annual reunion of the employees of Alfred Dolge was held on January 26, 1895. It was, as always, a large-scale production, full of good cheer, witty speeches, and various forms of entertainment, all designed to inspire the workers on for the next year. Another satirical publication, similar to *The Autoharp*, appeared. This one, called *The Scrutinizer: A yearly publication devoted to everybody's business* (January 26, 1895) related the progress of the Autoharp over the previous year:

> The New York store has pushed that new American instrument, the Autoharp, to such an extent that the clerical force had to be largely increased and ten typewriters are busy from morning to night attending to the correspondence. The Autoharp seems to have become a formidable rival to our felt department as regards volume and profit . . . . Although temptation was great during these hard times to try for an extra dollar by shading the quality of our goods, we have strictly adhered to the maxim to produce nothing but the very best in our line, and we can point to great improvements in the quality of our goods. We can proudly say that our customers never received better value in quality and quantity from us than during 1894.

The evening's entertainment for the reunion included the first presentation of "Count Cavalli and the Blue Felt Cats." It was an elaborate and whimsical performance that was certainly entertaining, but was also a thinly veiled advertising gimmick.

The blue felt was the newest product from the piano manufacturing company. It was, of course, also used on the Autoharps. Alfred Dolge had already engineered a very successful marketing campaign through the

CAVALLI AND THE CATS AT THE
DOLGEVILLE REUNION

THIS was the gem of the programme. Everybody in Dolgeville knows the handsome Count Ludovico Cavalli and to know him is to love him. But Dolgeville people are not as well acquainted with the Count's cats as they are with the Count himself. It is known that he has a large maltese cat farm (the farm is not so large, but the cats are immense) somewhere near the village, where he raises felines of the maltese variety, the hair of which, according to the veracious nobleman, is used extensively in the manufacture of the famous blue felt. When the announcement was made that Count Cavalli would give a public exhibition of the sagacity of some of his pets that he had specially trained for the purpose, the people of Dolgeville rejoiced exceedingly, for none of them had ever visited the farm, and even suave and plausible Karl Fink had never been able to persuade his confrère to show him over the place. The reunion was selected as the most appropriate opportunity for the exhibition, and the following poster, doubtless, drew many curious villagers to the hall:

THE WONDER OF THE AGE
FIRST APPEARANCE OF
COUNT CAVALLI AND HIS CELEBRATED BLUE FELT
CATS
A Triumph of Fin-de-Siecle Animal Training

CAST OF CHARACTERS:
Count Ludovico Cavalli de Hoboken, Trainer
Mr. Buffer-(Felt)................... Leading Tommy
Miss Lever (Felt) .... Leading Prima Donna
Mr. Under-(Felt) .... A Very Essential Feature
Mr. English-(Glass-Felt).......... A "polished" young
Tommy who makes himself felt
Mr. Fancy Upper-(Felt) .... A "Green" (& Co.)
Tommy who makes himself heard
Mrs. Export-(Felt)........ An Export from 13th St., N.Y.
alias "The old anti-fire office cat"
Mr. Lining-(Felt) .... Her oldest offspring, another
of "Green" (& Co.)
Mr. Tracker-(Felt, style 146).......... Her "youngest,"
Little, but—Oh, My!

PROGRAMME
Part I
(a.) Grand March and Military Drill.
(b.) Hoboken Star Atheneum Eccentricity—By the entire Troupe.
(c.) A Hoboken Love Tragedy.
    1.—The Serenade.
    2.—"The Rivals"—(No connection with other local talent).
    3.—"The Duel."
    4.—Finale.
    Five Minutes for Refreshments.
Part II
HOW THE BLUE FELT HAMMERS ARE MADE.
With an Interesting Lecture
and Many Illustrations.
BY COUNT CAVALLI

The audience watched the curtain rise with almost breathless curiosity. A great scampering was heard in the wings, accompanied by loud meowings and the cracking of a whip. A moment later Count Cavalli stepped upon the stage, followed by eight of his sagacious pets. Before the performance began the audience had time to observe the occupants of the stage closely, and the brief inspection sufficed to prove that there was no deception. It was the Count sure enough. No one could counterfeit that round and robust form, that heavy mass of dark hair, slightly tinged with gray, surmounting a brow like unto which that of Jove was

commonplace; that luxuriant beard which puts to shame the hirsute glory of the Prince of Wales: those rosy cheeks and those keen but kindly eyes.

As for the cats—well, they were rather large,—for cats, but not much larger than ordinary school boys. They were all blue, and all had red tails. This surprised the audience until the Count explained that he had succeeded in changing the color of the breed from the regulation mouse color to the exact hue of blue felt by feeding the animals upon minced coney rabbit seasoned with cayenne pepper. The pepper, he said, accounted for the red tails. It was discovered that each animal had a white letter branded on its back, a different letter on each cat. This, the Count explained, was the result of another experiment. When he wanted a line of cats branded with the letter F he fed the parents on minced lamb F-requently; when he wanted a line branded with E he served the lamb E-very E-vening; for an L he gave it for L-unch; for a T it was used at T-ea time, and so on. With these explanations the performance began.

The Count snapped his whip and the cats formed in line, standing on their hind legs. After going through the various evolutions of a grand march, the cats formed in line with their backs to the audience, when it was seen that the branded letters formed the words BLUE FELT.

The audience cheered heartily, for this was recognized as a specimen of *fin-de-siecle* advertising. Again the whip cracked, and the cats marched around in response to an encore, but they became somewhat unruly and mixed, and when they lined up once more the letters spelled FELT BLUE. When the Count saw this he became very angry, and snapped his whip savagely. Two of the animals became frightened, and ran off the stage. The others stuck to their posts, and lined up the best they could, when it was seen that the cats had somehow saved their trainer the trouble of swearing in his usual happy way, for the letters spelled TEUFEL.

The performance of the Count's pets closed with an exhibition of the manner in which piano hammers are covered with blue felt. A large box-like contrivance, filled with machinery operated by concealed shafting, occupied the center of the stage. On its front it bore this inscription:

COUNT LUDOVICO CAVALLI'S PATENT
MACHINE FOR MAKING BLUE FELT FOR
PIANO HAMMERS.

The cats were grouped about the machine as the Count came on the stage with his arm full of kittens. These he dumped into the machine, which ground away at a fearful rate. After several armfuls had been placed in the hopper, piano hammers covered with blue felt began to pour forth.

They were followed by several strings of real nice-looking sausages, which would seem to indicate that the Count is of an economical disposition, and has perfected a machine that will not only utilize the hair of the maltesians, but all of their parts as well. In this the machine is unique. You see the cats go in and the sausages come out. Hitherto we have only been aware of the disappearance of our felines just prior to the arrival of a fresh supply of sausages at the market.

In his eagerness to make the exhibition a success, the Count seized one of the trained cats to throw him into the hopper, but all the sagacious ones rebelled as if by magic, and in a trice the Count himself had been tossed into the machine, the grinding of which now became terrific.

A few minutes later there emerged one gigantic sausage, the exterior of which bore an outline of Cavalli's Apollonic figure. It was followed by a great sheet of blue felt in the form of a memorial slab.

The piano hammers thus produced were distributed among the guests as souvenirs of the occasion.—*Dodgeville Herald.*

music trade journals. According to the *Music Trades* (October 19, 1895), "Urged on by the determined efforts of [Dolge's] unequaled corps of salesmen, most of the leading [piano] makers took up the new felt." All the publications lauded the amazing and wonderful "Blue Felt," which quickly became the current fad. The *Music Trade Review* (December 28, 1895) reported, "The Dolge blue felt, particularly is one of the greatest successes of our day, and it is used not only by the manufacturers in this country, but in England and Germany."

Eventually the piano makers realized that the felt was really not any better (and some said it was worse) than Dolge's regular felt, and the fad passed. But by using gimmicks and heavy advertising, Dolge had drawn attention to his felts, and the article in the *Music Trades* pointed out that many piano makers simply substituted Dolge's regular felts when they decided to stop using the blue felt.

46

The young man and woman in this picture are probably missionaries. Her Autoharp is a Dolgeville Model #2¾, ca. 1895.

The reunion also featured the newest addition to the Autoharp family, the concert model Autoharp. A grand performance was given by Autoharp virtuoso Aldis J. Gery. Gery had been employed in the Philadelphia factory and had come to Dolgeville as the head of the finishing department. He was proficient enough on the instrument to find a place in the celebrated Gilmore Band led by Victor Herbert. He played the new and magnificent "Concert Grand" Autoharp, which he had designed and patented with Rudolf Dolge (U.S. Patent #521,109, filed in December 1893 and issued June 5, 1894). Single-handedly Gery did more to change the image of the Autoharp from that of a toy to a serious concert instrument than anyone could have imagined. In the first season with Gilmore's Band, Gery played in over one hundred concerts throughout the country.[11]

Gery received accolades for himself and the Autoharp everywhere he played. For example, the *Indicator* (December 7, 1895) described Gery:

> He brings out a delicious quality of tone and demonstrates to the satisfaction of everyone that it is capable of the most striking harmonies. Such work as Mr. Gery does is of the missionary kind, because no one that ever hears him can question the place of the Autoharp in the musical world.

Much of the credit, of course, should go to Alfred Dolge's marketing and promotional genius. This was acknowledged in the *Indicator* (January 5, 1895):

> The Autoharp is generally conceded by those who have watched its evolution and the careful manner in which it is handled by Alfred Dolge & Son, to be a musical instrument of superior quality. That fact has been demonstrated in the most satisfactory manner. The appearance of the Autoharp in the Victor Herbert concerts in the N.Y. Academy of Music settled the point beyond all dispute.

It was a marvelous circle: the success of the Autoharp got it into Gilmore's Band, and the Gilmore Band's playing in turn made the Autoharp even more popular. After the band played in a certain part of the country, the number of Autoharp orders from that area would markedly increase. The Dolges took advantage of that whole situation by getting the band's schedule and personally writing to every dealer to invite them to the concerts. Gery, still on Dolge's payroll and active in product development, naturally took every opportunity to expound upon the wonders of this marvelous instrument.[12]

The promotion of new products continued through 1895. Ads began to appear both in music publications and journals and in magazines for the general public. By 1895 the ads were everywhere, proclaiming the Autoharp to be "America's Favorite Instrument." A splendid glass cabinet designed for displaying the various Autoharp models traveled around the country, and a contest was held for the best Autoharp advertisement. Enticed by a thousand dollars in prizes, several thousand contestants entered. First prize went to Granville Smith, a graphic artist whose works previously had appeared in publications as well known as *Life* and *Harpers*.[13]

In 1895 the C. F. Zimmermann Company held eleven patents on the Autoharp, many developed by its own employees. Every new model came onto the market with a massive advertising campaign. The popularity of the instrument soared. According to the *Music Trades* (exact date unknown), "It has won this place on legitimate lines, by the adoption of two principles which insure success in any undertaking, namely: Intelligent advertising and constant experiments tending to the perfection and improvement of the instrument. It is an instrument of the future as well as to-day." The rage spread over the

47

This Autoharp display traveled around the country in 1895.

COMPANIONSHIP

Youth's Companion, February 21, 1895.

Youth's Companion, November 19, 1896.

Youth's Companion, January 6, 1898.

Youth's Companion, November 12, 1896.

48

continent and abroad. The C. F. Zimmermann Company started manufacturing the instrument for the American Autoharp Company of Toronto, Canada. These instruments were decorated with elaborate decals, a design feature that would soon be used on the U.S. models.

49

The building at 91 Niagara Street, Toronto, Canada, was occupied by the American Autoharp Company from 1895 to 1911. This photo was taken in July 1982.

With the Autoharp's commercial success, a part of Charles Zimmermann's dream was coming true. In 1895 many music books were published that used his figure system of notation. Although all these books were for the Autoharp, he had at least established his notation system in one small part of the music world. Even those Autoharp books published in foreign countries used Zimmermann's system.

In the United States orders continued to grow. A special "Autoharp Studio" was established in New York City to display all the models of Autoharps and to give lessons

on them. It was also the site of the semi-monthly meeting of the New York Autoharp Club. The interest in ensemble playing spread to all parts of the country. A new club was formed in Sitka, Alaska, with an initial order of six Autoharps![14]

In December 1895 the *Journal and Courier*, printed in nearby Little Falls, devoted most of its "industrial edition" to the Dolgeville factories, including, of course, the C. F. Zimmermann Company:

The popularity of the instrument has become phenomenal, and it is now to be found in every part of the civilized world. One hundred men are employed in the factory, the output of which is about 3,000 harps a week. In spite of the hard times the output of the factory has steadily increased, as has also the number of men employed. New machinery has been added and new styles of Autoharps have been launched since the beginning of the business. Although the present factory was built only two years ago, and numerous additions have been made thereto, a new and much larger structure is required and will be built early next year.

The article stated that the new factory was to be a four-story brick building, 60 by 180 feet.

This photograph of the new Autoharp Studio at 28 E. 23rd Street, New York, is from the 1896 company catalog. The building is no longer standing.

Sales of sheet music rose along with the harp's popularity. The *Journal and Courier* continued:

> Another prominent feature of the business is the arrangement and publication of figure music, written in the celebrated Zimmermann system of notation. Mr. Zimmermann spent many years in perfecting his system of notation. . . .With each Autoharp the company furnishes a book of instructions together with a collection of favorite melodies that are written in this system. Their sales of sheet music amounted to over 300,000 last year, and the indications are that the total will be double that this year.
>
> This unprecedented growth of business and the enormous popularity of the Autoharp are in great measure due to the wise management of the wholesale agents, Messrs. ALFRED DOLGE & SON, 110 East 13th St., New York, and it is safe to say that this industry will grow to immense proportions because it can be truly said that it is as yet in its infancy.

Not all the Dolge management was wise, however. The Autoharp company was still under the direction of Rudolf Dolge, who perhaps lacked the experience to have attained his father's business skills. At the same time as the local papers were praising Dolges and their successes, the *Music Trades* (December 21, 1895) (edited by the former editor of the *Dolgeville Herald*, John C. Freund) gave a different point of view:

> The rage for the Autoharp spread. Every jobber and dealer in musical merchandise wanted it. An assured fortune seemed in sight when Mr. Dolge, or some new manager whom he had appointed, lost his head, and conceived a scheme whose results have been disasterous.
>
> This scheme was nothing more nor less than to force all the dealers, by means of an ironclad agreement, to do business on a 10 percent margin, and to sell at certain figures specified in the contract.
>
> A general revolt was the result, and hundreds of dealers, many of them the largest in the country, refused to handle the Autoharp at any price whatever.
>
> The situation was aggravated by an interview with the manager of the Autoharp business (published in a certain musical sheet), who stated that Mr. Dolge had no use for the dealer, and intended to sell to the public directly.

It is surprising that the business-wise Alfred Dolge could have allowed such an uncharacteristic blunder to be made, and the scheme severely hurt the Dolge business. The proposed new factory was never built, and despite over $70,000 spent on advertising in 1895, one source stated that the Autoharp company would not show a profit for the year. In an attempt to rectify the damage done, radical policy changes were made early in 1896 to induce dealers to stock the Autoharp once again.[15]

In January Rudolf Dolge went to Chicago to close a deal with the W.W. Kimball Company, a large piano manufacturer with over five hundred stores, which planned to carry the Autoharp in all of them! Lyon & Healy (also of Chicago) ordered an entire carload of harps, an order estimated to be between two and three thousand instruments. The outlook for 1896 had definitely improved.[16]

An impressive catalog was printed for the dealers. A gold-embossed eagle carrying an Autoharp graced the cover, and a tissue sheet was inserted between all the pages. All the models were shown, as well as accessories, music (over four hundred pieces), and advertisements for dealers to use. The Dolges were trying to impress dealers with the product, and also to pass on some of the advertising expense to the dealer. The catalog offered the dealer a choice of advertising cuts which the Autoharp company would provide free upon assurance that the cuts would be used in local advertising. The catalog reads:

> Advertising must be looked upon, not as an unnecessary expense, but as an investment; part of the stock in trade. The Autoharp advertising has generally been commented upon as being among the most successful and effective in the world of advertising, and in the following pages we have endeavored to give a few hints on advertising based on our own experience, and that of enterprising dealers, and which we are sure will bring excellent returns if properly followed up.

Rudolf Dolge became very active in product development, too. Six new patents were

A SVMMER SIREN

-and · her · Avroharp

Advertising cuts from the 1896 company catalog.

THE
Zimmermann
AUTOHARP

on   Sail

At (Mortised for Name)

51

A · MODERN · ROMEO ·

AND · HIS · AVTOHARP.

MUSICAL INSTRI

obtained by the company in 1896, and Rudolf Dolge's name is on all of them. But despite the young man's full attention to the business, a personal rift between father and son ended the partnership of Alfred Dolge & Son at the end of 1896. Rudolf Dolge left with his family in January 1897 for Venezuela, where he became the manager of a warehouse for the National Association of Manufacturers.[17]

Rudolf Dolge had headed the Autoharp company for the previous four years. He had made some mistakes in management when he was running the business, but he had, or so it seemed, rectified them. The same year as his departure, however, Autoharp sales began to decline, and the company hired traveling salesmen to try to give sales a boost. One of these, Robin S. Tracy, vowed he could teach anyone to play the Autoharp. He also transcribed many pieces of music for the Autoharp instruction books and songbooks.[18] (His books were to be sold for years to come by Alfred Dolge & Son, the Phonoharp Company, and Oscar Schmidt-International, Inc.) Once again, almost overnight, the Autoharp company's fortunes had turned around!

Some advertising continued through 1897, but to a lesser extent than had been used in previous years. Four more patents were issued to the company, including the one assigned to them by C. F. Zimmermann himself! Even after he had sold his company, Zimmermann continued to work on his "best work" back in Philadelphia. The man who had been declared of "unsound mind" less than five years earlier was still improving the Autoharp at nearly eighty years of age! But there were no major new developments with the Autoharp that year. The last patent received by the C. F. Zimmermann Company of Dolgeville, New York, was filed on September 23, 1897, and issued in January 1898.

The beginning of the end for the C. F. Zimmermann Company and for all of the Dolge businesses was 1897. Details of the complex events that occurred in the final years of the Dolge industries are thoroughly chronicled in *Dolge*, by Eleanor Franz. With an almost unbelievable rapidity, Alfred Dolge went from riches to rags.

Dolge owned every industry in Dolgeville and had an enormous payroll. Money was tight, and Dolge took out some large loans

NO ROOM FOR THE OLD MAN

52

From the Cosmopolitan, December 1895.

From the cover of a German music book for Müller's Accord-zither, ca. 1896. Everything a man needs to go hunting: a walking stick, jacket, boots, hat, gun, and, of course, . . . an Autoharp!

53

during the year. He began to worry about his finances, but managed to continue to raise enough money throughout the year to prevent foreclosure on his factories. He was under constant pressure from two of his closest friends and advisors, Schuyler R. Ingham and Judge George Anson Hardin, who also, as two of Dolge's creditors, were trying to convince him to go into insolvency.[19]

Through a series of financial and personal problems the situation finally became critical, and on April 11, 1898, Alfred Dolge declared bankruptcy. Workers were sent home from all the factories, where one foreman had announced, "Alfred Dolge has failed, and we don't know when or if the factory will run again."[20]

By September, Schuyler Ingham had been made Receiver, and the factories reopened with Ingham in charge. Later it appeared that Ingham and Hardin had carefully

planned to take over Dolge's businesses. But that the astute Alfred Dolge could have been naive enough to play into their hands seems rather unrealistic. He lost his businesses, his home, his possessions, and many of his former friends, who now turned against their "town hero." Incredible as it seems, however, the facts as presented by Eleanor Franz do indicate that Dolge's "friends" simply outwitted him, maneuvering him into a completely vulnerable position.

In June, charges of fraud were brought against Alfred and Rudolf Dolge and the two banks that held the mortgages on the factories. The hearing was begun in February 1899, but fraud was never proved. On March 24, 1899, all the Dolge properties were sold off, some for less than one-tenth their value. All the industries continued to operate, except for the Autoharp factory, where thousands of Autoharps, lacking only their strings, were burned. No more harps would be made in Dolgeville.[21] Eventually the old Autoharp factory was bought by the Daniel Green Felt Shoe Company, which converted it into what became their Factory #2.[22]

"How the Brownies Captured the Autoharp"

From the 1896 company catalog.

54

The Autoharp Resounds Through Pike's Peak

Inventor Tesla Taps the Earth Current. Interesting Experiments in Which the Autoharp Plays a Prominent Part.

TESLA'S MARVELOUS ACHIEVEMENT.

AUTOHARP COMMUNICATING FOUR MILES THROUGH PIKE'S PEAK WITHOUT WIRES.

55

Drawing from the Musical Age, ca. March 1896.

The Autoharp has become the favorite of two continents, and has been the companion of travelers in their journeyings through foreign lands, but we doubt if it was ever played upon at such an altitude or occupied in such an important service to science, as it has been recently by Nikola Tesla, the distinguished inventor, who claims to have discovered a way to harness free electric currents. The Autoharp played no unimportant part in the proceedings, as can be seen from the following account in last Sundays' *World*:

The world is on the eve of an astounding revelation. The conditions under which we exist will be changed. The end has come to telegraph and telephone monopolies with a crash. Incidentally, all the other monopolies that depend on power of any kind will come to a sudden stop. The earth currents of electricity are to be harnessed. Nature supplies them free of charge. The cost of power and light and heat will be practically nothing.

The scientist-electricians who have for years been trying to master the mystery of electrical earth currents with which the ground beneath your feet is filled, are on the threshold of success. The success of the experiments they have under way means much to them, but vastly more to the people. It means that if Nikola Tesla succeeds in harnessing the electrical earth currents and putting them to work for man there will be an end to oppressive, extortionate monopolies in steam, telephones, telegraphs, and the other commercial uses of electricity, and that the grasping millionaires who have for two decades milked the people's purse with electrical fingers will have to relinquish their monopoly.

Nikola Tesla has discovered the secret of the electric earth currents of nature, and they will be adapted to the uses of man. He has succeeded in transmitting sound by the currents that make an electric net of the earth. The transmission of power will follow. His experiments reduced to commercially practicable uses will mean that men will be able to tap the electric currents of the earth and make them serve the purposes of industry and of trade just as a well-digger over on Long Island taps water, or a Pennsylvania miner opens a vein of coal. The mighty electrical energy that has been stored up in the earth for ages will be harnessed and made to move the machinery of men.

Electricity will be as free as the air. For the privilege of its use legislatures will not have to be bribed or men corrupted at the polls, and public boards will not have to be "seen" to bestow exclusive franchises upon corporations organized to use public property for purposes of private gain, and make the people pay the original cost of their investment and excessive charges for service in order to squeeze dividends out of copiously watered shares.

Monopolies for purveying steam power, too, will be forced to capitulate to free electricity, for with the latter manufacturers will only have to connect their dynamos with the earth current to set their machinery in motion. The successful adaptation of Tesla's discovery will administer a death blow to the most galling slavery that has ever yoked the activities of men to the treadmill of monopoly. Tesla is the wizard who is going to emancipate modern industries from the shackles of corrupting, dividend grabbing, monopolistic corporations.

Sound travels with amazing speed, but electrical vibrations travel so swiftly that it is difficult to conjure up a figure which will graphically illustrate their speed. Here is one that will, perhaps, convey a vivid and lucid impression. In fancy place yourself at a table with a revolver in one hand and a finger of the other hand on the key of a telegraph instrument connected with a wire that girdles the globe seven times and laps over on the eighth turn a distance equal to 11,000 miles. Pull the trigger of the pistol and simultaneously press the telegraph key. While the sound of the report of the revolver is traveling 1,250 feet the electrical impulse imparted by the pressure on the key will pass seven and a half times around the world through the wire with which the key is connected.

Sound travels 1,250 feet a second, an electric impulse 186,000 miles a second. If the electrical currents with which the earth is filled can be harnessed and put to work, a new era in electricity will have dawned. It is to the mastering of the mystery of these earth currents and their adaptation that scientists like Tesla have been striving.

In the course of Tesla's experiments it is reported he found that in the vicinity of large cities there were so many conflicting earth currents that satisfactory results could not be obtained. So he went out to Denver, and near there found a better field for experimenting. There he met a friend interested in electrical research. They went to Pike's Peak. Conspicuous among their baggage were two Autoharps.

Tesla and his friend scaled the rugged sides of the peak. At an elevation agreed upon they separated. Tesla skirted the peak and, on reaching a point precisely opposite the place at which he left his friend, he stopped. The two experimenters, on a line drawn straight through the peak, were thus separated by four miles of stratified rock. The two Autoharps had been very delecately attuned before the scientists parted, and a time fixed for Mr. Tesla's comrade to play an air (also agreed upon) on the Autoharp.

Tesla waited patiently the arrival of the appointed time. Then he connected his Autoharp with the ground in such a way as to secure harmonic resonance with the earth current. The manner and medium of this connection are secrets. The receiving Autoharp was equipped with a microphone. As the time approached for his friend on the other side of the peak to strum the appointed tune Tesla listened with rapt attention.

At last, as a tuning-fork responds to its harmonic note sounded on the strings of a piano, the Autoharp in Mr. Tesla's hand gave out the harmonic tones of "Ben Bolt," which his companion at his station four miles away straight through the peak was plucking from the tense wires of his instrument. The experiment was a success. After many tunes had been played Tesla and his companion descended the peak. A statement of the facts and results of the experiments was written and attested before a notary public as a matter of scientific record.

The electric currents are in the earth. Their strength is great enough to furnish all the power and light man needs. Mr. Tesla has overcome the initial difficulty, and has located and tapped the earth currents. The rest will follow, as followed the telephone, Prof. Bell's discovery of how to transmit speech over a wire.

The *Music Trade Review*,
exact date unknown
(Based on the story in the
New York World, March 8, 1896.)

Alfred Dolge prepared to leave the town he had built and loved. In April eight hundred former employees and loyal friends gathered for a big farewell party. A glorious era in Dolgeville was at an end. The new owners of the factories had no use for profit-sharing plans, and all that Dolge had put into the pension plans for his employees was lost. When Dolge spoke at the farewell party he explained, "I trusted my 'friends' implicitly. They have done their work well . . . with cunning which would be a credit to Lucifer himself. I leave Dolgeville a poor man, saddled with an enormous indebtedness; but I go away, head erect, knowing that not all my labor has been lost. I leave my footprints here which cannot be erased whatever may come. Goodbye! Goodbye!"[23]

Alfred Dolge went to Southern California. He took with him two carloads of wine from New York and immediately started a wholesale wine business. With some of the friends who left Dolgeville with him, he started a new felt factory specializing in covering piano hammers. He named the location of his new factory Dolgeville, which eventually became part of Alhambra, California. Later he sold pianos, had an interest in an orange grove near Covina, California, and again became a successful businessman.[24]

In October 1920 Alfred and Anna Dolge set out on a tour around the world.[25] While on a train in Italy, Alfred Dolge died on January 5, 1922.[26] His ashes were brought back to the original town of Dolgeville, New York, where they were buried at the highest point of the cemetery. The inscription on the monument reads "The Founder of Dolgeville." His wife died in 1941, and her ashes are buried beside her husband's.[27]

Rudolf Dolge did well in South America. The Dolgeville library has papers he sent them detailing his career there: a founder of the Sociedad de Sciencias Naturales, first president of the Venezuelan section of the Pan American Society, and a managing representative of the Standard Oil Company.

Advertisement, ca. 1895.   56

He died in 1950 and is buried near his parents, along with his wife, who died in 1953, and their son, Alfred Dolge, Jr. (1893–1918.)[28]

At the burial ceremony for Alfred Dolge there was a brief speech by Dr. Rudolf Ruedemann of Albany, New York. Reprinted in the *Little Falls Evening Times* (July 6, 1922), part of his speech was designed to balance the scales of Dolge's successes and failures:

Before we return his mortal remains to our Mother Earth, from whom all life springs, it behooves us to review briefly what this man accomplished, to see wherein his greatness rested, to ask ourselves why he, who once was the center of both admiration and attack, is, now that the book of life is closed, still beloved of his friends and without enemies.

Let us be frank and just as to [his] failure, and acknowledge that he may have overreached himself in his ambitious plans and enterprises, as a genius often does; but we also know that, idealist that he was, he considered everybody as true and honest as himself and thereby failed to distinguish false friends and flatterers from the true ones.

A great man is greatest in misfortune and adversity. And so was Alfred Dolge. ... The world loves a good fighter and Alfred Dolge was a brave, foursquare fighter, who knew no foul blows and did not protect himself against them.

He loved the village that bears his name. He loved its citizens and he loved his adopted country with every fibre of his great heart; and, great and noble as he was, he did not forget, much less belittle, the old fatherland from which he had come. He was an honor to the country of his birth and to the country of his adoption.

Great and good man, rest in peace!

No. 101

UNCLE SAM—Well, neow, that there Autoharp music's got into my legs; I can't keep still. It's like everything else my boys have invented, it's got the "git there" in it, strong.
MISS COLUMBIA—"Your boys?" What do you mean by that?
UNCLE SAM—Why, don't you know that the Autoharp is an American invention?

57

From the 1896 company catalog.

58

Aldis J. Gery

Solo autoharpist of Gilmore's 22nd Regiment Band.

CHAPTER 5

THE CONCERT GRAND AUTOHARP

Had someone dared prophesy a few years ago that the Autoharp would reach such a state of development or enjoy such a wide popularity as it enjoys to-day that man would have been voted an imbecile, unless he could have foreseen the hands into which the Autoharp was destined to fall.

The invention of the Autoharp was similar to a great many other things. In its earliest state of development it was considered a toy, fit companion to the good little girl's imitation piano at which she would set her doll. The Autoharp was then a toy in every sense of the word.

The Autoharp of ten years ago was looked on with contempt by musicians; to-day a great composer has written for it. Why?

That question was raised in the March 27, 1895, issue of the *Musical Courier*. The article went on to explain that it was the "development of the musical possibilities" and the "artistic qualities" of the Autoharp that began to change the "toy" image of the Autoharp:

The great strides in development have culminated in the present large size concert Autoharp, an instrument of wonderful musical possibilities. The toy of a few years ago has become a musical instrument for which great musicians of the calibre of [Xavier] Scharwenka have written charming works and on which artists like Aldis J. Gery play in such concerts as those given by Gilmore's Band. Musicians no longer speak slightingly of the Autoharp, and it has come to claim a place in the orchestra.

The popularity of the instrument is so enormous that already a larger factory is proposed and will be built when present plans are matured. And this in view of the artistic progression of the instrument, which was ten years ago looked on as a toy of the people of no musical attainment.

The concert model Autoharp was a subject of great interest to the music trade journals of the late nineteenth century. News of the Autoharp, the Dolgeville factory, and the families of Alfred Dolge and his son Rudolf seemed to be favorite topics with these publications. But it was indeed the concert model Autoharp that caused the biggest commotion. The instrument was extremely expensive for its day, and no expense was spared by the Dolges for its promotion.

What was so different about this large Autoharp? Why was it promoted so heavily by Aldis Gery? Was this Autoharp really as successful as the press releases claimed? Some answers are clear, other still cloudy.

First, let's look at the harp itself and how it worked. Probably the finest known, extant example of this Autoharp model is currently owned by Gryphon Stringed Instruments in Palo Alto, California. It is in excellent condition. The only restoration needed was to the back of the harp, and that was done at the very capable hands of Jose Mario Martello of Concord, California.

The harp is very large: 30 inches long at the bass end and 20½ inches across at the chord bars. It's 1¾ inches thick. The soundboard is spruce, but the rest of the top side of

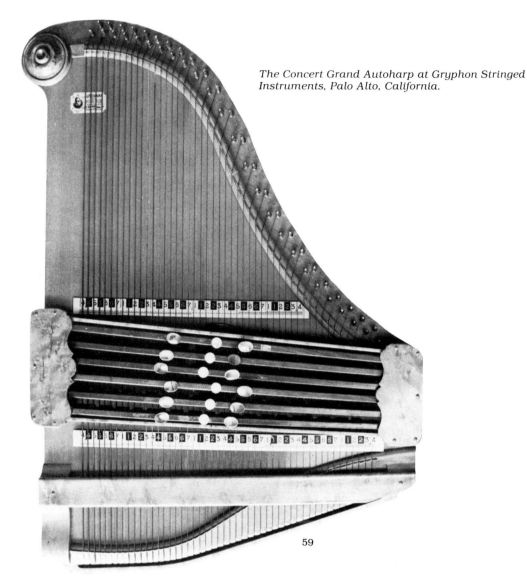

59

the harp is birdseye maple with an ivoroid binding. The buttons on the bars are celluloid. The craftsmanship is high quality with considerable attention given to artistic details such as the scroll at the upper left and the two chord bar holders.

There are six chord bars with metal shifters on each side of the chord bar button. However, these shifters are "fake" on the top bar (#1 position). They don't actually do anything on that bar except give a uniform appearance to the bars. The bars can all be moved into three different positions. By changing the positions and depressing the shifter levers, sixty-three different combinations are possible, producing all sixty major, minor, dominant seventh, minor seventh,

and diminished chords. The forty-nine strings are tuned in four *complete* chromatic octaves.

First consider the three positions for each of the bars. In the photograph you can see that the bars (from top to bottom) are in a right position, center position, and the left position, respectively. The sequence is repeated for the bottom three bars. Each bar (except the #1 bar, which will be discussed separately) makes a major chord based upon a different tonic note. When the bar is shifted to the left (toward the bass end of the harp), the felt pads simply move one note down the scale to make the chord "flat." In the right position (toward the treble end), the chord becomes "sharp." For example, the bar in

66

the #2 space makes an A-major chord when in the center position. Move it to the left and it is A-flat major; to the right, A-sharp major. The other bars make chords based on D, G, C, and F major (#3 to #6, respectively).

The #1 chord bar is for the diminished seventh chords. Since these chords are built from the root tone in such a way that there are actually only three different combinations of notes for all twelve chords, only one bar is needed to produce the twelve diminished chords (four chords with identical notes in them are made from each of the three positions).

The bar is moved into the three positions by just sliding the bar in the proper direction with the finger on the chord bar button. The bar is supported on the bass end by a pointed peg which can fit into any one of three notches on that end of the bar. A flat-top peg supports the treble end. The peg slips easily from one notch to the other when the button is pushed. Each of the two pegs is set into a hole in the frame of the harp with a spring underneath it. This, of course, allows the bar to be lowered onto the strings. See Figure 1.

Each bar also has two metal levers which when depressed (alone or in combination) shift *some* of the dampers to new positions. Figure 1 shows the entire bar viewed from the side that has the left shifter mechanism. The closeup drawings in Figures 2 and 3 are also of the left shifter mechanism. The right shifter works on the other side of the chord bar in a similar manner.

The shifting mechanism consists of the lever attached to a metal strip set into a routed groove on the side of the bar. A small metal "stop" in the treble end of the groove prevents the strip from going too far. A spring at the bass end brings the strip back to its original position when the lever is released. Individual rubber dampers are attached to a metal shaft which in turn is soldered to the metal strip. When the strip moves, the damper moves with it.

Figure 2 shows a closeup of the shifter at rest. When the chord bar is depressed, the rubber damper mutes the string indicated by the second dot from the left. However, when the lever is depressed on the bar, the damper moves. The shaft of the lever is attached to the bar by a nail, and the shaft pivots at this point. It goes behind the metal strip and attaches to another metal piece that in turn is attached to the metal strip.

Figure 3 shows what happens when the lever is depressed. The shaft pivots on the nail, allowing the shaft to swing out to the right in its routed slot. The shaft then pushes the other metal piece and the metal strip. The damper now moves over toward the treble end and mutes a string one semitone higher than before (the third dot from the left). This is the shifter that changes the major chord to a minor chord. The original position allows the third note of the chord (third dot from the left) to sound for the major chord. When the lever is depressed, however, the damper moves over to *mute* the

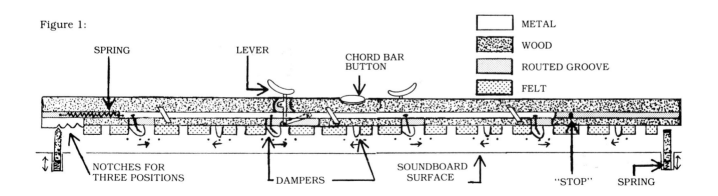

Figure 1:

METAL

WOOD

ROUTED GROOVE

FELT

SPRING LEVER CHORD BAR BUTTON

NOTCHES FOR THREE POSITIONS DAMPERS SOUNDBOARD SURFACE "STOP" SPRING third tone and *open* the string one semitone below. Since a minor chord has a flatted third, the chord is now a minor chord.

The right shifter uses the same mechanism, but with a slightly different result. The arrows in Figure 1 show that the left shifter moves the dampers to the right (treble end) and the right shifter moves them to the left (bass end). The difference in the shifters is that the dampers for the right shifter are thinner; while they move away from a string to *open* it up, they do *not* in turn *mute* a new string. The strings on both sides of the moveable damper pad are always muted by the permanent felt pads. This is the shifter that adds (opens) the seventh note of the chord. When the right shifter is used alone, a dominant seventh chord results. If the left shifter is also depressed, a minor seventh chord is produced. Four possible chords (major, minor, dominant seventh, and minor seventh) can be made in each of the three positions (left, center, and right): twelve chords off of each bar. Figure 4 shows all the possibilities.

Although this harp was advertised as producing seventy-two chords, several chords are different in name only (e.g., D-flat and C-sharp). The notes contained in these chords are enharmonically the same, and the two chord bars mute exactly the same strings. Eliminating these duplications leaves a total of sixty chords.

The harp examined here is basically the same model shown in 1895/96 ads. The shifter levers are different, and this model shows a logo decal on the soundboard, absent in the drawings in the ads. It was probably made in early 1895. Production was said to have begun on this model in December 1894, but the design is considerably different from that shown in the original patent (#521,109, issued June 5, 1894). The original design features are visible in the photograph of Aldis Gery.

A close look at the harp Gery is holding reveals a fretboard at the bass end. While the patent mentions that the strings over the fretboard could be used "so as to correspond with the melody strings or finger board of a zither or other instrument," the drawing and text of the patent suggest just one string over the fretboard for tuning! If the string is stopped at each of the frets, a complete octave of a chromatic scale can be played and those notes used to tune the forty-nine strings on the harp.

The patent also suggests that slight openings were made in the cover plate over the treble ends of the chord bars. This was to allow marks to be put on the bars indicating "the position to which the bar has been shifted." The bass end cover plate also shows openings in the shape of a lyre to allow for the "ready escape of sound."

Although these features were eliminated from the standard production model concert harps, the design was still sufficiently elaborate to warrant a selling price of $150 in 1895 and $250 in 1896! If the Dolges were

Figure 2:

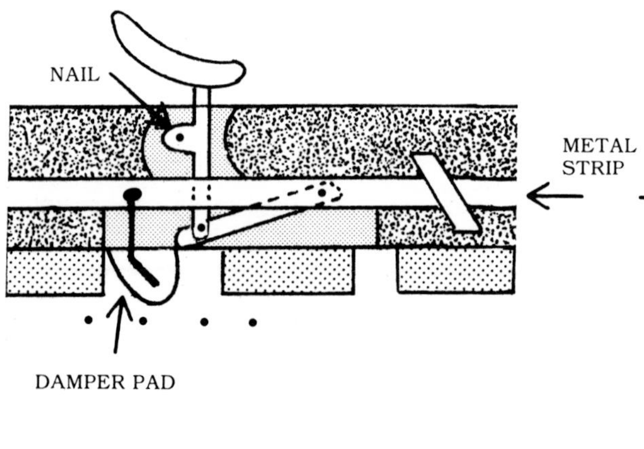

NAIL

METAL STRIP

DAMPER PAD

Figure 3:

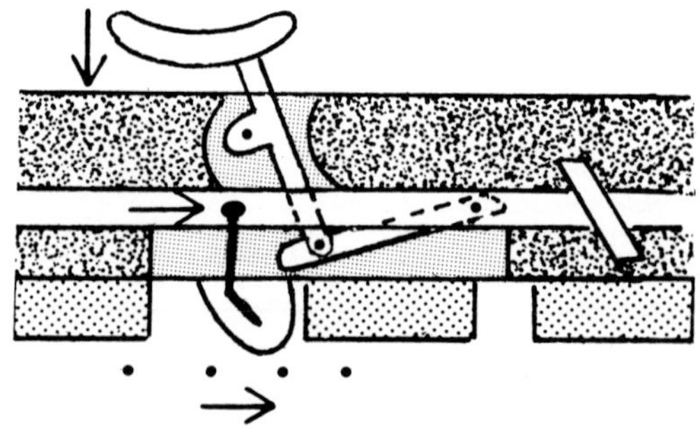

successful in marketing this instrument, it was no doubt due to the massive promotion program they developed to present this model to their dealers and the public. Foremost in this scheme were the concerts performed by Aldis J. Gery with Gilmore's 22nd Regiment Band led by Victor Herbert. These shows and recitals went so far as to inspire the classical composer Xavier Scharwenka to write several selections specifically for this Autoharp model. Even Charles F. Zimmermann, the inventor of the Autoharp, was surprised at the progress of the instrument he had created. The *Music Trade Review* (August 3, 1895) gives the following account of the impact of the concert model harp:

> When the Autoharp with all its interests, passed into the hands of Alfred Dolge & Son, some two years ago, it was a successful musical novelty. No one at that time looked upon the Autoharp as an instrument which had a great future as a musical instrument. Immediately upon the transfer of the manufacturing plant to Dolgeville, experiments were made to perfect the Autoharp. A complete chromatic scale correctly drawn, a body on the lines of the most approved piano construction, a new and ingenious action, resulted in the Concert Autoharp. This instrument has awakened the interest of our leading musicians, and the great artist and composer, Xavier Scharwenka, has composed several selections for it.
>
> Recently Mr. Aldis J. Gery, when on his tour with Gilmore's Band, called upon Mr. Zimmermann, in Philadelphia, and played the Concert Autoharp. The inventor scarcely recognized this perfect instrument, as the "Autoharp idea" had been developed so far beyond his original invention.

Music trade publications made a big to-do over the performances of Aldis Gery. The fervor with which he spoke of this harp and its possibilities as an orchestral instrument was a clear indication of his commitment. His connection with the Dolge Company was no secret, but no one pointed out that one of the reasons for his interest in this instrument was that the inventors of this model were Aldis Gery and Rudolf Dolge!

Freund's Musical Weekly (May 15, 1895) gave this account of the effects of Gery's playing the concert harp in one hundred performances while on tour with Gilmore's Band:

> This trip has done much for the popularity of the Concert Autoharp, and everywhere it went Mr. Gery's performance elicited unbounded enthusiasm from the audience and the most favorable criticisms from the press.
>
> It has been clearly demonstrated what effects the larger sized Concert Autoharp can produce in conjunction with a full band, and a new field — the concert-room — has opened for the instrument which has already achieved such marked popularity in the home.
>
> When we called at the Autoharp studio . . . some time ago, to examine the Concert Autoharps that were at that time almost fresh upon the market, Mr. Barry

Figure 4:

BAR #1 (FAKE SHIFTERS)	LEFT POSITION				CENTER POSITION				RIGHT POSITION			
SHIFTERS USED:	(F#/G♭), A, C, (D#/E♭) Diminished Seventh				G, (A#/B♭), (C#/D♭), E Diminished Seventh				(G#/A♭), B, D, F Diminished Seventh			
	NONE	LF.	RT.	BOTH	NONE	LF.	RT.	BOTH	NONE	LF.	RT.	BOTH
BAR #2	A♭	A♭m	A♭7	A♭m7	A	Am	A7	Am7	A#	A#m	A#7	A#m7
BAR #3	D♭	D♭m	D♭7	D♭m7	D	Dm	D7	Dm7	D#	D#m	D#7	D#m7
BAR #4	G♭	G♭m	G♭7	G♭m7	G	Gm	G7	Gm7	G#	G#m	G#7	G#m7
BAR #5	C♭	C♭m	C♭7	C♭m7	C	Cm	C7	Cm7	C#	C#m	C#7	C#m7
BAR #6	F♭	F♭m	F♭7	F♭m7	F	Fm	F7	Fm7	F#	F#m	F#7	F#m7

Owen, the manager, was brimful of enthusiasm and predicted a wonderful future for the concert instruments. How far his predictions were true the close of the present season of Gilmore's Band fully demonstrates.

Mr. Aldis Gery . . . is a modest, unassuming young man, undeniably talented, and capable of drawing some marvelous effects from his instrument; and he is a hard worker besides. But he will have to look to his laurels now, for the Autoharp has now won its place on the concert stage, and ere long Autoharpists will be as thick as the leaves in Vallombrosa.

The *Presto* (November 28, 1895) went so far as to venture the prediction "that the Autoharp would deprive the guitar, mandolin, and banjo of their popularity. It ought to, for it is as far superior to [those instruments], as an electric light is to a tallow dip."

It did seem that the Autoharp was about to take over the musical world. A record eight thousand Autoharps were sent out in one shipment, and the new and popular #2⅞ model was "selling like hot cakes in winter time." Factory output was five hundred harps per day by the end of 1895. The *Indicator* (November 16, 1895) continues its report:

> The demand for the concert Autoharp has increased so rapidly that it became necessary not long ago to purchase a building opposite the factory and fit it up for the exclusive making of the Concert Autoharp. This work is an art in itself because the Concert Autoharp as a musical instrument is of a higher grade than the other harps and hence in making the Concert Autoharp only the most skilled artisans are employed in the manufacture of the large harp. A new lot of Concert Autoharps, and a fine assortment of instruments they are, are about ready for the trade. They will show some improvements, especially in the action, that will make them superior to any that have been so far put upon the market.

That's all very impressive, but these glowing accounts of the sound of the concert harp and its success in the market place raise more questions than they answer. First, although the concert model harp always is mentioned as the highest-priced model, it's hard to realize just how expensive it was in terms of 1895/96 incomes. *The Historical Statistics of the United States Part 1: Colonial Times to 1970* (published by the U.S. Department of Commerce/Bureau of the Census, Bicentennial Edition, p. 168) gives average annual earnings for all industries and occupations in 1895/1896 as $145/$411. That couldn't leave a lot left over from daily necessities to buy a musical instrument that cost $150/$250. Even the highest-paid workers of the day (unsurprisingly, Executive Department Federal Employees) had yearly incomes of only $1,104/$1,084. The concert model could amount to almost 25% of one's annual income!

Could Dolge possibly have sold enough concert harps to justify an entire building devoted to the exclusive production of this model? It seems unlikely, despite a possible explanation from the *Musical Courier* (March 27, 1895) that "the great increase in orders for large size and expensive Autoharps shows the strides the instrument has made among musicians, as well as music loving people of wealth." It would appear that the key is in the last five words.

But even if there were enough music lovers to spend that much money on an instrument, where are all those concert model harps today? They wouldn't simply have been thrown out in the garbage or burned as firewood if the owner tired of the novelty of the instrument. They were beautiful enough that they would have at least been preserved as art objects, sold to someone else, given to a favorite niece, or as a last resort put away in Aunt Emily's attic. In any case, if they had existed in any quantity, logic dictates that more of them would be around today. The consensus among those persons familiar with the history of the Autoharp is that probably few of these harps were made. The factory building set up for the "exclusive making of the Concert Autoharp" must have been small indeed!

INTERVIEW WITH ALDIS J. GERY

The following interview was conducted for a nineteenth-century publication called *Strings*, which was published in Dolgeville, New York, and apparently was used to let the trade know what was new (and news) at Alfred Dolge & Son Company.

Reprinted in *The Presto* (January 3, 1895), another publication for the music trade, the interview began with an introduction explaining that Mr. Gery had first become "interested in the Autoharp by working for the C. F. Zimmerman [sic] Co., in Philadelphia. He was employed by them when quite young, in the factory at first, making instruments; in fact, he helped to make some of the first instruments which were put on the market. Mr. Gery is also an accomplished violinist and was the leader of an orchestra in Philadelphia."

Your familiarity with the instrument, Mr. Gery, has no doubt, made you enthusiastic concerning it, but is this enthusiasm such as may be shared by any conscientious student of the instrument and its scope?

Oh, yes, yes, indeed. The instrument is so fascinating that even if one begins with one of the smaller instruments he will become so interested that there will be a constant desire to increase his facility and perfect himself in performance.

What can be done, in your opinion, on the smaller instruments; are they susceptible of solo work?

Oh, yes, just as much as the concert harp, save that they are limited, of course, in reference to scale and chords.

Is the concert harp the next thing to the No. 6?

No, we have a No. 7, which comes between, but is not as complete as the concert harp.

The concert harp has as great a variety of chords as a piano, has it?

Oh, yes; every chord in music.

How do you regard it as compared with the grand harp?

It is a different instrument entirely: It is not to be compared with the grand harp at all; it cannot take its place; it is so much an instrument by itself that it will find its own place, I believe.

It is susceptible of being used and it is of value in an orchestra aside from the harp and with the harp?

Yes, indeed.

The concert Autoharp is comparatively a recent development, is it not?

Oh, yes; it only came out last December. I have only been playing the concert Autoharp myself since that time.

Are there a number of people studying it in a careful way and with a view of becoming soloists on the Autoharp?

Oh, yes. We have quite a number of people studying it most enthusiastically. Of course, my familiarity with the smaller instrument gave greater facility with the concert harp, and yet it is so much more complete in itself as to cause me to have to study hard in order to become proficient.

Yes, but does this last expression of opinion conflict with the Messrs. Dolge & Son's statement about the Autoharp being "Easy to play"?

Not at all. It is impossible by the use of the chord bars on a well-tuned instrument to obtain other than a harmony, and so it can be used after a very few months intelligent practice in connection with the instruction book as an accompaniment for simple airs, so that it is in truth "Easy to play." But at the same time, to secure the most elaborate effects in connection with the more elaborate music, the higher grade Autoharps must be used and a degree of proficiency acquired in the use of the instrument which can only be attained by considerable study.

What was your opinion of the success of the experiment at the Academy of Music the other night?

A good impression was certainly made. The musicians, one and all, spoke well of it. They all examined the instrument after I was through playing and were very curious concerning it and seemed to thoroughly admire it.

How did the public receive it?

First rate, it took well.

Mr. Herbert has been correctly quoted in reference to the Autoharp, has he?

Oh, yes, entirely so; he seems to be an enthusiastic believer in the instrument from what he has said.

Let me see, what were his words?

"The Autoharp is a practical musical instrument of unique tone-quality and possessed of every musical advantage."

What about the Autoharp music, the "figure notation" as it is called; is it practicable for a person to study music from this notation alone and become proficient as a general musician?

Oh, yes, for the figure music is also used in connection with the names of the notes on the usual staff, and therefore while learning the one system one is practically acquiring the other. And, by the way, let me say here that I regard the Autoharp as the greatest harmony teacher of any instrument in existence.

Indeed! You mean to say that the variety of chords is such as to very quickly teach music?

Yes, that is the idea.

Did you learn to play the Autoharp from figure music or from the ordinary staff?

I commenced with the figure music on the Autoharp, but before that time I understood the usual music.

Do you consider that figure music is an aid in the development of the Autoharp?

Indeed I do; the notation is so simple and its application to the Autoharp is so perfect that after very little practice accompaniments and even solos can be perfectly learned so as to give pleasure to those who listen, and that too, even on one of the cheaper grade of instruments.

CHAPTER 6

AUTOHARPS 1893 to 1899

Autoharps made by the C. F. Zimmermann Company (The Zimmermann Autoharp Company), Dolgeville, New York. (Includes harps made for the American Autoharp Company, Toronto, Canada.)

MODELS

Harmonette	#2⅞	#6	#72
#1	#3	Parlor Grand	#72⅞
#2	#4	Concert Grand	#73
#2¾	#5	#71	Unknown model number

FEATURES

Logo: Five types. All say "Dolgeville, New York"
Label: Four types.
Holders: Wood. Painted black. Glued or screwed onto soundboard.
Bars: Wood. Painted black.
Buttons: Round, slightly concave, cream-colored celluloid, except #73, which has raised, black wood buttons.
Bar labels: Celluloid.
Music scale: Celluloid. Zimmermann figures for string names.
End cover: Detachable type or none.
Feet: Three brass nailheads.
Music stand holes: Two on slanted edge.
Bridges: Wood. Painted black. Single metal rod inset.
Tuning pins: Angled backward slightly.
Strings: Loop-end strings attach over hitch pins.
Soundboard, back and sides: Natural finish or painted black.
Decorations: Lines painted on natural finishes. Decals on some black harps.
Prices: September 1896 company catalog (or Sears catalog where specified).

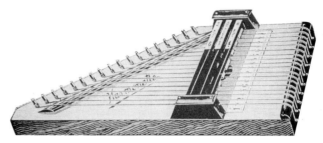

60

Catalog drawing.

18 strings.
3 bars.
3 chords: F, B-flat, C7.

Harmonette model. Note tuning pins all on one diagonal line. Bars not original.

Logo: "Harmonette" painted on the soundboard.
Label: Special "Harmonette" label.
Holders: Natural finish.
Bars: Original bars missing.
End cover: None.
Music stand holes: None.
Bridges: Natural finish.
Soundboard: Natural finish.
Back and sides: Dark stained.
Size: 17 inches by 8¼ inches.
Price: $2.50
Introduced: ca. 1895.
Discontinued: ca. 1897.

Special "Harmonette" label. Says "Patented May 9, '82" at top.

61

62

#1

21 strings.
3 bars.
3 chords: C, F, G7.

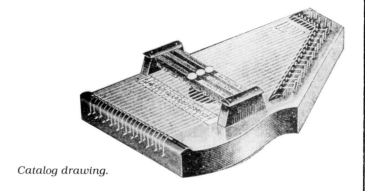

Catalog drawing.

Model #1 with first logo, first label.

Logo: Decal with original patent date.
Label: Script style letters.
End cover: None.
Soundboard: Natural finish.
Back and sides: Black.
Size: 18 inches by 10 inches.
Price: $6.00.
Discontinued: ca. 1897.

First label: Script style letters. Same as last Philadelphia label, but on cream-colored paper (ca. 1893 to early 1895).

63

64

#2

23 strings.
4 bars.
4 chords: C, F, G7, C7.

No example of this model available.
Shown in booklet "How the Autoharp Captured the
Family" (ca. 1893-1894).
Also in Sears catalog 1894. (Price: $3.25.)
Probably discontinued when Model #2⅞ introduced in 1895.
Not in 1896 catalog.

65

First logo: Decal with original patent date (ca. 1893 to mid 1894). This type of logo is clearly shown in the drawing below from "How the Autoharp Captured the Family."

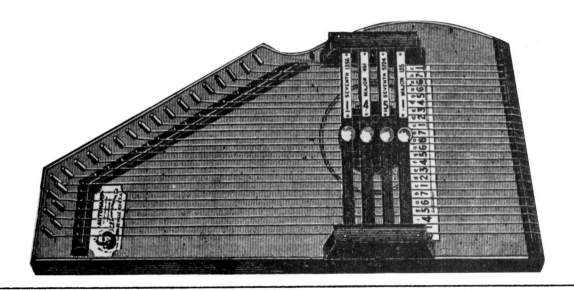

#2¾

23 strings.
5 bars.
5 chords: C, F, B-flat, G7, C7.

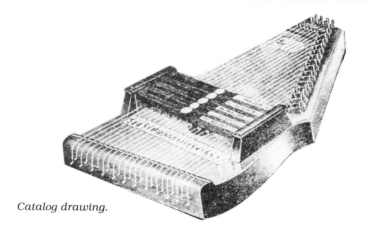

Catalog drawing.

Early model #2¾ with second logo, first label.
Note placement of treble side holder.

Logo: Celluloid plate with dates to July 1894.
Label: Script style letters.
Holders: Glued to soundboard.
Felts: Purple.
End cover: None.
Feet: Pointed brass nailheads.
Soundboard: Natural finish.
Back and sides: Black.
Special features: Harp is wider than earlier Philadelphia model, allowing the treble end holder to be placed to the right of the top bridge, rather than below it.
Size: 18 inches by 10 inches.
Price: $8.00.

Second logo: Celluloid plate with patent dates to July 1894 (ca. mid-1894 to early 1895).

66

67

68

69

Philadelphia Model #2¾ on top of back of early Dolgeville Model #2¾. Note difference in width.

The wider spacing of the holders required longer bars, which became the standard size. Bottom to top: B-flat chord bars for Models #2¾ made in Philadelphia (ca. 1891), Dolgeville (ca. 1895), Boston (ca. 1920), and Jersey City (1964).

70

Holder for Model #2¾. Brass strip holds springs in place. Holder is glued to soundboard as were Philadelphia chord bar holders. Hole in soundboard is from nail for celluloid music scale.

Third logo (below left): Decal with patent dates to July 1894 (ca. early 1895 to late 1895).

Second label (right): Patent dates to December 1894 on cream-colored paper (ca. early 1895 to 1897).

71

72

The C. F. Zimmermann Company made special Autoharps for the American Autoharp Company of Toronto, Canada. The decal of the woman with one breast bared (#1001) must have been too daring, for it was soon changed (by #2155) to a lady in a dress with a more conservative neckline. That decal became the first decal to be used on the Zimmermann Company's own Model #72⅞. Closeup photographs of both decals appear in the color section.

73

Fourth logo: Decal with patent dates to July 1895 (ca. late 1895 to ca. 1897).

Model #2¾ (#1001) with fourth logo, special label.

Logo: Decal with dates to July 1895.
Label: Special for #1001.
Felts: Blue.
Soundboard: Black.
Decorations: Soundboard decal. ''The Favorite'' in gold lettering.
Special features: Back of harp has seven screws spaced evenly along the bottom, curved side, and top edges.

Special label for #1001.

74

75

Fifth logo (left): Black letters on gold background (ca. 1897 to 1899). Catalog drawing (ca. 1898) shows new decal and "The Favorite" on Model #2¾ (below).

76

Model #2¾ with fifth logo, third label. After 1896 Model #2¾ was painted black and became "The Favorite."

Third label (below): "Genuine Zimmermann Autoharp" on cream-colored paper (ca. 1897 to 1898). Note company name now reads "The Zimmermann Autoharp Company" instead of the "C. F. Zimmermann Co."

77

78

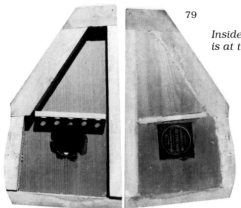

79

Inside a Model #2¾ (left). Note single brace with holes. Lower joint is at the sides.

Very late Model #2¾ (ca. 1898) with fifth logo, fourth label turned sideways (below).

80

Fourth label: Silver letters on black paper (ca. 1898 to 1899).

81

Newer holders had wooden strip to hold springs in place, and holders were attached with long screws running through the holders to the frame.

82

#2⅞

28 strings.
7 bars.
7 chords: C, F, B-flat, G7, C7, Am, Dm.

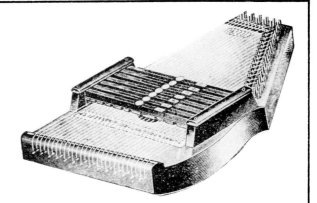

Catalog drawing.

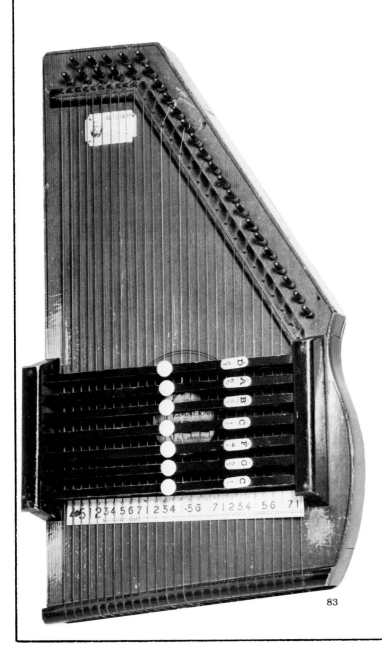

Logo: Celluloid plate with dates to July 1894.
Label: "Genuine Zimmermann Autoharp" on cream-colored paper.
Bar labels: Standard letter names for chords in addition to the Zimmermann figures. Seventh chords say "sept."
End cover: None.
Soundboard: Natural finish.
Size: 20 inches by 12 inches.
Price: $12.50.
Introduced: 1895.
Discontinued: ca. 1897.

Model #2⅞ with second logo, second label from collection of the Smithsonian Institution. Note standard letter names for chords.

83

#3

28 strings.
4 bars, 5 shifters.
9 chords: C, F, B-flat, G, G7, C7, D7, Am, Dm.

Catalog drawing.

No example of this model available.
Shown in "How the Autoharp Captured the Family" (ca. 1893-1894) and in 1896 catalog.
Bars: Shifters change chords.
End cover: Slotted wooden strip in booklet. None in catalog.
Soundboard: Natural finish.
Size: 20 inches by 12 inches.
Price: $17.50
Discontinued: ca. 1898.

Drawing of Model #3 from booklet "How the Autoharp Captured the Family."

#4

28 strings.
5 bars, 6 shifters.
11 chords: C, F, B-flat, G, D,
G7, C7, D7, Am, Gm, Dm.

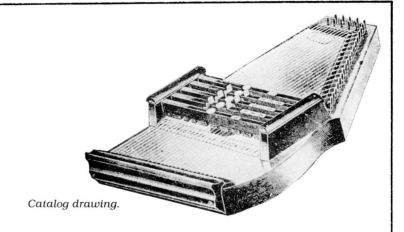

Catalog drawing.

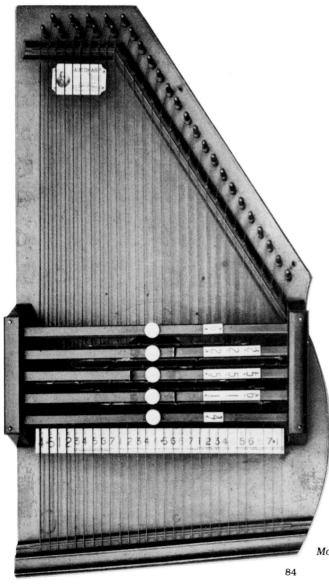

Logo: Celluloid plate with dates to July 1894.
Label: Script style letters.
Bars: Shifters change chords.
Felts: Green.
End cover: Detachable.
Soundboard: Natural finish.
Back and sides: Painted black.
Binding: Inlaid wood.
Size: 21 inches by 12 inches.
Price: $23.00.
Discontinued: ca. 1899.

Model #4 with second logo, first label.

84

#5

28 strings.
5 bars, 8 shifters.
13 chords: C, F, B-flat, G, D, G7, C7,
D7, Am, Gm, Dm, Em, Bm.

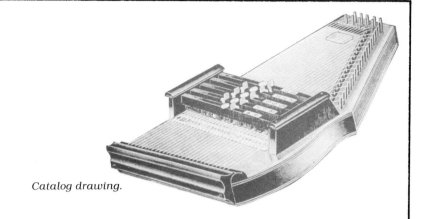

Catalog drawing.

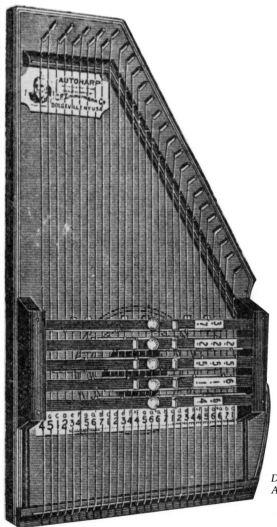

No example of this model available.
Shown in "How the Autoharp Captured the
Family" (ca. 1893-1894) and in 1896 catalog.
Bars: Shifters change chords.
End cover: Slotted wooden strip in booklet.
Detachable in catalog.
Soundboard: Natural finish.
Back and sides: Rosewood veneered or "imitation ebony" (black paint).
Binding: Inlaid wood.
Size: 21 inches by 12 inches.
Price: $28.75.
Discontinued: ca. 1899.

*Drawing of Model #5 from booklet "How the
Autoharp Captured the Family."*

#6

32 strings.
6 bars, 10 shifters.
16 chords: C, F, B-flat, G, D, A, G7,
C7, D7, A7, Am, Gm, Dm, Em, Bm,
C-sharp diminished seventh.

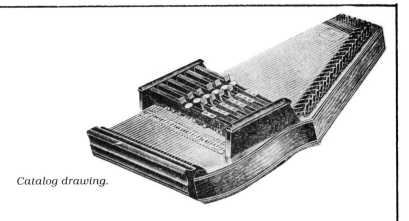

Catalog drawing.

Logo: Decal with original patent date.
Label: Script style letters.
Bars: Shifters change chords.
End cover: Detachable.
Soundboard: Natural finish.
Back and sides: Imitation rosewood.
Binding: Inlaid wood.
Size: 22 inches by 13 inches.
Price: $40.50.

Model #6 with first logo, first label.

85

The back and sides of Model #6 were imitation rosewood. The inlaid edge binding was white maple with a narrow strip of black between.

86

The slotted wooden strip (an extension of the bridge) was replaced by a detachable cover which had to be removed to change strings.

87

Catalog drawing (ca. 1898) shows the words "Modèle de Luxe" on the slanted side. These words also appeared on the Model #6 harps in the Sears catalogs after 1903.

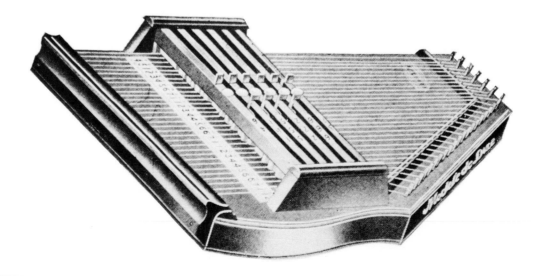

Parlor Grand

39 strings.
10 bars, 13 shifters.
38 chords: C, G, B-flat, G, D, A, E, B, G7, C7, D7, A7, E7, B7, Am, Gm, Dm, Em, Bm, Cm, and a number of compound chords.

No example of this model available.
Shown in 1896 catalog.
Bars: Seven bars with shifters to change chords. Three thin bars probably made "compound chords" (diminished seventh chords?).
End cover: Detachable.
Music stand holes: None.
Soundboard: Very choice grained red wood.
Sides: Mahogany or birdseye maple.
Binding: Inlaid wood.
Special features: Hand-rest.
Size: 24½ inches by 15½ inches.
Price: $125.00 with wood case.
$170.00 with fine soleleather case.
Introduced: ca. 1895.

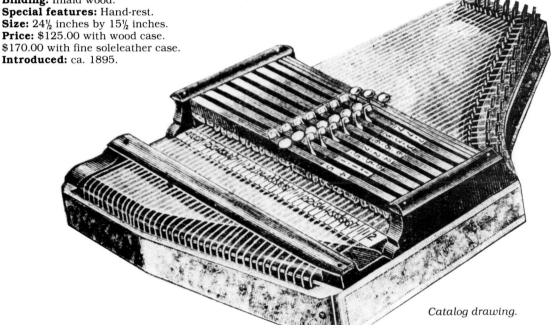

Catalog drawing.

The catalog description states, "This instrument is the largest and finest Autoharp made, with the exception of the Concert size. It is designed to produce the finest musical tone, and no expense has been spared to achieve that result.

"The Parlor Grand is now used by the students of five leading colleges: University of Pennsylvania, Amherst, Williams, Princeton, and Columbia, in connection with their regular mandolin, banjo and guitar clubs. As a solo instrument it has proved an enormous success wherever played by Mr. Aldis J. Jerry [sic], the Autoharp soloist with Gilmore's famous band. As an accompaniment instrument it stands unrivaled, the great facility with which it can be played by any one, even those who are not especially gifted in a musical way, its sweet tone and wonderful volume, commend it at once to every lover of music."

Concert Grand

49 strings.
6 bars, 10 shifters.
60 chords: All major, minor, dominant seventh, minor seventh, and diminished seventh chords.

Catalog drawing.

Logo: Decal with dates to July 1894.
Label: Dates to December 1894.
Holders: Birdseye maple.
Bars: Shifters change chords. (Two shifters "fake.") Bars move to three positions each.
Felts: Green.
Shifter pads: Sheepskin or buckskin.
Bar labels: None.
Music scale: Two strips, one above chord bars. Resembles keyboard.
End cover: Detachable.
Music stand holes: None.
Soundboard: Spruce. Natural finish.
Back and sides: Birdseye maple.
Binding: Edges inlaid.
Special features: Hand-rest.
Size: 30 inches by 20½ inches.
Price: $250.00.
Introduced: 1894.
Discontinued: 1899.

See Chapter 5 for complete description.

59

Concert Grand Autoharp with third logo, second label at Gryphon Stringed Instruments, Palo Alto, California.

#71

20 strings.
3 bars.
3 chords: C, F, G7.

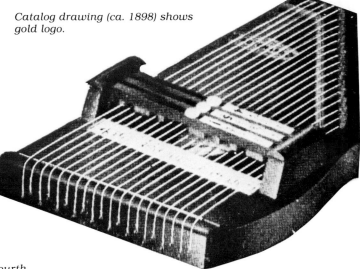

Catalog drawing (ca. 1898) shows gold logo.

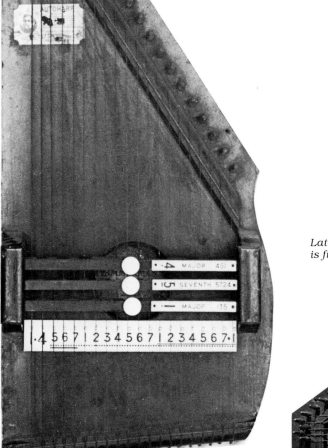

Very early Model #71 with fourth logo, second label from the collection of the Musical Museum, Deansboro, N.Y.

Logo: Decal with dates to July 1895.
Label: Dates to December 1894.
Felts: Green.
End cover: None.
Soundboard, back and sides: Black.
Special features: No bridge pins on upper bridge.
Size: 17¼ inches by 7½ inches.
Prices: (1899 Sears catalog) $1.95.
Introduced: ca. 1897, probably replacing Model #1. (Not in 1896 catalog.)

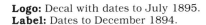

Later Model #71 with fifth logo, third label. (The music scale is from a Model #2¾ and does not belong to this harp.)

88   89

#72

32 strings.
6 bars, 10 shifters.
16 chords: C, F, B-flat, G, D,
A, G7, C7, D7, A7, Am, Gm,
Dm, Em, Bm, and C-sharp
diminished seventh.

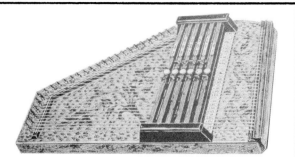

Catalog drawing.

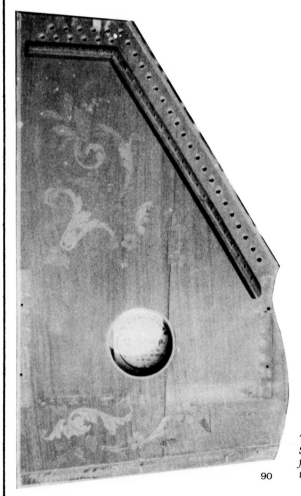

Logo: None.
Label: Script style letters.
Bars: Shifters change chords.
End cover: Detachable.
Music stand holes: None.
Soundboard: Natural finish with marquetry.
Binding: Inlaid wood.
Decorations: Floral design created by marquetry (wood veneer inlaid into soundboard).
Size: 22 inches by 13 inches.
Price: Unknown.
Introduced: ca. 1894.
Discontinued: By 1896.

This special Model #72 with first label was shown in the September 1896 catalog, but was not offered for sale. Except for the marquetry it is the same as the Model #6. A closeup of the marquetry design is in the color section.

90

#72⅞

32 strings.
8 bars.
8 chords: C, F, B-flat,
G7, C7, A7, Dm, Gm.

The griffin decal.

91

Logo: Gold decal.
Label: ''Genuine Zimmermann Autoharp'' on cream-colored paper.
Felts: Green.
Bar labels: Standard letter names for chords in addition to the Zimmermann figures.
End cover: None.
Soundboard, back and sides: Black.
Decorations: Fancy decals on soundboard. (All in color section.)
Size: 21 inches by 10½ inches.
Price: (1899 Sears catalog) $5.45.
Introduced: ca. 1897 (replacing Model #2⅞).

The most common examples of the Model #72⅞ have the fifth logo, the third label, and the griffin decal.

92

93

The earliest known Model #72⅞ with the fourth logo, second label. Still visible on the soundboard is the outline of the same decal that was used on the special Model #2¾ (#2155 and #6693) made for the American Autoharp Company.

A very late Model #72⅞ with the fifth logo, fourth label. This decal would be used again in the twentieth century by the Phonoharp Company and by Oscar Schmidt-International.

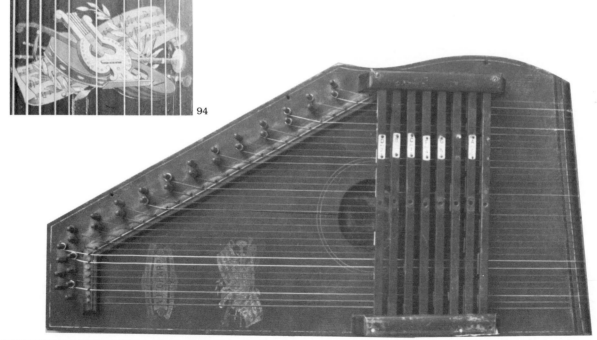

94

95

#73

37 strings.
12 bars.
12 chords: C, F, B-flat, G, G7,
C7, D7, A7, E7, Am, Gm, Dm.

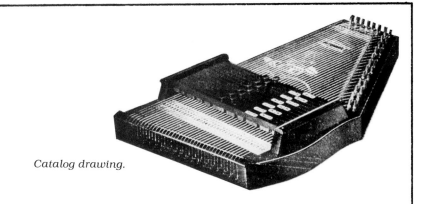

Catalog drawing.

Logo: Gold decal.
Label: "Genuine Zimmermann Autoharp"
on black paper.
Holders: Thin wood slats between bars.
Bars: Placed close together.
Buttons: Raised, black wood. Arranged in
two rows.
Felts: Green.
Bar labels: Standard letter names for
chords in addition to the Zimmermann
figures.
Music scale: Octaves are indicated.
End cover: Detachable.
Soundboard, back and sides: Black.
Decorations: Soundboard decal. (In color
section.)
Size: 21 inches by 11¾ inches.
Price: (1900 Sears catalog) $6.95.
Introduced: ca. 1898.

*All known examples of Model #73 have the fifth
logo, fourth label.*

*The larger Model #73 required two interior braces,
both drilled with holes similar to the brace in the
Model #2¾.*

96

97   98

Model number unknown

41 strings.
13 bars.
48 chords: All major, minor, dominant seventh, and diminished seventh chords.

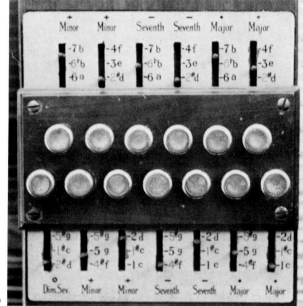

The chord bar mechanism showing three positions for each chord bar.

Logo: Decal with dates to July 1895.
Label: Dates to December 1894.
Bars: Move to three positions.
Music scale: Has standard music scale in addition to the Zimmermann figures.
End cover: Detachable.
Music stand holes: None.
Soundboard: Natural finish.
Binding: Inlaid wood.
Special features: Wooden chord bar cover. Wider frame (to allow bars to move into three positions). Label sideways. This model does not appear in any catalogs, but several examples exist. It may have been a limited production model or the Model #7 mentioned in the interview with Aldis Gery.

Summary: Autoharps 1893 to 1899

Autoharps made by the C. F. Zimmermann Company (The Zimmermann Autoharp Company), Dolgeville, New York. (Includes harps made for the American Autoharp Company, Toronto, Canada.)

Models: Harmonette, #1, #2, #2¾, #2⅞, #3, #4, #5, #6, Parlor Grand, Concert Grand, #71, #72, #72⅞, #73, one unknown model number. Special models #2¾ made for the American Autoharp Company.

Introduced: #1, #2, #2¾, #3, #4, #5, and #6 from Philadelphia, 1893. Concert Grand and #72, ca. 1894. Harmonette, #2⅞, and Parlor Grand, 1895. #71 and #72⅞, ca. 1897. #73, ca. 1898. American Autoharp Company models, ca. 1896-1897.

Discontinued: #2, ca. 1895. #72, by 1896. Harmonette, #1, and #2⅞, ca. 1897. #3, ca. 1898. #4, #5, and Concert Grand, ca. 1899.

Logo: 1) Decal with only the original patent date. 2) Celluloid plate with dates to July 1894. 3) Decal with dates to July 1894. 4) Decal with dates to July 1895. 5) Black letters on gold decal. Logos #1-4 say "C. F. Zimmermann Company." Logo #5 says "Zimmermann Autoharp Company." All say "Dolgeville, New York."

Label: 1) Script style letters, same style as last Philadelphia label, on cream-colored paper. No company name or place of manufacture. 2) Patent dates listed to December 1894, cream-colored paper. "C. F. Zimmermann Company" and city given. 3) "Genuine Zimmermann Autoharp" cream-colored paper. Company name changed to "Zimmermann Autoharp Company." 4) "Genuine Zimmermann Autoharp," black paper.

Holders: Wood. Painted black or natural finish. Early ones glued to soundboard, later attached by long screws. Model #73 has thin slats between the bars.

Bars: Wood. Painted black or natural finish. Some have metal shifters to change chords. Some move to three positions.

Buttons: Round, slightly concave, cream-colored celluloid arranged in single row. Model #73 has raised, black wood buttons arranged in two rows.

Felts: Purple, green, or blue.

Shifter pads: Sheepskin or buckskin.

Bar labels: Celluloid strips. Some have both Zimmermann figures and letter names for the chords.

Music scale: Celluloid with Zimmermann figures for string names. Fancier models have variations.

End cover: Smaller models have none. Others have detachable type.

Feet: Three pointed brass nailheads on standard models.

Music stand holes: Two holes on the slanted edge of the harp on most standard models. More expensive models have no holes.

Bridges: Wood. Painted black or natural finish. One metal rod inset.

Tuning pins: Angled backward slightly.

Strings: Loop-end strings wrap around lower end and attach over hitch pins.

Soundboards: Natural finish or "imitation ebony" (black paint).

Back and sides: Most painted black. Some have natural finish.

Binding: Inlaid wood edges on more expensive models.

Decorations: Varied. Some have fancy decals on the soundboard.

Special features: Parlor Grand and Concert Grand have hand-rests. Model #71 has no bridge pins.

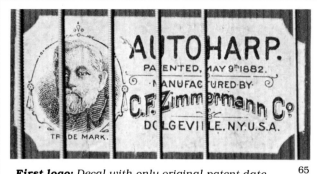

First logo: *Decal with only original patent date (ca. 1893 to mid-1894). Note company name is "C.F. Zimmermann Company."* 65

Second logo: *Celluloid plate with patent dates to July 1894 (ca. mid-1894 to early 1895).* 67

Third logo: *Decal with patent dates to July 1894 (ca. early 1895 to late 1895).* 71

Fourth logo: *Decal with patent dates to July 1895 (ca. late 1895 to 1897).* 73

Fifth logo: *Gold decal without patent dates (ca. 1897 to 1899). Company name is changed to "Zimmermann Autoharp Company."*

76

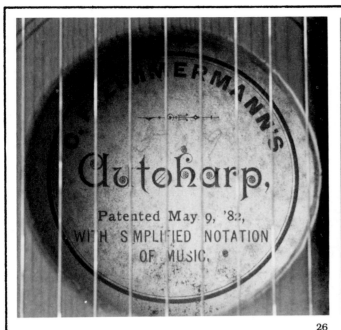

26

72

First label: *Script style letters on cream-colored paper (ca. 1893 to early 1895).*

Second label: *Patent dates to December 1894 on cream-colored paper (ca. early 1895 to 1897). Note company name is "C.F. Zimmermann Company."*

Third label: *"Genuine Zimmermann Autoharp" on cream-colored paper (ca. 1897 to 1898). Company name is changed to "Zimmermann Autoharp Company."*

Fourth label: *"Genuine Zimmermann Autoharp" in silver letters on black paper (ca. 1898 to 1899).*

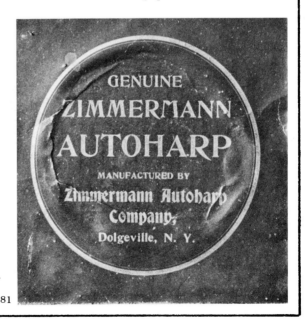

78   81

101

Oscar Schmidt

## CHAPTER 7

THE PHONOHARP COMPANY AND
INTERNATIONAL MUSICAL CORPORATION

> In presenting this Catalogue we feel that the Zimmerman [sic] Autoharp needs no special introduction. The instrument has been well-known for many years. It is identified by a gilt, black-lettered label near the upper end, bearing the name of the Company and the trademark. Be sure to get the genuine "Autoharp" and thus be assured of satisfaction.
> Catalog of the Phonoharp Company,
> East Boston, Massachusetts

After the Dolgeville Autoharp factory closed in 1899, the Autoharp entered a dormant period of about ten years. Autoharps could still be purchased through the Sears catalogs during this time, but the number of available models diminished until by 1910 only three models were offered in the catalog: the #2¾ (five-bar), the #72⅞ (eight-bar), and the #73 (twelve-bar). Probably the Autoharp continued being listed all these years because there was a substantial 1899 inventory and/or a dramatic drop in sales.[1]

The once-popular Autoharp did not easily fade into obscurity, however, for sometime around 1910, the Phonoharp Company of Boston, Massachusetts, began to make Autoharps once again.[2] The Phonoharp Company had been incorporated on April 27, 1892, in Maine, where it did business both in Berwick and Portland. Within a year the company had opened offices in Boston, moving into its factory at 150 Liverpool Street in 1897. The Phonoharp Company manufactured a variety of zither-type instruments, including the Phonoharp and the more popular Columbia Zither. Later additions included the Marxophone, the

Celestophone, and the Pedoplane-brand velodipede. Many of these items can be found advertised in magazines and mail-order catalogs right beside the Autoharp.

Exactly how Phonoharp secured the rights to the Autoharp is unknown, but the process involved some familiar names. After buying the trademark from Charles Zimmermann, Alfred Dolge transferred the trademark registration filed under his own name to the C. F. Zimmermann Company on February 7, 1894. However, when the trademark was later reregistered in 1927, the list of previous owners comprised C. F. Zimmermann, Alfred Dolge, the C. F. Zimmermann Company, Theodore Roth, and the Phonoharp Company. The key name here may very well be Roth, who headed the business department for the C. F. Zimmermann Company.

Roth was very active in the C. F. Zimmermann Company. His signature appears on several company documents, and he is the co-owner of one of the company's patents. Apparently he obtained the rights to the Autoharp trademark after the failure of the company in 1899, although how he came into its possession is not known. Roth does seem to be the likely connection between the C. F. Zimmermann Company and the Phonoharp Company, however, since he moved from Dolgeville to Boston.

In a 1962 interview with Mr. E. Stone, a ninety-two-year-old resident of Dolgeville, A. Doyle Moore asked about Roth. Stone recalled that after the Autoharp company closed, Roth went to some "felt works in

Boston."[3] Although the 1927 registration of the trademark states that the mark "has been continuously used . . . since on or about May 9, 1882," there is no evidence to indicate that Roth actually ever produced any Autoharps himself. Eleanor Franz seems to agree: "I doubt that Roth ever made autoharps after leaving here, but did go to Boston to work in a felt company."[4] However it happened, the Autoharp trademark passed from the C. F. Zimmermann Company to the Phonoharp Company through Theodore Roth.[5]

Phonoharp registered the trademark in its name on March 9, 1911, in California (#4775). Why it chose to register the Autoharp name in California rather than with the U.S. Patent and Trademark Office is unknown, but it probably had something to do with Alfred Dolge's starting his new business there.[6]

A manufacturer's catalog shows the new Phonoharp-brand Autoharps, which are the same five basic models as were offered by

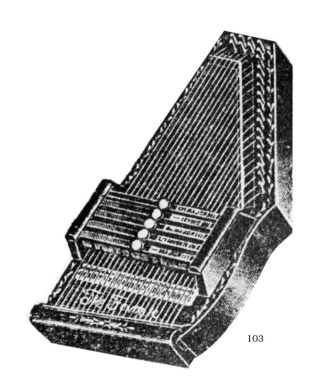

103

Wards catalog, Spring-Summer 1918. Note the flower and vine pattern around the edge.

102

The building at 150 Liverpool Street, East Boston, was occupied by the Phonoharp Company from 1897 to 1926. This photograph was taken in 1983.

Dolge: the #71 (three-bar), the #2¾ (five-bar), the #72⅞ (eight-bar), the #73 (twelve-bar), and the #6 (six bars with shifters). The Parlor Grand model was available by custom order only, but no new standard models were added during the Phonoharp years, possibly because the Autoharp was only one of many products sold by this company.[7] Only one new Autoharp patent was obtained during the years in Boston.

After 1916 both the Sears-Roebuck and Montgomery Ward catalogs offered three models of Phonoharp Autoharps with five, eight, and twelve bars. Although these three models continued to sell, the Autoharp did not regain its former popularity. In time, space in the catalogs began to be devoted more to the other Phonoharp instruments, and less to the Autoharp. The eight-bar Autoharp was discontinued in the early twenties, and by the mid-twenties the Autoharp had disappeared completely from the catalogs.[8] For the next fifteen years most Autoharp sales were made by door-to-door salesmen.[9]

Phonoharp duplicated other efforts of the earlier manufacturer of the Autoharp. For example, they continued to use Robin Tracy's music arranged for Autoharp, which was contained in the instruction book packaged with each instrument. For the #6 model the book was the *Zimmermann Instructor* and for the other models *Tracy's Improved Method for Autoharp*. The description of the contents of the book for the #2¾ model is identical to the contents of *The Zimmermann Autoharp Instructor* (subtitled "arranged in connection with the Zimmermann System of Figure Music for the Zimmermann Autoharp") by R. S. Tracy, for which no publisher or facts of publication are given. Since all the Dolgeville music bears the name of Alfred Dolge & Son and printed matter from Oscar Schmidt-International always has Zimmermann's name spelled with only one "n," the latter instructor was most likely published during the Phonoharp period. Phonoharp itself was probably the publisher.

Interestingly, it was the Phonoharp Company's error that resulted in the misspelling of Zimmermann's name for so many years. The early Phonoharp Autoharp models had the Zimmermann name on them twice, once in the logo on the soundboard and once on the label in the soundhole. The logo had the correct spelling, but the label had the name with the single "n." Either this went

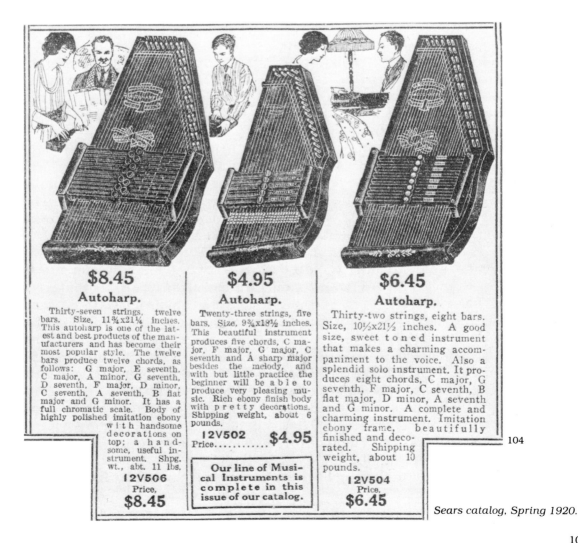

$8.45

Autoharp.

Thirty-seven strings, twelve bars. Size, 11¾x21¼ inches. This autoharp is one of the latest and best products of the manufacturers and has become their most popular style. The twelve bars produce twelve chords, as follows: G major, E seventh, C major, A minor, G seventh, D seventh, F major, D minor, C seventh, A seventh, B flat major and G minor. It has a full chromatic scale. Body of highly polished imitation ebony with handsome decorations on top; a handsome, useful instrument. Shpg. wt., abt. 11 lbs.
12V506
Price,
$8.45

$4.95

Autoharp.

Twenty-three strings, five bars. Size, 9¾x18½ inches. This beautiful instrument produces five chords, C major, F major, G major, C seventh and A sharp major besides the melody, and with but little practice the beginner will be able to produce very pleasing music. Rich ebony finish body with pretty decorations. Shipping weight, about 6 pounds.

12V502 **$4.95**
Price............

Our line of Musical Instruments is complete in this issue of our catalog.

$6.45

Autoharp.

Thirty-two strings, eight bars. Size, 10½x21½ inches. A good size, sweet toned instrument that makes a charming accompaniment to the voice. Also a splendid solo instrument. It produces eight chords, C major, G seventh, F major, C seventh, B flat major, D minor, A seventh and G minor. A complete and charming instrument. Imitation ebony frame, beautifully finished and decorated. Shipping weight, about 10 pounds.

12V504
Price,
$6.45

104

Sears catalog, Spring 1920.

Instruction book, ca. 1925, probably published by the Phonoharp Company.

unnoticed by the company or it was simply not regarded as serious enough to correct by reprinting all the labels. Then the Phonoharp Company changed the logo from 'The Zimmermann Autoharp" to " The Original Autoharp." Now the only place the name appeared was on the label where it was spelled incorrectly, and from that time on the name was consistently misspelled on most Autoharps. In fact, the name is still frequently misspelled.

Despite the careless error and the lack of any new models, the Phonoharp Company did leave its mark on the development of the Autoharp. By concentrating on just a few models, it was able to make some improvements in the design. All models except the three-bar #71 were given end pin covers, for example, and both the covers and the soundboards were decorated with decals and gold-leaf logos. Models #72⅞ and #73 sported the special decal found on the last Dolgeville model #72⅞. This decal also was used on most of Phonoharp's other instruments (e.g., the Marxophone) and has come to be identified as the "Phonoharp" decal, despite its Dolgeville origin.

During this time the Autoharp gained a solid foothold in the mountain and rural areas of the southern and eastern seaboard states.[10] Still available through catalogs, the instrument found a place in the chruch, in the schools, and in the home, where music was an important form of family entertainment. Social events would invariably include music, and the ease with which the Autoharp could be played enabled everyone to join in.

In the mid-twenties and the thirties a series of corporate changes occurred which eventually brought the Autoharp into the hands of its current owners. The first was in 1926 when the International Muscial Corporation was formed on April 26th by Alfred F. McCabe, William Banker, and John R. Turner. One day later the shares in the corporation were transferred to Oscar Schmidt, his son, Walter Schmidt, William A. Copeland, and Harold G. Finney.

Oscar Schmidt already owned Oscar Schmidt, Inc. (incorporated March 31, 1911), which manufactured zithers, guitars, banjos, mandolins, and other stringed instruments, and Copeland and Finney were officers in the Phonoharp Company. This was not a merger of the two corporations, however, but the formation of an entirely new corporation. Although both Oscar Schmidt, Inc., and the Phonoharp Company continued to exist in their own right, the

Phonoharp Company did little or no business on its own after the creation of International Musical Corporation. The Phonoharp Company was finally dissolved by the Supreme Judicial Court of the State of Maine on November 5, 1928, by the petition of Harold G. Finney. Oscar Schmidt continued to manufacture guitars, banjos, etc., and actually did much of the mill work for the instrument bodies under contract to the new International Musical Corporation.

The articles of incorporation for International Musical Corporation state its object:

> To manufacture, purchase or otherwise acquire, to import, export, lease, sell, and generally deal in and with, both wholesale and retail, talking machines, phonographs, graphophones, gramophones, pianos, player pianos, automatic pianos, organs, hand organs, pipe organs, zithers, Hawaiian art violins, ukelins, autoharps, calliopes and any and all other sound reproducing instruments, whether operated by hand, by electricity, mechanically, by means of pedals or otherwise.

> To engage in and conduct a general phonographic and talking machine supply business and especially to manufacture or acquire by purchase, lease or otherwise to dispose of by sale, lease, or otherwise cylinder and disc records, music rolls, or other devices for recording sound, whether manufactured of paper, fibre, metal, composition or combination of materials and all supplies, appliances, apparatus, attachments, parts, accessories, machinery or other articles necessary or convenient for use in connection with phonographs, gramophones, talking machines, pianos, organs and all other sound producing and reproducing machines and devices.

The two stringed-instrument manufacturers were obviously ready to ride with the popular tide of the day. The Autoharps, zithers, and other zither-type instruments were still to be sold, but the emphasis is clearly on the newer and more successful talking machines.

The first board meeting of the International Musical Corporation was held on May 1, 1926. William Copeland was elected

Prints made from the original metal plates, now in the collection of Oscar Schmidt-International, Inc.: Model #71 (three chord) and Model #72⅞ (eight chord).

chairman of the board; Oscar Schmidt, president; Walter Schmidt, vice president; and Harold Finney, treasurer. (At a later date Finney also became secretary.) The meeting was held in the Oscar Schmidt, Inc., offices at 87 Ferry Street, Jersey City, New Jersey. The officers voted to establish and maintain an office of the corporation here as well as the registered office at Hoboken Factory Buildings, Fifteenth and Bloomfield Streets in Hoboken, New Jersey.[11]

Oscar Schmidt and William Copeland, who were the major stockholders, had entered into a contract on January 27, 1926, in which they agreed to combine their two businesses, which was immediately done at this first board meeting. The Phonoharp Company sold and transferred "all the patents and applications therefor, and copyrights used in and relating to its business," and Oscar Schmidt, Inc., sold and transferred "that part of its business which consists in the manufacture of zithers of all descriptions, Hawaiian Art Violins and accessories therefor, and publishing and selling certain books for use in connection therewith, as well as the trade-marks, copyrights, letters patent and applications therefor relating to said business" to International Musical Corporation.

Specifically, Phonoharp transferred twenty-eight patents (including its one Autoharp patent) and the trademark registrations for "Autoharp," "Columbia," "Celestophone," "Marxophone," and "Pedoplane." The transfer document cites U.S. trademark registrations for the last four trademarks, and the California registration for the Autoharp, making it clear that Phonoharp never obtained a U.S. trademark registration for the Autoharp. Oscar Schmidt, Inc., transferred several zither and stringed instrument patents, but retained the main part of the business dealing in guitars, banjos, mandolins, and ukuleles, including such well-known trade names as "Stella," "Sovereign," and "La Scala."

Little is known about William Copeland, the top man at the new International Musical Corporation. He was not one of the original men involved in the incorporation of the Phonoharp Company but by 1909 was on its board of directors as treasurer. He must have risen to the top position on the board to be the one to negotiate the 1926 business deal with Oscar Schmidt.[12]

Oscar Schmidt was a German immigrant who had come to the United States after going bankrupt as a bookbinder in Germany. He first went into music publishing and later started a retail music business. Eventually he went into the manufacturing of musical instruments, and by the time he helped form International Musical Corporation he owned seven factories in the United States and abroad. He had eleven children with his first wife, but only four survived: his son, Walter, and three daughters: Hanna, Clara, and Elsa.[13]

As with many new businesses, the first year for International Musical Corporation showed a loss, but by the middle of 1927 things were looking brighter. The company had cut back on the quantity of instruments produced from thirty-one models requiring twenty-five different body styles to eighteen models requiring only fourteen different bodies. Most of these instrument bodies were supplied by Oscar Schmidt, Inc., and Finney reported at an April meeting that there had been a "vast improvement in delivery of zither bodies by Oscar Schmidt, Inc." and commented "upon the extra fine quality and workmanship, this together with the prompt deliveries being very satisfactory."

One of the "zither bodies" was surely the Autoharp, but it's likely that few Autoharps were produced. Only one Autoharp by International Musical Corp. is included in this study, a five-bar model #2¾.[14] Its soundboard logo, the same design as the Phonoharp logo, says "International Musical Corporation," and the inside label lists the place of manufacture as Hoboken, New Jersey. No new Autoharp patents were issued to this corporation. The closest thing was a "stringed instrument" (Patent #1,799,172 issued April 7, 1931) that bears a remarkable resemblance to the future Guitaro (patented by Oscar Schmidt-International in the mid-sixties).

In the last four months of 1927 business began to decline and production decreased in volume. The company did manage to show a profit in 1927, however, but although several new instruments were being developed for 1928, the outlook for the coming year was not very promising. Some in-house quarreling began late in the year, which was to drag on for several years. There were accusations of overcharges on the cost of the mill work done by Oscar Schmidt, Inc. In March 1929 International Musical Corp. considered initiating a suit against Oscar Schmidt, Inc., "for the purpose of determining the reasonableness and exactness of the cost of the mill work supplied by Oscar Schmidt, Inc. to this concern during the years 1926-1927-1928." This March 28 board meeting was the last one attended by Oscar Schmidt himself.

Nineteen twenty-nine was a devastating year for International Musical Corporation and for Oscar Schmidt, Inc. Not only did the stock market crash in October, plunging the country into the Great Depression, but Oscar Schmidt died while on a business trip to Czechoslovakia. It is ironic that the man whose name is so closely associated with the Autoharp today died several years before the name "Oscar Schmidt" was to appear on the instrument.

Oscar Schmidt's shares in International Musical Corporation went to his son, Walter, and Oscar Schmidt, Inc., was held in trust by the bank on behalf of Oscar Schmidt's second wife, many years his junior. She was to be supported by the company's earnings until her death, at which time the shares would be inherited by Schmidt's son.[15]

What was generally referred to in the board meeting minutes in 1929 and 1930 as "the Oscar Schmidt, Inc., overhead dispute" continued into 1931. On December 30, 1931, the board voted to dissolve International Musical Corporation and join with Oscar Schmidt, Inc. to form another new

corporation. Oscar Schmidt-International Corporation was incorporated on December 31, 1931, with offices at the 87 Ferry Street, Jersey City, New Jersey, address of Oscar Schmidt, Inc. The new company took over the zither-making business of the International Musical Corporation, while Oscar Schmidt, Inc., continued its guitar/banjo/mandolin business.

Oscar Schmidt, Inc., managed to survive the collapse of the bank that held it in trust, but the Schmidt estate dwindled considerably.[16] The company that had been one of the world's premier guitar makers in the twenties finally fell apart in the thirties and was forced to sell the guitar business (with trademarks "Stella" and "Sovereign") to the Harmony Company.[17] Oscar Schmidt, Inc., finally was dissolved on May 18, 1937.

Oscar Schmidt-International Corp. began making zithers in 1932, and although recovery from the dormant and transition years would be slow, in the next fifty years the Autoharp was to stage a comeback.

106

The popularity of the original Carter Family helped bring the Autoharp back into vogue. Sara Carter's harp is a Phonoharp Model #72⅞.

## CHAPTER 8

AUTOHARPS 1910 to 1931

Autoharps made by the Phonoharp Company, Boston, Massachusetts (1910 to 1926), and the International Musical Corporation, Hoboken, New Jersey (1926 to 1931).

MODELS

#71	#73
#2¾	#6
#72⅞	Parlor Grand

FEATURES

Logo: Black letters on gold background, similar to last Dolgeville design. Two Phonoharp logos. One International Musical Corporation logo.

Label: Gold letters on black paper. Zimmermann name misspelled. Same design used for International Musical Corporation. Both give company name and place of manufacture.

Holders: Wood. Painted black. Attached with screws.

Bars: Wood. Painted black.

Buttons: Round, slightly concave, cream-colored celluloid, except #73, which has raised, black wood buttons.

Bar labels: Celluloid.

Music scale: Gold decal with Zimmermann figures for string names.

End cover: Detachable type, except #71, which has no cover.

Feet: Three brass nailheads.

Music stand holes: Two on slanted edge.

Bridges: Wood. Painted black. Upper bridge has one metal rod inset. Lower bridge has two rods.

Tuning pins: Angled backward slightly.

Strings: Loop-end strings attach over hitch pins.

Frame: Phonoharp models have lower joint on the sides of the harp. International Musical Corporation models have lower joint on the bottom.

Soundboard, back and sides: Painted black.

Decorations: Decals on some models.

Prices: Company catalog, ca. 1912 (or Sears catalog where specified).

#71

20 strings.
3 bars.
3 chords: C, F, G7.

107

Second logo: "The Original Autoharp" (ca. 1917 to 1926). Note that the #71 harp still has no bridge pins.

Logo: "The Original Autoharp."
Label: Standard #71.
Felts: Green.
End cover: None.
Special features: No bridge pins.
Size: 17¼ inches by 8¼ inches.
Price: $2.50.
Discontinued: ca. 1918-1919.

Model #71 with second logo. Note music scale is now a gold decal. This was the only Phonoharp model made without an end cover.

108

#2¾

23 strings.
5 bars.
5 chords: C, F, B-flat, G7, C7.

Catalog drawing.

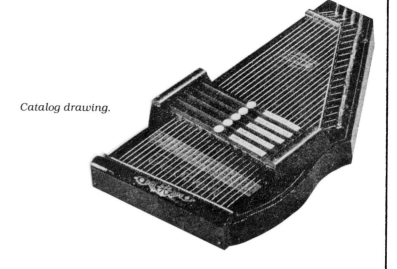

Logo: "The Zimmermann Autoharp."
Label: Standard #2¾.
Felts: Green and purple.
End cover: First type of decal.
Decorations: "The Favorite." Early models with first logo have a delicate flower and vine pattern around the outer edge.
Size: 17¾ inches by 9¾ inches.
Price: $4.00.

Model #2¾ with first logo (ca. 1910 to 1917) and first end cover decal. "Zimmermann" is spelled correctly. Note flower and vine design at edge.

110

111

109

113

Interior of Model #71 shows crude brace made of wood strip with two small blocks glued to it. The joint between the lower frame piece and the side pieces is still on the side of the harp.

112

Labels inside the soundhole have Zimmermann's name misspelled with a single "n." It would be misspelled for years to come.

114

115

Phonoharp added a second metal rod below the lower bridge to hold the strings above the wood surface.

Model #2¾ with second logo, third end cover decal. The flower and vine pattern has been replaced by a single gold line.

116

#72⅞

32 strings.
8 bars.
8 chords: C, F, B-flat,
G7, C7, A7, Gm, Dm.

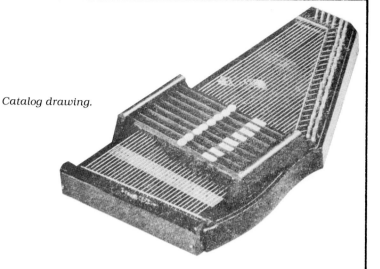

Catalog drawing.

Logo: "The Zimmermann Autoharp."
Label: Standard #72⅞.
Decorations: Soundboard decal. (In color section.) Flower and vine pattern.
Size: 21 inches by 10½ inches.
Price: (1918 Sears catalog) $6.25.
Discontinued: ca. 1922.

Early Model #72⅞ with first logo. End cover decal has worn off or end cover replaced. One chord bar is missing. Soundboard decal is the same as that used on the last Dolgeville Model #72⅞. Purchased ca. 1910 from Sears catalog.

Played by Sara Carter with the original Carter Family, this harp is on exhibit in the Country Music Hall of Fame and Museum.

117

111

Early models with first logo and flower and vine pattern have the first type of end cover decal (above and right).

118

Logo: "The Original Autoharp."
Label: Standard #72⅞.
Bar labels: Zimmermann figures and letter names for chords.
End cover: Second type of decal.
Decorations: Soundboard decal. (In color section.) Single gold line around edge.

Later Model #72⅞ with second logo, second end cover decal (left and below). Note bar labels have letter names for chords.

119

120

#73

37 strings.
12 bars.
12 chords: C, F, B-flat, G, G7,
C7, D7, A7, E7, Am, Gm, Dm.

Catalog drawing.

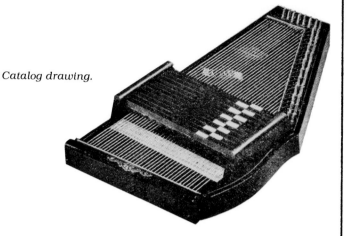

Logo: "The Original Autoharp."
Label: Standard #73.
Holders: Thin wood slats between bars.
Bars: Placed close together.
Buttons: Raised, black wood. Arranged in two rows.
Felts: Green.
Bar labels: Standard letter names for chords in addition to the Zimmermann figures.
Music scale: Octaves are indicated.
End cover: Second type of decal.
Decorations: Soundboard decal. (In color section.) Single gold line around edge.
Size: 21¼ inches by 12 inches.
Price: $10.00.

Model #73 with second logo. Close placement of chord bars is different from the wider placement of bars on Model #72⅞.

121

122

All Phonoharp Autoharps have the same label design with the model number in the middle.

The third type of end cover decal has a more flowing design than the geometric patterns of the earlier decals.

123

Closeup detail of a Model #73. The joint between the lower frame piece and the side frame piece is visible on the side of the harp. The chord bar assembly has been moved closer to the end cover and is not in the original position.

124

#6

32 strings.
6 bars, 10 shifters.
16 chords: C, F, B-flat, G, D, A,
G7, C7, D7, A7, Am, Gm, Dm, Em, Bm,
and C-sharp diminished seventh.

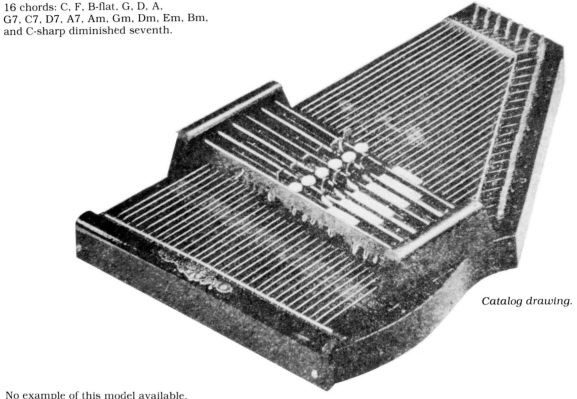

Catalog drawing.

No example of this model available.
Bars: Shifters change chords.
End cover: Shows second decal in
drawing.
Decorations: Soundboard decal in drawing appears to be the same design as that used on the Dolgeville Model #73.
Size: 21½ inches by 13 inches.
Price: $20.00.
Discontinued: ca. 1918.

PARLOR GRAND

39 strings.
10 bars, 13 shifters.
38 chords: C, G, B-flat, G, D, A, E, B, G7, C7, D7, A7, E7, B7, Am, Gm, Dm, Em, Bm, Cm, and a number of compound chords.

The Parlor Grand Model is offered in the Phonoharp catalog, but was made by custom order only. No examples of this model have appeared in this research.

INTERNATIONAL MUSICAL CORPORATION (1926-1931)

#2¾
(Shown)

23 strings.
5 bars.
5 chords: C, F, B-flat, G7, C7.

#73
(Not shown)

37 strings.
12 bars.
12 chords: C, F, G, B-flat, G, G7, C7, D7, A7, E7, Am, Gm, Dm.

Logo for International Musical Corporation.
125

Label for International Musical Corporation still has Zimmermann's name misspelled.

127

End cover: No decal.
Music stand holes: None.
Special features: Frame design changed. Joint between lower frame piece and side frame pieces is now visible on the lower end of the harp (detail below).

126

128

Summary: Autoharps 1910 to 1931

Autoharps made by the Phonoharp Company, Boston, Massachusetts (1910 to 1926), and International Musical Corporation, Hoboken, New Jersey (1926 to 1931).

Models: #71, #2¾, #72⅞, #73, #6, and Parlor Grand.
Introduced: All models from Dolgeville, reintroduced ca. 1910.
Discontinued: Models #71 and #6, ca. 1918. Model #72⅞, ca. 1922.
Logo: 1) Phonoharp with "The Zimmermann Autoharp" 2) Phonoharp with "The Original Autoharp" 3) International Musical Corporation.
Label: 1) Phonoharp with gold letters on black paper. 2) International Musical Corporation. Both give model numbers and place of manufacture. Both have "Zimmermann" misspelled.
Holders: Wood. Painted black. Attached by screws. Model #73 has thin slats between the bars.
Bars: Wood. Painted black. Some have metal shifters to change chords.
Buttons: Round, slightly concave, cream-colored celluloid arranged in single row. Model #73 has raised, black wood buttons arranged in two rows.
Felts: Green or purple.
Bar labels: Celluloid strips. Some have both Zimmermann figures and letter names for chords.
Music scale: Gold decal with Zimmermann figures for string names.
End cover: Model #71 has no cover. Other Phonoharp models have detachable end covers with decals (three types). International Musical Corporation harps have plain end covers without decals.
Feet: Three round brass nailheads.
Music stand holes: Two holes on slanted edge of harp on most models.
Bridges: Wood. Painted black. One metal rod inset in upper bridge. Two metal rods at lower bridge.
Tuning pins: Angled backward slightly.
Strings: Loop-end strings wrap around lower end and attach over hitch pins.
Frame: The joint between the lower frame and side frame pieces is at the side on Phonoharp models. It is on the bottom on International Musical Corporation harps.
Soundboard, back and sides: Painted black.
Decorations: Varied. Some models have fancy decals on the soundboard.

First logo: "The Zimmermann Autoharp" with name spelled correctly (ca. 1910 to 1917).

129

Second logo: "The Original Autoharp" (ca. 1917 to 1926).

130

112

122

Label: Phonoharp Autoharp label is the same design, 1910 to 1926: gold letters on black paper with the model number in the middle. Says "Zimmermann [sic] Autoharp Manufactured by The Phonoharp Co., Boston, Mass. U.S.A."

Label: International Musical Corporation label is the same design as the Phonoharp label, with only the name and location changed. Gold letters on black paper. Says "Zimmerman [sic] Autoharp Manufactured by International Musical Corp., 15th and Bloomfield Sts., Hoboken, N.J."

127

Logo: Design for International Musical Corporation is a variation of the previous Phonoharp design (1926 to 1931).

125

Harold Finney   **Walter Schmidt**

131

This photo with two unidentified employees was taken sometime in the 1930s at the Oscar Schmidt office in Jersey City, New Jersey.

## CHAPTER 9

OSCAR SCHMIDT-INTERNATIONAL, 1932 to 1963

The Autoharp is not new. For more than 50 years it has stood the test of time with ever increasing popularity. It is used in schools and colleges, by churches and missionaries in far off lands, in homes and group singing, in theaters and night clubs . . .

> *Instructor for the Zimmerman* [sic] *Autoharp No. 73.* (Oscar Schmidt-International, Inc., 1947)

The first "Oscar Schmidt"–brand Autoharps appeared after the dissolution of the International Musical Corporation at the end of 1931. The newly formed Oscar Schmidt-International Corporation was owned by Oscar Schmidt's widow, Elizabeth, his son, Walter, and Harold Gordon Finney. Most of the daily business was in the hands of Finney, who was the plant manager. During the next thirty-one years, Finney was the person who held the company together through its most difficult years.

Harold Finney had worked for William Copeland at the Phonoharp Company in Boston. He had been there only a few years when, with the creation of the International Musical Corporation, the company moved to Hoboken, New Jersey. Finney served as both treasurer and secretary of International, and although he was only a minor shareholder in the company, he was Copeland's right-hand man, taking care of most of the latter's corporate business. When the International Musical Corporation dissolved, Copeland appears to have withdrawn from the partnership with the Schmidts (probably a result of the long-term overhead dispute), but Finney became one of the major shareholders in

the new Oscar Schmidt-International Corporation and continued to handle the financial and business side of the company.[1]

Although several patents for zither-type instruments bear Finney's name, he was not particularly involved in product development or other musical aspects of the company. His daughter Barbara remembers that her father could play one piece on any instrument — "Ramona" — but that that was the only tune he could play. His expertise was in accounting and finance, two vital areas for any company trying to survive the Great Depression.

As with most businesses in the thirties, times were rough for the Oscar Schmidt-International Corporation. The company was restructured once more, when on February 24, 1936, Oscar Schmidt-International, Inc., was formed, and on October 21, 1936, the Oscar Schmidt-International Corporation was dissolved.[2] In order to keep the payroll small, the company drastically reduced the work force and discontinued all products that weren't competitive, concentrating on the popular zither models. The Autoharp was kept, though its sales represented only about five percent of the business, in part because manufacturing Autoharps was far more labor intensive than manufacturing ordinary zithers. Sales were conducted mostly by door-to-door salesmen,[3] and it wasn't until 1939 that the Autoharp reappeared in the Montgomery Ward catalogs.

During the 1930s the Autoharp was a strong presence in the schools, and in

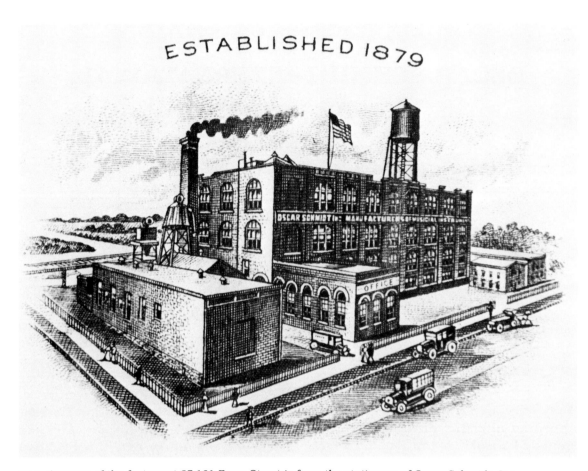

ESTABLISHED 1879

This drawing of the factory at 87-101 Ferry Street is from the stationery of Oscar Schmidt, Inc.

churches and rural homes, even though production was still quite limited. Some twelve-chord harps made in the early years of the decade had fancy soundboard decal decorations (reminiscent of the earlier Dolgeville and Phonoharp models), but within a few years the Autoharp was stripped bare of frills, leaving the plain, basic black body that was to remain the standard style for more than thirty years.

Many Autoharps survive from the days of Dolge and the Phonoharp Company, but few from the days of Oscar Schmidt-International, Inc., prior to 1945. The Schmidt harps had four-digit numbers stamped into the back of the harp until 1964, giving a clue to the production levels. Two early harps with the ornate decals have numbers 0589 and 0686, the latter purchased in 1936. No "07" series harps have surfaced, but the several "08" series harps (up to 0858) available are the plain black ones without the decals.[4]

Later numbers were change so that the first two digits indicated the year of manufacture. From the many harps extant from the period 1945 to 1964 we know that twelve-chord and five-chord Autoharps were continuously manufactured during those years. However, few harps survive that were made by Schmidt prior to 1945. The numbers were not unique to each harp and represented a "batch" number, not the number of the individual harp. Quite possibly prior to 1945 fewer than nine hundred batches of Autoharps were made, and the batches may simply have been numbered in sequence.

During the Second World War, the company was unable to obtain the metals needed to produce Autoharps and other zithers as well as parts such as strings. After all, musical-instrument manufacturing was a "nonessential" industry. The result was a drop in total factory production of about sixty percent, and according to Finney's wife

120

and daughter, a situation for the company worse than during the Depression. There was little or no production of new Autoharps during this time, since Autoharp sales still amounted to only a small percentage of the total company sales. What little inventory Oscar Schmidt had remaining from the thirties had to last through most of the war. Some accessories were manufactured in small quantities, while others were dropped altogether.[5]

Autoharp price lists confirm the hardships imposed by the war. A mid-thirties price list shows thirteen different sets of Autoharp music available. A 1945 list shows all but three of those sets sold out. The sets were not reprinted. Another list, which comes between the two others (ca. 1942), shows that all types of metal fingerpicks were discontinued, and prices on other metal products were as much as one hundred percent higher than the mid-thirties prices. However, prices on this list are also absolutely identical to those on the 1945 list, a result of strict wartime price controls.

In the late forties, when price controls had been lifted and raw materials were available again, Oscar Schmidt-International, Inc., began to grow again. Having sold out the instruction books by R.S. Tracy, Oscar Schmidt now began to print its own publications. The first one was *Instructor for the*

This photograph (ca. 1944) shows "Uncle Bill" playing the Autoharp "Appalachian-style," but below the chord bar assembly. Note the decal on the soundboard.

132

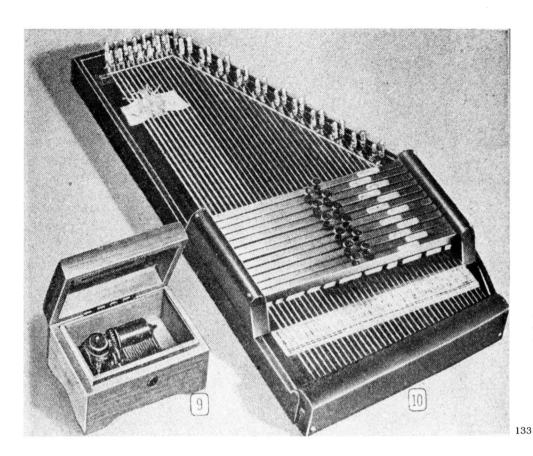

Wards catalog, Spring-Summer 1944. Note the decal is the same as that on Uncle Bill's harp.

133

Zimmerman [sic] *Autoharp* (1947), whose introduction tells us that the Autoharp had enjoyed more than fifty years of "ever increasing popularity" — an inaccurate though prophetic observation.

During the war the Autoharp had been used in hospital wards to accompany songs, by both the Gray Ladies and the wounded soldiers themselves. The harp was still used as the "mountain piano" of rural missionaries and had all but replaced the far too expensive piano in the classroom.

Teachers continued to use the Autoharp in place of a piano after the war, for a variety of reasons. For one thing, the Autoharp was inexpensive enough that every classroom teacher could have one: the piano became the tool of the music specialist. For another, no special training was required to play the harp, making it ideal for accompanying classroom singing of all types. And lastly, children could play the Autoharp, too. Simple songs were easily taught to children who were excited by their immediate success. As long as the harp was in tune, and the correct

bar depressed, a child could play a song without hitting any sour notes.

Not only was the Autoharp good for teachers; teachers were good for the Autoharp. In fact, the expanding educational market was what put the Autoharp company back on its feet. Postwar music programs began to emphasize the Autoharp more and more. Teachers' songbooks, instruction manuals, filmstrips, records, and training films were developed to open up the possibilities of using the Autoharp in the classroom. Advertising was begun again in publications such as the *Music Educators Journal*.

The Autoharp still had a long way to go, however, before its popularity would increase enough to put its production on par with the zither division of the Oscar Schmidt company. Its minimal importance to the total business is evidenced in an article on the Jersey City factory printed in a local newspaper sometime around 1950, in which the zither business is described in detail and Harold Finney is referred to as "Mr. Zither."

134

The Autoharp became popular with school children in the fifties.

Nowhere in the two-column story does the word "Autoharp" appear.[6]

The much-needed additional impetus came in an unusual form, however. In 1949 an insurance executive named L.H. Martin of Des Moines, Iowa, was introduced to the Autoharp. Besides enjoying playing it, he saw some business possibilities in the instrument. Martin, corresponding with Harold Finney at the Schmidt factory, apparently came to a mutually satisfying agreement with Finney. He founded the National Autoharp Sales Company, which initially sold mostly through Sunday newspaper mail-order sections, with modest results.[7]

Soon Martin realized that the Autoharp's use was most widespread in the public schools. According to Martin's daughter, Sally Paul, during the early fifties her father and mother conceived the idea of an Autoharp with a gold finish. They felt it would look and wear better than the black harps and would be a good promotional device, so Finney agreed to manufacture harps with a gold finish. In return for meeting an annual sales quota, National Autoharp Sales Company was given the exclusive distribution rights on the "New Golden Autoharp," as it was advertised in such publications as *Music Educators Journal*.

With the success of the Golden Autoharp, National Autoharp Sales enlisted the aid of music educators to prepare an entire classroom music program based on the use of the Autoharp. Two books, *Golden Autoharp Harmonies* and *A Teacher's Guide for the Golden Autoharp*, were published by National Autoharp Sales in 1953 and 1955. The company also produced "practice Autoharps," cardboard facsimiles for each pupil to "play" on the desktop, while one pupil or the teacher played a real Autoharp.

A "Practice Autoharp" made by National Autoharp Sales Company.

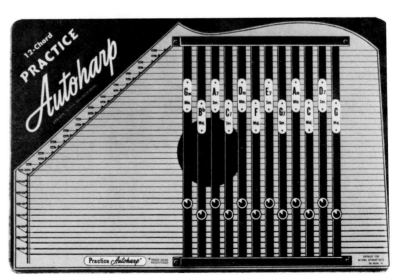

135

National Autoharp Sales was responsible for the first major change in the Autoharp made in the twentieth century: the development of a fifteen-chord Autoharp, first introduced around 1961. Although the new model was well received, its price made it less popular than the standard twelve-chord model. A seventeen-chord model Autoharp was made briefly by custom-order only, but soon dropped. Both models were Golden Autoharps.

The small distribution company continued for several years at about the same level of sales. In 1962 Martin died, leaving the company to his daughter, Mrs. Paul. She operated the company from the basement of her parents' house, later from a warehouse. Health problems prevented her from devoting herself full time to the business, however, and slowly the company began to falter. After 1963, the annual sales quota for National Autoharp Sales was set so high that the small company could no longer meet it, and the era of the Golden Autoharp was over.

While sales to schools in the fifties had boomed, consumer sales also rose. The Autoharp soon surpassed the zither in popularity, and production increased until it overtook the zither to become the major product from Oscar Schmidt-International, Inc. In 1955 the Autoharp reappeared in the Sears-Roebuck general catalogs, where it is still included today. Other than through the catalogs of Sears and Montgomery Ward, little consumer advertising was done: Autoharps were sold by traveling salesmen or directly from the company.

Oscar Schmidt's widow died in 1958, and her company shares passed on to Walter Schmidt. Just one month later, Walter died. With his sister Hanna deceased and his sister Clara married, he had left his shares in the company to his third sister, Elsa, who

136

Teachers began to use the Autoharp extensively after the Second World War. This photograph was taken sometime during the mid-fifties.

was unmarried. Elsa wasn't interested in the business, however, and although she was now the major shareholder, she left the company to be run by Finney, who was nearly seventy years old, and his production manager, Henry Ruckner. For the next several years, the factory continued to run completely under the control of Finney, who had supervised its operation for over twenty-five years.[8]

With the beginning of the sixties came the "folk revival," renewed interest in traditional American music inspired by such popular performers as the Kingston Trio, the Limelighters, and Peter, Paul, and Mary. As old-time music became more popular, so did the Autoharp. Mother Maybelle Carter was now playing the Autoharp when she performed with her daughters at the Grand Old Opry. More national exposure was coming through Mike Seeger, who played Autoharp with the New Lost City Ramblers. Seeger also traveled into the mountain regions of Virginia to record the playing of several old-time musicians: Ernest "Pop" Stoneman, Kilby Snow, and Neriah and Kenneth Benfield. The subsequent release of the 1962 Folkways album *Mountain Music Played on the Autoharp* enabled musicians all over the country to hear the Autoharp used primarily as a melody instrument. The instrumental tunes on this album revealed that the Autoharp can be used to play a solo as well as provide a rhythm back-up for vocal songs.

It was also in 1962 that a University of Illinois graphic arts instructor, led by his interest in the Autoharp, began researching the history of the Autoharp. A. Doyle Moore started with the Oscar Schmidt factory in Jersey City and worked his way back in time to the invention of the Autoharp in Philadelphia. The publication of his findings in an article in the December 1963 issue of the *New York Folklore Quarterly* aroused more interest in the Autoharp among folk music enthusiasts and paved the way for the research presented here.

On February 16, 1963, Harold Finney died at the age of seventy-two, and Elsa Schmidt suddenly found herself in charge of the company. Having been completely uninvolved with the daily business of the company since her brother had left it to her, she knew she had to get some assistance. She turned to her nephew, Glen Peterson, Jr., the son of her sister Clara and grandson of Oscar Schmidt.

137

As the Autoharp became increasingly popular in the schools, it once again became a favorite for home entertainment.

## CHAPTER 10

AUTOHARPS 1932 to 1963

Autoharps made by Oscar Schmidt-International Corporation and Oscar Schmidt-International, Incorporated, Jersey City, New Jersey. (Includes harps made for National Autoharp Sales Company, Des Moines, Iowa.)

MODELS
#2¾ (5 chord)   #73 (12 chord)

FEATURES
Logo: One type. Some harps have no logo.
Label: Two types. Gold letters on black paper. Some harps have no label.
Holders: Wood or bakelite plastic (12-chord model only).
Bars: Wood. Painted black.
Buttons: Raised, round. Wood or plastic. Black or white.
Bar labels: Celluloid or paper.
Music scale: Decals, gold leaf or white paper. Zimmermann figures for string names. Some have standard notation added.
End cover: Detachable. Wood or extruded plastic.
Feet: Felt pads or wood.
Music stand holes: Two on slanted edge.
Bridges: Wood. Upper bridge has one metal rod inset. Lower bridge has two rods.
Tuning pins: Angled backward slightly.
Strings: Loop-end strings attach over hitch pins.
Soundboard, back and sides: Black. Batch numbers stamped into wood on back (from 1945 to 1964 the first two digits indicate the year, with some exceptions). Golden finish made for National Autoharp Sales Company.
Decorations: Decals on some harps.
Prices: Sears or Wards catalogs.

#2¾
(5 chord)

23 strings.
5 chords: C, F, B-flat, G7, C7.

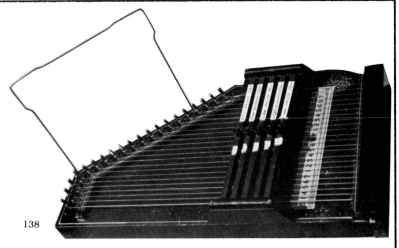

138

A 1946 Model #2¾ (#4627) with music stand in place.

MAJOR 24

SEVENTH 1356

MAJOR 461

SEVENTH 5724

MAJOR 135

Logo: None.
Label: Standard #2¾.
Holders: Wood.
Buttons: Black wood.
Felts: Green.
Bar labels: Celluloid strips with Zimmermann figures.
Music scale: Gold decal with Zimmermann figures.
End cover: Wood.
Feet: Felt, nailed to harp back.
Decorations: Single gold stripe at edge.
Size: 17 inches by 9 inches.
Price: (1945) $11.95.

A 1945 Model #2¾ (#4591). Bar labels (inset) are missing from this harp. Note shape of wooden buttons below.

139

140

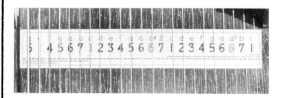

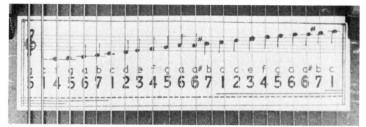

The first music scale for Model #2¾ is a gold decal with the Zimmermann figures (ca. 1932 to 1947).

141

The second music scale has notes in the standard music notation added to a white paper decal (ca. 1947 to 1952). Yellowing varnish often gives the white decals a golden tint.

142

In 1950 the wood buttons were changed to plastic, and in 1952 the chord bar labels were changed to oval celluloid pieces with the standard letter names for the chords.

143

Early Models #2¾ have two small holes for the music stand. The unreinforced holes are between pins #7 & #8 and between pins #19 & #20 (ca. 1932 to 1947). In 1948 metal eyelets were added to reinforce the holes, and in 1950 the holes were moved closer together between pins #7 & #8 and between pins #14 & #15.

144

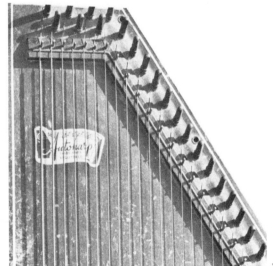

145

146

The logo designed like a scroll was
added to the soundboard in 1951.

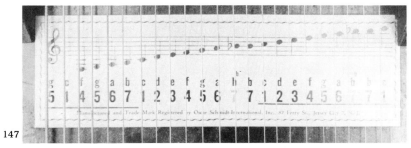

147

A third music scale was introduced in 1952. The manufacturer's name
and address have been added. The dotted staff line and leger lines of the
Zimmermann system have been eliminated and the a-sharp has been
changed to the more logical b-flat. The corresponding Zimmermann
figure has been changed from a dotted six to a dotted seven.

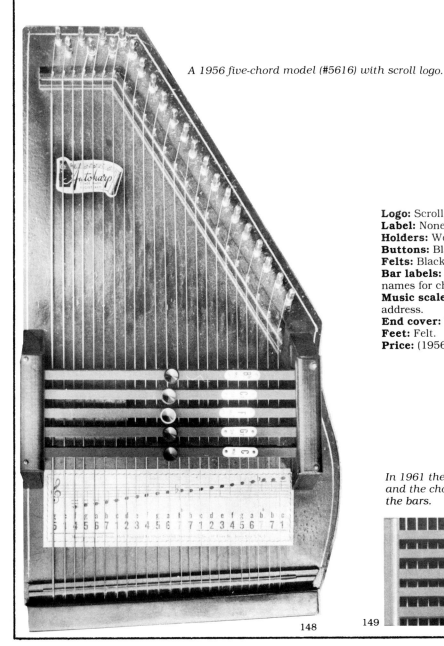

A 1956 five-chord model (#5616) with scroll logo.

Logo: Scroll decal.
Label: None.
Holders: Wood.
Buttons: Black plastic.
Felts: Black.
Bar labels: Celluloid ovals with standard letter
names for chords.
Music scale: Has manufacturer's name and
address.
End cover: Wood.
Feet: Felt.
Price: (1956) $16.95. (1960) $17.95.

In 1961 the buttons were changed to white plastic,
and the chord bar labels changed to paper glued to
the bars.

148   149

#73

(12 chord)

37 or 36 strings.
12 chords: C, F, B-flat, G, G7, C7, D7, A7, E7, Am, Gm, Dm.

Decal from Model #73 (#0589), ca. 1935.

150

Logo: None.
Label: Standard #73.
Holders: Wood with thin slats between the bars for close spacing of bars.
Buttons: Black wood.
Bar labels: Celluloid ovals with Zimmermann figures and standard letter names for chords.
Music scale: Gold decal.
End cover: Wood.
Strings: 37.
Decorations: Early models had ornate soundboard decals. (In color section.)
Size: 22 inches by 11 inches.
Price: (1934) $8.98. (1939) $11.95.

Model #73 (#0589, ca. 1935). Note decal, but no logo.

151

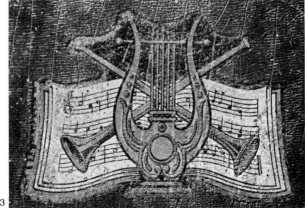

152   153

The decal from the last Dolgeville Model #72⅞ (which was used on the Phonoharp Models #72⅞ and #73) was used once again in the mid-1930s (left). It is found on a Model #73 (#0686) purchased in 1936. The decal shown on the harp played by "Uncle Bill" appeared on the harps in the Montgomery Ward catalogs, late 1942 to early 1944. The decal in the photograph (right) is from a Model #73 (#0757).

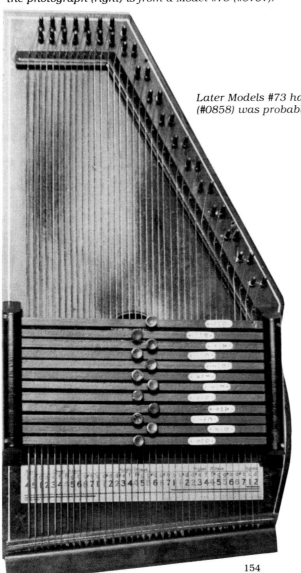

Later Models #73 have plain soundboards with no decals. This harp (#0858) was probably made in the early forties (ca. 1944).

Price: (1942) $13.45.

The standard Oscar Schmidt-International label still has Zimmermann's name misspelled.

154

155

156

All harps made by Oscar Schmidt-International (1932 to 1962) have the double metal rod at the lower bridge.

157

The first music scale for Model #73 is a gold decal with the Zimmermann figures (1932 to 1947).

By 1945 the four-digit batch number began to indicate the year of manufacture (the first two digits). This harp (#4594) shows virtually no change from the "08" series harps.

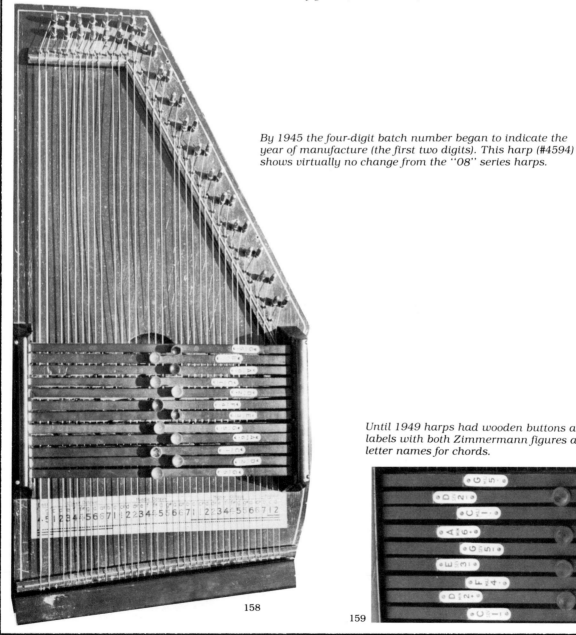

Until 1949 harps had wooden buttons and celluloid labels with both Zimmermann figures and standard letter names for chords.

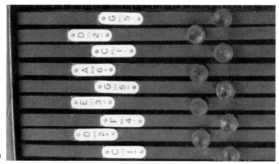

158

159

The wooden chord bar holders for the Model #73 has thin slats between the bars to allow a tighter spacing of the bars. A wooden strip holds the springs in place. By the late forties the green felt was replaced by black felt.

160

The second music scale has notes in the standard notation added to a white paper decal (ca. 1947 to 1952). The dotted staff line and leger lines of the Zimmermann system have been eliminated.

161

Music scale: White paper decal.
Price: (1948) $16.75.

A 1948 Model #73 (#4805).

162

By 1950 the chord bar buttons were changed from wood to plastic. Note the shape of the buttons is different from the shape of the wooden buttons. (See detail of wooden buttons on Model #2³/₄.)

163

In 1950 the two holes for the music stand were moved closer together. On a 1949 Model #73 (#4903) the holes are between pins #17 & #19 and between pins #31 & #33 (right). After 1950 they were between pins #25 & #27 and pins #33 & #35 (below).

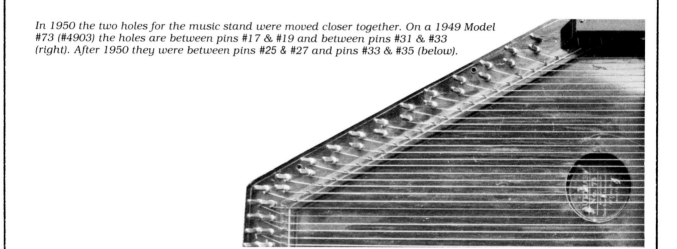

164

This 1950 harp (#5044) shows an early attempt at amplification. A microphone was put inside the harp with the cord coming out through a hole drilled in the treble side of the harp.

165

166

A soundboard logo reappeared in 1951. The scroll design is printed on a white paper decal. Yellowing varnish often gives the white decals a golden tint.

A 1951 twelve-chord model (#5115) shows the new logo and the new label. The sixteen-chord unit is not the original unit.

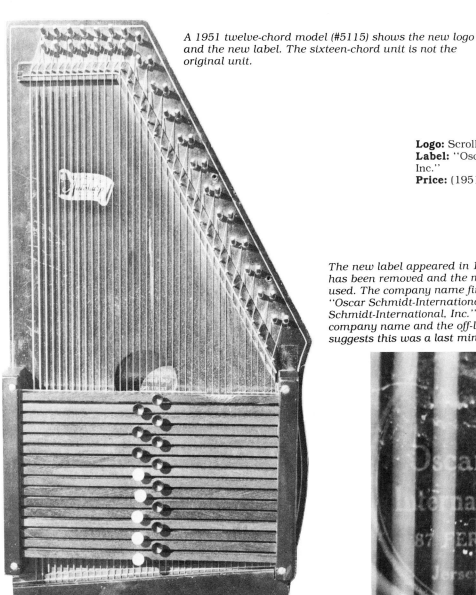

Logo: Scroll decal.
Label: "Oscar Schmidt-International, Inc."
Price: (1951) $19.98.

The new label appeared in 1951. The Zimmermann name has been removed and the model numbers are no longer used. The company name finally has been changed from "Oscar Schmidt-International Corp." to the correct "Oscar Schmidt-International, Inc." The word "the" before the company name and the off-line placement of "Inc." suggests this was a last minute change.

167   168

135

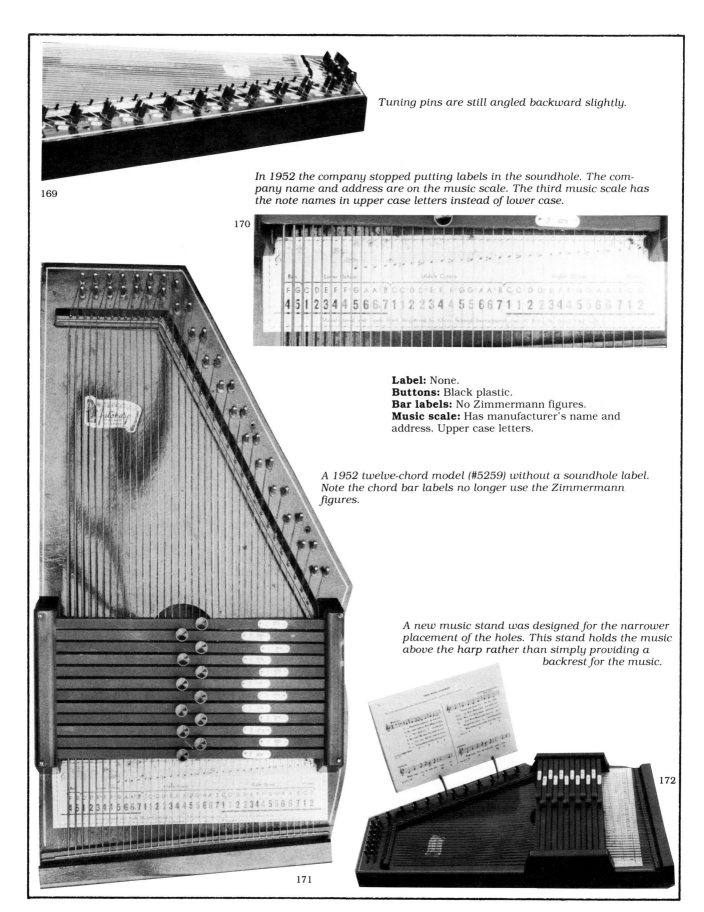

Tuning pins are still angled backward slightly.

169

In 1952 the company stopped putting labels in the soundhole. The company name and address are on the music scale. The third music scale has the note names in upper case letters instead of lower case.

170

Label: None.
Buttons: Black plastic.
Bar labels: No Zimmermann figures.
Music scale: Has manufacturer's name and address. Upper case letters.

A 1952 twelve-chord model (#5259) without a soundhole label. Note the chord bar labels no longer use the Zimmermann figures.

A new music stand was designed for the narrower placement of the holes. This stand holds the music above the harp rather than simply providing a backrest for the music.

172

171

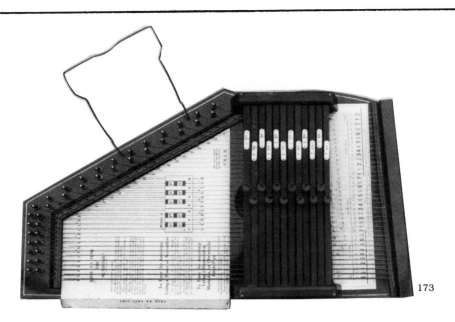

173

A paper tuning guide in place under the strings of a 1952 harp. It has tuning instructions as well as the note name for each string.

174

In 1953 a plastic chord bar holder was made for the twelve-chord models. The molded bakelite plastic holders are attached to the harp with screws at each end. A 1953 model (#5352) shows the new holders. The closeup view shows the inside details.

175

By 1959 the end cover was changed from wood to extruded plastic. The plastic cover at right has a different appearance from the wooden cover below.

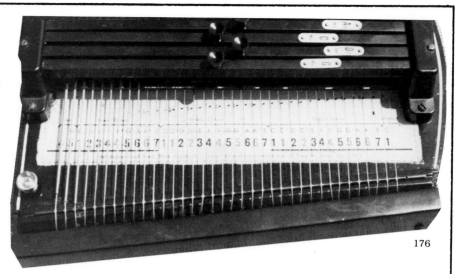

176

By 1955 the harp had been changed from thirty-seven strings to thirty-six strings. The name of each string is printed by the tuning pins on a paper decal. The decal covers the entire tuning pin area, and it was printed with dots to use as a guide for drilling the holes for the tuning pins and music stand.

Holders: Plastic.
Strings: 36.
Special features: Note names by tuning pins.
Price: (1955) $21.95. (1962) $24.95.

A 1956 harp (#5612) owned by Pop Stoneman is on exhibit in the Country Music Hall of Fame and Museum. Note that Stoneham amplified his harp with a pickup attached to the bass side.

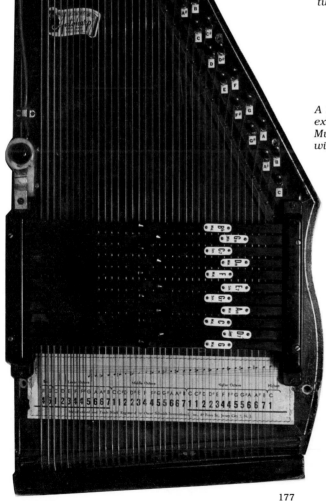

In 1961 the chord bar buttons were changed from black plastic to white plastic. The celluloid bar labels were replaced by oval paper labels glued to the bars.

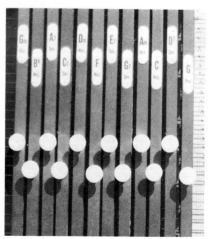

177   178

179

NATIONAL AUTOHARP SALES CO.

180

37 or 36 strings.
12 chords: C, F, B-flat, G, G7, C7, D7, A7, E7, Am, Gm, Dm
15 chords: C, F, B-flat, G, G7, C7, D7, A7, E7, Am, Gm, Dm, and C, C-sharp and D diminished seventh.

A wooden fifteen-bar holder from a 1962 model (#6245).

Logo: "The New Golden Autoharp."
Label: None.
Holders: Wood on fifteen-chord model. Twelve-chord model used bakelite plastic holders after they were introduced.
Special features: Golden finish. (Golden harp included in color section.)
Price: (1958) 12-chord: $26.75. (1964) 12-chord: $32.98. 15-chord: $36.98.
Introduced: ca. 1952.
Discontinued: ca. 1964.

The holders on this 1956 model (#5612) have been lowered for more playing room and are not in the original position.

A special seventeen-chord Golden Autoharp was made for Maybelle Carter in 1958 (#5808). It is on display in the House of Cash Museum.

181

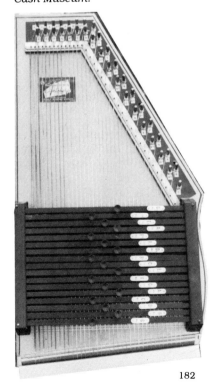

182

Summary: Autoharps 1932 to 1963

Autoharps made by Oscar Schmidt-International Corporation (1932 to 1936) and Oscar Schmidt-International, Incorporated (1936 to 1963), Jersey City, New Jersey.
(Includes harps made for National Autoharp Sales Company, Des Moines, Iowa.)

Models: #2¾ (5 chord) and #73 (12 chord). Special 12-chord and 15-chord models made for National Autoharp Company.

Introduced: Both standard models from International Musical Corporation. Golden Autoharps for National Autoharp Sales Company, ca. 1952.

Discontinued: Golden Autoharps, ca. 1964.

Logo: 1) None. 2) Scroll decal. 3) Special logo for National Autoharp Sales Company.

Label: 1) Gold letters on black paper with model number and place of manufacture. Has "Zimmermann" still misspelled. 2) Zimmermann name and model numbers removed. "Corp." changed to "Inc." 3) None.

Holders: Wood, painted black, on all five-chord and fifteen-chord models. Twelve-chord harps had black wood holders until 1953 when they were replaced by bakelite plastic holders.

Bars: Wood. Painted black.

Buttons: 1) Raised, black wood (1932 to 1949). 2) Black plastic (ca. 1950 to 1961). 3) White plastic (1961—).

Felts: 1) Green (ca. 1932 to 1949). 2) Black (ca. 1949—).

Bar labels: 1) White celluloid labels with both Zimmermann figures and letter names for chords (1932 to 1950) 2) White celluloid labels with standard letter names for chords (ca. 1951 to 1961). 3) White paper labels.

Music scale: 1) Gold decal with Zimmermann figures for string names (1932 to 1947). 2) White paper decal with standard notation added (1947 to 1952) 3) Company name and address added to white paper decal (1952—).

End cover: 1) Black wood (1932 to 1958) 2) Extruded black plastic (1959—).

Feet: Felt or wood.

Music stand holes: Two holes on slanted edge. 1) Unreinforced holes with wide spacing: 5 chord between pins #7 & #8 and #19 & #20, 12 chord between pins #17 & #19 and #31 & #33 (1932 to 1947). 2) Wide spacing with holes reinforced by metal eyelets (ca. 1948 to 1949). 3) Narrow spacing of holes: 5 chord between pins #7 & #8 and #14 & #15, 12 chord between pins #25 & #27 and #33 & #35 (1950—).

Bridges: Wood. Painted black. One metal rod inset in upper bridge. Two metal rods at lower bridge.

Tuning pins: Angled backward slightly.

Strings: Loop-end strings wrap around lower end and attach over hitch pins. Twelve-chord model was changed from 37 strings to 36 strings by 1955.

Frame: Joint between bottom and side frame pieces is at the bottom.

Soundboard, back and sides: Black.

Decorations: Early models (1932 to ca. 1944) have soundboard decals. Later models have single stripe (gold or white) around edge. Note names added by tuning pins, ca. 1955.

Special features: Batch numbers stamped into back of harp, usually four digits (sometimes five digits). From 1945 the first two digits indicate the year of manufacture.

Logo: *Early harps by Oscar Schmidt-International have no logo (ca. 1932 to 1950). In 1951 the decal with the scroll design was introduced.*

183

The New Golden Autoharp logo: *Decal on harps made by Oscar Schmidt-International for National Autoharp Sales Company (ca. 1952 to 1964).*

179

First label: *Oscar Schmidt-International Corporation used the same design as that used by International Musical Corporation (ca. 1932 to 1950). Gold letters on black paper. Says "Zimmerman [sic] Autoharp Manufactured by Oscar Schmidt-International Corp., 87 Ferry Street, Jersey City, N.J."*

155

Second label: *Gold letters on black paper. Zimmermann name and model numbers removed (1951 to 1952). Says "Manufactured by the Oscar Schmidt International Inc., 87 Ferry Street, Jersey City, N.J." In mid-1952 the soundhole label was eliminated.*

168

184

Glen Peterson, Jr.

Meg Peterson

185

## CHAPTER 11

OSCAR SCHMIDT-INTERNATIONAL, 1963 to 1978

Lastly, but not leastly, they look lovely. All of these technical and engineering improvements, made possible by the design of an Autoharp body that is a masterpiece of good taste, modern design, and a warm concern for tradition.
The All New "B" Model Autoharps, booklet 1967

Shortly after the early 1963 arrival of Glen Peterson, Jr., at Oscar Schmidt-International, Inc., a new program of product development began, which would culminate in the creation of the B-model Autoharps. After reaching an agreement with his Aunt Elsa whereby the shares in the company would be gradually turned over to him in the next few years, Peterson immediately initiated an active marketing and promotion campaign. The last three door-to-door salesmen were fired, and serious attention paid to increasing the output from the factory.[1]

Changes in the instrument itself also appeared as Peterson set out to completely redesign the instrument that had shown little change for over sixty years. These changes and the many others that would be made in the next fifteen years were all made to facilitate production and reduce manufacturing costs.[2] The first change was the elimination of the soundhole. At the time the inside of the Autoharp had interior braces glued to both the top and the back of the harp. The braces were near the soundhole, making the air cavity inside the harp small and virtually ineffective. The braces also prevented the top of the harp (the soundboard) from vibrating independently of the back. According to Peterson, the soundhole did little to increase the volume of the instrument and contributed to cracking and warping. Without a soundhole, the Autoharp had fewer production problems and drew fewer consumer complaints.[3]

Peterson continued to make changes in the appearance of the instrument. Realizing that much of the interest in the Autoharp came from traditional musicians, he consulted with the popular performers of the day, Maybelle Carter, Mike Seeger, and Cecil Null. They told him what they would like to see in the Autoharp, and by the end of 1963 the first "Appalachian"-model harp was ready for the market. This harp did have a soundhole in its spruce soundboard, and although the interior braces were spaced farther apart to create a larger air cavity, the braces still connected the soundboard to the back of the Autoharp. The Appalachian model also had fifteen chords, but the three new chords were not the diminished seventh chords of the fifteen-chord Golden Autoharps. Instead, they were E, A, and D major, chords frequently used in traditional and folk-style music. The first ad for the Appalachian model appeared in the December 1963 – January 1964 issue of *Sing Out!* magazine.

Meanwhile, Peterson's wife, Meg, a classical violinist, began to learn to play the Autoharp in order to develop some instructional materials for it. With guidance from Maybelle Carter and Cecil Null, Meg Peterson began to write the first of what would be a long series of Autoharp instructional books.[4] Since the 1964 publication of *Music*

Maybelle Carter and Cecil Null were the popular Autoharp players in the early sixties and helped design the "Appalachian" model held by Maybelle. Cecil is holding a Golden Autoharp made for National Autoharp Sales Company.

for Everyone, Meg Peterson has written dozens of books for the Autoharp.

By 1964 an entire new line of Autoharps was under way. A fifteen-chord molded-plastic styrene chord bar holder brought the standard fifteen-chord model's price down into direct competition with the twelve-chord model. The old bakelite plastic twelve-chord holders were also replaced by styrene ones, and the old extruded-plastic end-pin covers were replaced by molded-plastic covers with rounded edges. Finally, the familiar scroll logo that had appeared on the harps since 1951 was replaced with a more modern, trapezoid-shaped design, and new rectangular buttons were put on the wooden bars.

The "standard"-model fifteen-chord Autoharp had the three diminished seventh chords, and in 1965 another fifteen-chord harp, with D, E-flat, and F7 chords, was introduced. With the Appalachian fifteen-chord harp, three fifteen-chord models were now on the market, and their popularity soon surpassed that of the twelve-chord model. The five-chord model was dropped in 1964. With the exception of the Appalachian

model, the harps still lacked soundholes, and a new music scale, designed to look like a keyboard, was added beneath the strings at the lower end of the harp.

When the new models went on the market, special models were developed for the mail-order catalogs of Sears-Roebuck and Montgomery Ward. Up until 1965 the harps in the catalogs were identical to those in music stores. After that year, however, harps purchased through Sears and Wards would be made especially for them. In 1964–65, Oscar Schmidt also built an "Electroharp" exclusively for Sears. The Electroharp was the forerunner to today's electric Autoharp.

Also in 1964, the "Guitaro" was introduced. The original patent for the Guitaro, filed on June 17, 1963 (U.S. Patent #3,237,503, issued March 1, 1966), was the first of numerous patents to be issued to the company through 1971. Designed by Glen Peterson and Henry Ruckner, the instrument came in two models. One model sported a resonator and had a soundhole in

An instruction book and record were made for the Guitaro, featuring Anita Carter. The drawing shows the model with the resonator.

Our other school...

had plenty of Autoharps

This 1965 advertisement with the sad-faced youngster was aimed at the educational market.

188

its back; the other had the soundhole in the front and no resonator. The resonator model was eventually dropped in the early seventies.

By mid-1966 the old Jersey City factory was seriously inhibiting the development of new products, so a modern plant was purchased on Garden State Road in Union, New Jersey. This factory remains the site of Autoharp production today. The old factory eventually was demolished, and the site is now occupied by a row of townhouses.

The new factory seemed to provide a good environment for creativity and product development, beginning with the design of a new chord bar (U.S. Patent #3,401,586, filed August 8, 1967, and issued September 17, 1968). The new bar was made of extruded aluminum with a styrene top; the rectangular buttons could now be chemically fused to the plastic top instead of glued. Production costs were cut considerably by the

elimination of the time-consuming and costly process of painting the three sides of the wooden bars. New Autoharps were equipped immediately with the new chord bars.

Glen Peterson also was interested in tapping new markets, and the popularity of the Lovin' Spoonful (with John Sebastian playing the Autoharp) turned Peterson's thoughts to designing a good solid-body electric instrument that could be used in rock music. The Electroharp made for Sears had used a microphone for amplification, but the chord-bar noise was amplified along with the music. Peterson set about developing a magnetic pickup. Meg Peterson also grew prolific after the move to Union, and soon her *The Many Ways to Play the Autoharp* instructional books were introduced.

The most significant changes ever to be made in the physical design of the Autoharp came in mid-1967 with the first "B"-model harps. An ad in the September 1967 issue of

145

Music Educators Journal proudly announced that the Autoharp had "been completely redesigned." The B model incorporated four major new features: (1) The pin block was made from laminated maple, originally four-ply, later eight-ply. (2) A slotted aluminum string anchor was fitted into a special groove routed into the lower frame of the harp, so that the strings no longer went around the end of the Autoharp to hook over the end pins. (3) The upper soundboard bridge was replaced by individual guide posts (bridge pins) for each string. (4) The tuning pins were perpendicular to the soundboard instead of slanted backward at an angle. A new machine accurately drilled all seventy-two holes for the tuning pins and guide posts at the same time . . . efficiently and precisely.[5]

The B-model harps came in the same four styles as the previous A-model harps: twelve-chord, two types of fifteen-chord standard models, and fifteen-chord Appalachian model. Only the Appalachian model had a soundhole, with braces still connecting top to back.

190

Glen Peterson, Jr., and Cecil Null playing Guitaros at a music trade show. Note the electric model at the far left.

189

This 1964 instruction book was one of the first written by Meg Peterson.

Special A-model harps were still produced for Sears and Wards. In 1968 Sears started using its own "Silvertone"-brand logo on the harps. In 1972 Sears began to offer the B models in its general catalogs, and no more A models were made. Wards also used its own "Airline" brand on its special A-model harps, beginning in 1965 and continuing until Wards, too, began to sell the B models in 1972. Special black-body B-model harps were made for J.C. Penney, and Autoharps also were offered in the Spiegel catalog.

During 1967–68 the solid-body electric models were developed and ready for the consumer market. On January 25, 1967, Summit Musical Instruments was incorporated, with the sole purpose of selling the new electric models. A brochure explained:

Instruments like these, and a market potential that big, called for the formation of a new marketing organization. Summit Musical Instruments is it.

Summit will market these Autoharps exclusively through musical instrument retailers. They will not be sold through any other outlets. Our goal is to build a dealer organization composed of wide awake hustlers who see the potential in these instruments and then go out and get fat selling them.

U.S. Patent #3,499,357 (filed July 21, 1967, and issued March 10, 1970) shows the Cutlass model with two pickups, one bass and one treble. Both the Cutlass and the single-pickup Lancer were twenty-one-chord models, the first models introduced with interchangeable chord bars and a plastic chord bar cover. The less-popular, more-expensive Cutlass model was dropped in the early seventies.

Two other patents were applied for in 1968, the first a logical follow-up to the new electric Autoharps: a pickup accessory that could be put on any acoustic Autoharp (U.S. Patent #3,548,067, filed September 27, 1968, and issued December 15, 1970). The second was for a specially designed styrofoam carrying case (U.S. Patent #3,596,754, filed December 11, 1968, and issued August 3, 1971).

Both the pickup accessory and the styrofoam case appear in the 1969 brochure for the new "BH" – model Autoharps. For all practical purposes the BH models were simply B models with soundholes. The soundhole "breakthrough" was attributed to the development of the trademarked "Acoustiwood," a hard maple plywood panel that facilitated the complete elimination of the structural braces, enlarging the air cavity to its maximum and enabling the

191

A company brochure (ca. 1968) reads, "The photo shows Chris Darway of the "CRITTERS" playing the camouflaged Electric. The pickup is there, but who can tell it?" [Author's note: I can!]

This 1969 advertisement reads, "No! We don't have a hole in our heads . . . just sound thoughts about the Autoharp."

192

soundboard and back to oscillate independently. The Appalachian model already had a soundhole, of course, but the soundboard was changed from solid spruce to laminated maple with a thin veneer of spruce on top and the interior braces removed. The first acoustic/electric instrument was offered as an option for the Appalachian fifteen-chord BH model, bringing the Autoharp line up to five models.

Advertisements were less frequent after 1969, the company feeling that ads were ineffective; most promotion efforts were done by direct mail from that time until 1978. In addition, much of the company's energy in the early seventies was spent dealing with the newly introduced Chromaharp, a Japanese import distributed in the United States by Rhythm Band, Inc., at prices substantially below those of the Schmidt Autoharp. The Chromaharp was the first serious competitor to the Autoharp and had an immediate effect on Autoharp sales, particularly in the large educational market.[6]

In order to meet this sudden competition, Oscar Schmidt-International increased its productivity and actively pursued sales to schools. On January 12, 1971, another corporation was formed, Music Education Group, more commonly known by its acronym MEG. MEG was formed to diversify "Oscar" and make full use of the factory. "Oscar" made most of the products for MEG, but MEG was a separate company whose aim was to directly reach music educators. It carried a full line of school musical instruments, including the ever-popular classroom Autoharp.[7] Harps marketed by MEG had the MEG logo on the soundboard but otherwise were the same as the standard Autoharps.

Two new models were introduced in 1971: an acoustic twenty-one chord and an acoustic/electric twenty-one chord. The body of the twenty-one-chord acoustic harp was the same as that of the standard BH model, but due to the unique chord bar assembly, the new harp was called a "C" model. Both models were made only for MEG and not available to regular music stores until 1975.

The fifteen-chord model with the three diminished seventh chords was dropped from the line, and around 1972 or 1973 MEG introduced the fifteen-chord "Attaché" model, designed for the teacher to play on top of the desk and featuring the MEG logo. In 1975 the MEG Autoharps were renamed the "Educator" models. A twenty-one-chord Attaché model was finally offered to the

193

The Many Ways to Play the Autoharp books were published in 1966 shortly after the move to Union, New Jersey.

general public that year, and the Appalachian model was changed from a fifteen-chord model to a twenty-one-chord model. The twenty-one-chord harps were now sold in retail music stores and in 1977 appeared in the Sears catalog. By 1978 the twenty-one-chord models would account for more than fifty percent of new Autoharp sales.[8]

In 1977 Schmidt continued to diversify its products. Dulcimers were added to the line, and in the June 1977 issue of *Musical Merchandise Review* Schmidt announced the new "Redondo" guitars. Reflecting on the original Schmidt corporation's selling its guitar business to the Harmony Company, the announcement continues with, "Now history has sort of come full circle. In March 1977 we acquired much of the fine guitar making machinery owned by Harmony, and moved it to our plant in New Jersey. Our affiliate company, OMNIGUITAR, is now in production on a full-line of the most beautiful, most saleable, economy guitars ever made in the U.S.A."

The company also purchased a smaller guitar company, the Codé Corporation, and was negotiating to purchase C.F. Martin/Netherlands. However, just when the company appeared to be growing by leaps and bounds, Glen Peterson suddenly found himself in the shoes of Alfred Dolge: his company overextended with a serious cash-flow problem. By the spring of 1978 the company was under the Chapter 11 controls of the court with production carefully regulated until a suitable buyer could be found. In October, Oscar Schmidt-International, Inc., was purchased by the owners of Fretted Industries, Inc., of Northbrook, Illinois: Rudolf Schlacher and Richard Johnstone.

194

Two unidentified young men play the new Lancer while a poster of the Cutlass hangs on the wall behind them. The Lancer appears to have a logo screened on the soundboard.

## CHAPTER 12

AUTOHARPS 1963 to 1967

Autoharps made by Oscar Schmidt-International, Inc., Jersey City, New Jersey (1963 to 1966), and Union, New Jersey (1966—   ). (Includes all "Silvertone" and "Airline" Autoharps and Guitaros.)

MODELS

#2¾ (5 chord)	#15E	Electro-harp
#12A	Appalachian (#45)	Silvertone
#15A	Guitaro (#55, #55B)	Airline

FEATURES

Logo: Two types for standard models. Special designs for special models.
Label: None.
Holders: Wood, bakelite plastic, or styrene plastic.
Bars: Wood or aluminum with plastic inset.
Buttons: Raised, round, white plastic or rectangular white plastic.
Bar labels: Paper labels or chord names imprinted on rectangular buttons.
Music scale: Paper decal with Zimmermann figures and standard notation or paper keyboard type decal with standard notation only.
End cover: Plastic. Extruded or molded.
Feet: Wood.
Music stand holes: Two on slanted edge or none.
Bridges: Wood. Upper bridge has on metal rod inset. Two rods at lower bridge.
Tuning pins: Angled backward slightly.
Strings: Loop-end strings attach over hitch pins.
Soundboard, back and sides: Painted black, except special models. After mid-1963 soundboards were made without soundholes (except Appalachian).
Prices: Sears or Wards catalogs unless otherwise specified.

AUTOHARPS 1967 to 1978

Autoharps made by Oscar Schmidt-International, Inc., Union, New Jersey. (Includes harps made by Summit Musical Instruments, Inc. "Silvertone" and "Airline" Autoharps and Guitaros are in the section above.)

MODELS

#12B	#15EBH	#21C, #21CE
#12BH	#15C	#21C/R, #21CE/R
#12BH/R	#15EBH/R	MEG
#12C	Appalachian (#45B)	Educator
#15B	Appalachian (#45BH, #45BHE)	Cutlass
#15EB	Appalachian (#45C, #45CE)	Lancer (#80)
#15BH	Appalachian (#45C/R, #45CE/R)	Attaché (#30C)

FEATURES

Logo: Two types for standard models. Special designs for special models.
Label: One type. Most harps have no label.
Holders: B models: Styrene plastic. C models: Plastic pegs under chord bar cover.
Bars: B models: Aluminum/plastic. C models: Aluminum.
Buttons: B models: Rectangular white plastic, fused to bar. C models: Moveable, oval white plastic.
Music scale: Plastic keyboard type, with or without music staff.
End cover: None.
Feet: Wood or rubber.
Bridges: None. Individual guide posts at top end, aluminum string anchor inset in rout at lower end.
Tuning pins: Perpendicular.
Strings: Ball-end strings hook into slots of string anchor.
Frame: Interlocking frame with laminated pin block on most models, four-ply or eight-ply.
Soundboard, back and sides: Natural finish or stained. A few painted. With or without soundhole.
Prices: Sears or Wards catalogs unless specified otherwise.

#2¾
(5-chord)

23 strings.
5 chords: C, F, B-flat, G7, C7.

195

The familiar scroll decal appears on all Models #2¾ made during this period.

Logo: Scroll decal.
Holders: Wood.
Bars: Wood.
Buttons: Round.
Bar labels: Paper ovals.
Music scale: Paper decal.
End cover: Extruded plastic.
Soundboard, back and sides: Black. No soundhole.
Size: 17 inches by 9 inches.
Price: (1960) $17.95.
Discontinued: 1964.

A late Model #2¾ made in early 1964.

196

#12A

36 strings.
12 chords: C, F, B-flat, G,
G7, C7, D7, A7, E7,
Am, Gm, Dm.

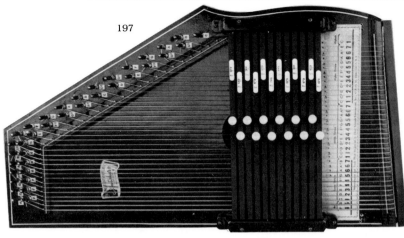

197

A very early 1963 Model #12A (#6325) still has the soundhole. Bar labels are ovals.

Later 1963 Model #12A (#6345) has no soundhole and rectangular bar labels.

198

Logo: Scroll decal.
Holders: Bakelite plastic.
Bars: Wood.
Buttons: Round.
Bar labels: Paper ovals, then rectangles.
Music scale: Paper decal with Zimmermann figures and standard notation.
End cover: Extruded plastic.
Soundboard: Black. No soundhole.
Size: 22 inches by 12 inches.
Price: (1963) $24.95.
Discontinued: 1967 with introduction of B-model Autoharps.

A 1964 model shows the soundboard without the soundhole.

199

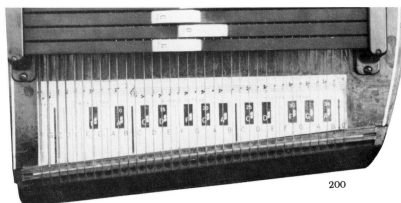

200

201

A new trapezoid-shaped logo was introduced in 1964 (top).

The tuning pins still slant backward slightly on the harps with the new design changes (bottom).

202

Closeup of the new "keyboard" design for the music scale, without Zimmermann figures. The music scale is paper glued to cardboard. This is covered with plastic and then attached to the soundboard by screws. Note rectangular buttons on wood bars and molded end pin cover with rounded corners (top left).

A 1964 model showing the design changes: 1) trapezoid logo, 2) keyboard music scale, 3) styrene plastic chord bar holders, 4) molded styrene plastic end pin cover, and 5) rectangular white plastic buttons with chord names. Batch numbers were no longer stamped on the back of the harp (left).

Closeup of the new styrene chord bar holder. After 1966 the wood bars were replaced by aluminum bars with plastic inserts (below).

203

204

#15A, #15E

36 strings.
15 chords: C, F, B-flat, G, G7,
C7, D7, A7, E7, Am, Gm, Dm, and
    #15A: C, C-sharp, and D diminished seventh.
    #15E: D, F7, and E-flat.

A very early Model #15A with scroll decal and round buttons. Note styrene chord bar holders and molded end cover.

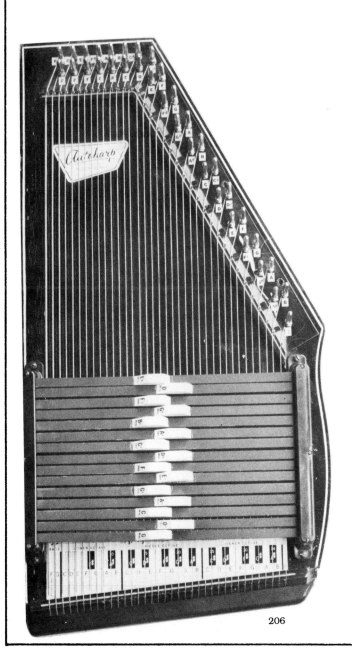

Logo: Trapezoid decal.
Holders: Styrene plastic.
Bars: Wood.
Buttons: Rectangular.
Bar labels: None. Chord names on buttons.
Music scale: Keyboard type.
End cover: Molded plastic.
Soundboard: Black. No soundhole.
Size: 22 inches by 12 inches.
Price: (1965) $34.95.
Introduced: Model #15A, 1964. Model #15E, 1965.
Discontinued: Both models in 1967.

Model #15E was introduced in 1965. Rectangular buttons are glued to wooden bars.

Two small white dots show where the holes were to be drilled for the music stand. After 1965 the holes were no longer drilled.

208

After the move of the factory to Union, New Jersey, in mid-1966, new chord bars were designed. Aluminum bars with plastic tops inset replaced the wooden bars. Buttons are chemically fused to the plastic. Other features remain the same: slanted tuning pins, keyboard scale, molded end cover.

209

A late Model #15A (ca. 1967) no longer has paper decal with note names by the tuning pins. The letters are screened onto the harp.

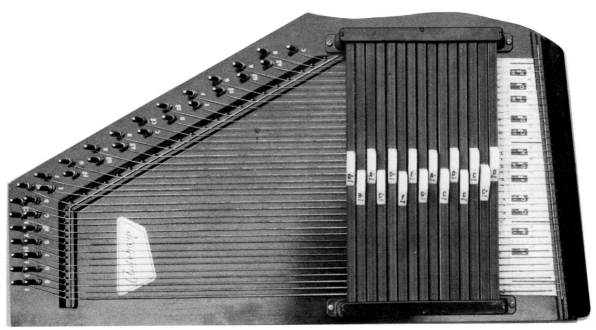

210

Appalachian
#45

36 strings.
15 chords: C, F, B-flat,
G, E, A, D, G7, C7, D7,
A7, E7, Am, Gm, Dm.

211

Special "Appalachian" logo.

212

Logo: Special "Appalachian" logo on gold decal.
Holders: Styrene plastic.
Bars: Wood. Natural finish.
Buttons: Rectangular.
Bar labels: None. Chord names on buttons.
Music scale: None.
End cover: Molded plastic.
Soundboard, back and sides: Spruce soundboard with soundhole. Natural finish.
Special features: No string names by tuning pins. Chord bar assembly set closer to end of harp for more playing room.
Size: 22 inches by 12 inches.
Price: (1963 company ad) $69.50.
Introduced: Late 1963.
Discontinued: 1967.

An Appalachian Model #45 with molded end cover (left). A catalog drawing clearly shows the extruded plastic end cover (below).

Guitaro
#55, #55B

24 strings.
15 chords: C, F, B-flat, G, D,
G7, C7, D7, A7, E7, B7,
Am, Gm, Dm, Em.

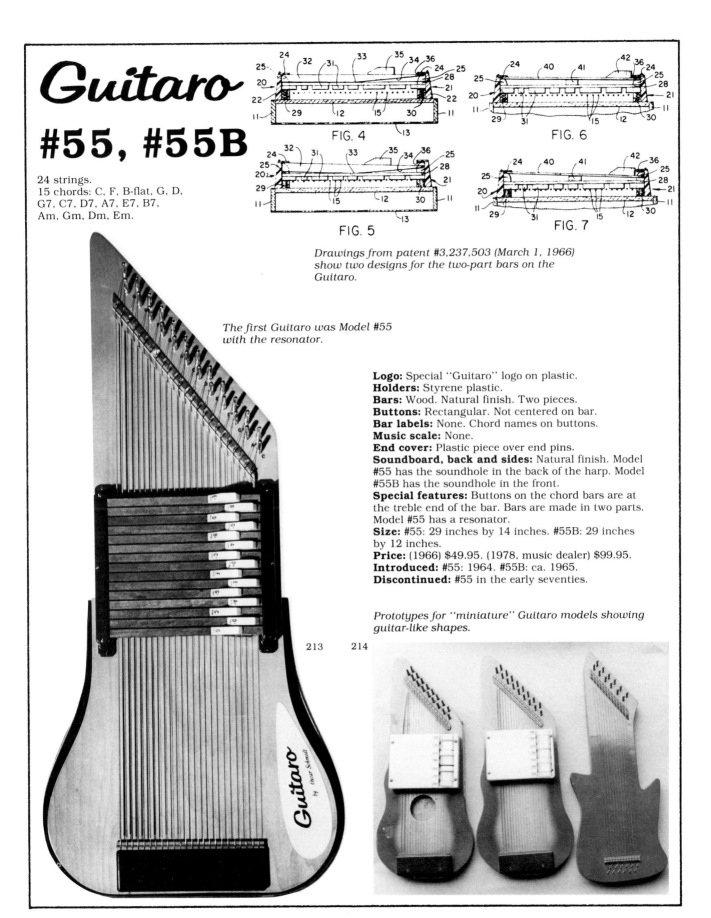

FIG. 4

FIG. 5

FIG. 6

FIG. 7

*Drawings from patent #3,237,503 (March 1, 1966)
show two designs for the two-part bars on the
Guitaro.*

*The first Guitaro was Model #55
with the resonator.*

Logo: Special "Guitaro" logo on plastic.
Holders: Styrene plastic.
Bars: Wood. Natural finish. Two pieces.
Buttons: Rectangular. Not centered on bar.
Bar labels: None. Chord names on buttons.
Music scale: None.
End cover: Plastic piece over end pins.
Soundboard, back and sides: Natural finish. Model
#55 has the soundhole in the back of the harp. Model
#55B has the soundhole in the front.
Special features: Buttons on the chord bars are at
the treble end of the bar. Bars are made in two parts.
Model #55 has a resonator.
Size: #55: 29 inches by 14 inches. #55B: 29 inches
by 12 inches.
Price: (1966) $49.95. (1978, music dealer) $99.95.
Introduced: #55: 1964. #55B: ca. 1965.
Discontinued: #55 in the early seventies.

*Prototypes for "miniature" Guitaro models showing
guitar-like shapes.*

213   214

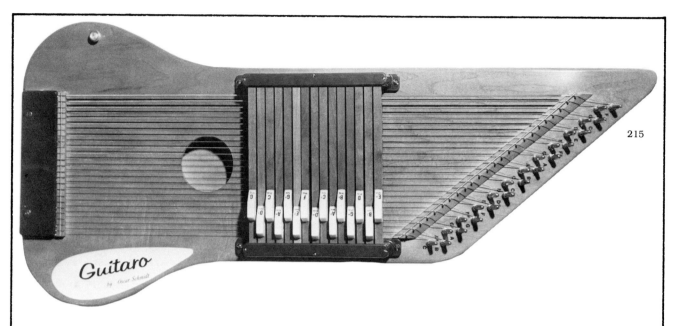

The second Guitaro Model #55B continued to be offered after the #55 was dropped.

215

SEARS, ROEBUCK COMPANY
Electro-harp

36 strings.
15 chords: C, F, B-flat, G,
G7, C7, D7, A7, E7,
Am, Gm, Dm, and
C, C-sharp, and D diminished seventh.

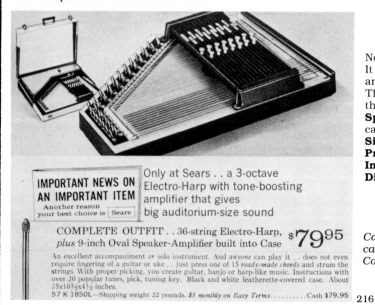

No example of this model available.
It appeared in the Sears catalogs in 1964 and 1965 and was made exclusively for Sears.
The first amplified Autoharp, it was the forerunner of the electric models.
Special features: Amplifier and speaker built into case.
Size: 25 inches by 16½ inches.
Price: (1964) $79.95.
Introduced: 1964.
Discontinued: 1966.

Catalog advertisement from Spring 1964 Sears catalog. Photo courtesy of Sears, Roebuck and Company.

216

SEARS, ROEBUCK COMPANY
"Silvertone" Autoharps

36 strings.
12 chords: C, F, B-flat, G, G7, C7, D7, A7, E7, Am, Gm, Dm.
15 chords: C, F, B-flat, G, D, E-flat, G7, C7, D7, A7, E7, F7, Am, Gm, Dm.

217

218

In 1968 the Silvertone logo was added to the soundboard. It was screened onto the harp, replacing the logo below the music scale. Chord bars were changed to aluminum/plastic.

Logo: "Autoharp" logo screened below music scale.
Holders: Styrene plastic.
Bars: Wood.
Buttons: Rectangular.
Bar labels: None. Chord names on buttons.
Music scale: Standard notation screened onto soundboard.
End cover: Molded plastic.
Soundboard, back and sides: Soundboard cream-colored. Back and sides are dark burgundy. No soundhole.
Size: 22 inches by 12 inches.
Price: (1966) 12-chord: $32.95. 15-chord: $36.95.
Introduced: 1965.
Discontinued: 1972.

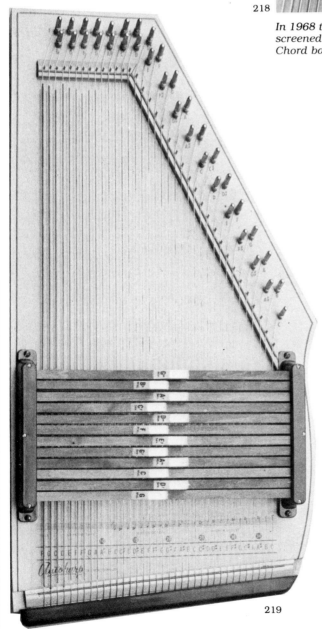

An early example of the special model harps made for Sears. Note the Autoharp logo below the music scale and no "Silvertone" logo on soundboard (left).

A-model Silvertone harps continued to be made for Sears after the introduction of the B-model harps. A later Silvertone model shows the special logo on the soundboard. In 1970 the soundboard was changed from basswood to maple with a natural finish (below).

219

220

MONTGOMERY WARD COMPANY
"Airline" Autoharps

36 strings.
12 chords: C, F, B-flat, G, G7, C7, D7, A7,
E7, Am, Gm, Dm.
15 chords: C, F, B-flat, G, G7, C7, D7, A7,
E7, Am, Gm, Dm, and C, C-sharp, and
D diminished seventh.

221

Airline logo was screened onto harp.

Logo: Special "Airline" logo screened onto harp.
Holders: Styrene plastic.
Bars: Wood. Natural finish.
Buttons: Rectangular.
Bar labels: None. Chord names on buttons.
Music scale: Plastic strip with standard notation.
End cover: Molded plastic.
Soundboard, back and sides: Dark mahogany finish. No soundhole.
Size: 22 inches by 12 inches.
Price: (1966) 12-chord: $28.95. 15-chord: $34.95.
Introduced: 1965.
Discontinued: 1972.

Airline harps were made for the Montgomery Ward Company. They were first introduced after the standard A-model harps were redesigned. These special A-model harps were still made after the introduction of the B-model harps, until 1972.

222

#12, #12BH, #12BH/R, #12C
Monterey

36 strings.
12 chords: C, F, B-flat, G, G7, C7, D7, A7, E7, Am, Gm, Dm.

223

The new logo on the B-model harps still has the trapezoid outline, but it is screened onto the soundboard, not a decal.

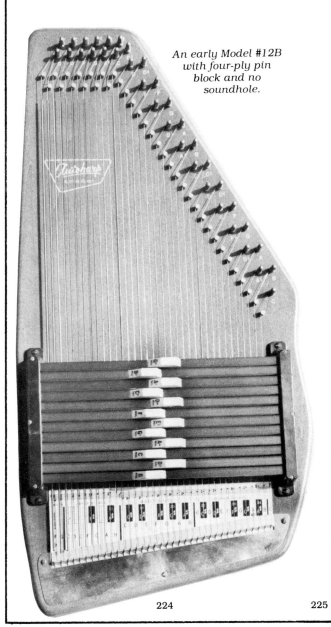

An early Model #12B with four-ply pin block and no soundhole.

Logo: Trapezoid outline.
Music scale: Plastic keyboard with music staff.
Frame: Four-ply laminated pin block.
Soundboard, back and sides: No soundhole. Light stain.
Special features: On early B-model harps the string anchor cover goes over the top of the string anchor. It has to be removed to change strings.
Size: 23½ inches by 12 inches.
Price: (1972) $39.49. (1978, music dealer) $110.00.
Introduced: 1967.

Closeup of the four-ply laminated pin block on early B-model harps. In 1968 it was changed to eight-ply.

224   225

226

Closeup of music scale on 1968 Model #12B. Harp has eight-ply pin block and darker stain. Note string anchor cover extends over the top of the slots in the string anchor. It must be removed to change strings.

227

In the early seventies the string anchor cover was redesigned so that the edge turned down into the string anchor rout. Now strings can be changed without removing the cover.

In 1975 the music scale was redesigned. The keyboard design remained the same, but the staff with notes was removed. The staff was included as a separate piece and could be attached by the owner if desired.

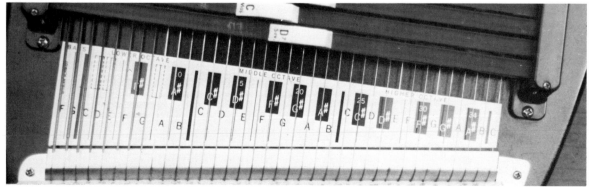

228

229

230

In 1975 the Autoharp logo was enlarged and the trapezoid outline removed.

231

The soundhole was reintroduced on all Autoharps in 1969. This dark dark-stained 1975 "Monterey" Model #12BH shows the new logo and the new music scale design. The chord bars have been modified. Note no label in the soundhole.

Some twelve-chord harps were made with the C-model chord bar cover. This Model #12C was made for the educational market. Note the staff has been attached to the soundboard.

In 1978 the Model #12BH/R was introduced. It had a new label in the soundhole, but was not significantly different from the Model #12BH.

232

#15B, #15EB, #15BH, #15EBH, #15C, #15EBH/R

Newport, Berkshire

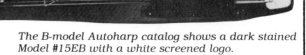

The B-model Autoharp catalog shows a dark stained Model #15EB with a white screened logo.

36 strings.
15 chords: C, F, B-flat, G, G7, C7, D7, A7, E7, Am, Gm, Dm, and
   (Newport) #15B: C, C-sharp and D diminished seventh.
   (Berkshire) #15EB: D, E-flat, F7.

A 1968 Model #15EB, with eight-ply pin block and no soundhole.

Logo: Trapezoid outline.
Music scale: Plastic keyboard with music staff.
Frame: Eight-ply laminated pin block.
Soundboard, back and sides: No soundhole. Natural finish.
Special features: String anchor cover goes over the top of the string anchor.
Size: 23½ inches by 12 inches.
Price: (1972) $53.95. (1978, music dealer) $105.00.
Introduced: 1967.
Discontinued: "Newport" Model #15BH, ca. 1972-73.

In 1968 the four-ply laminated pin block was changed to an eight-ply pin block.

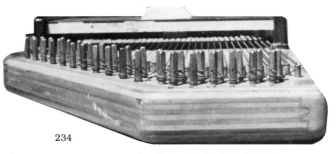

233

234

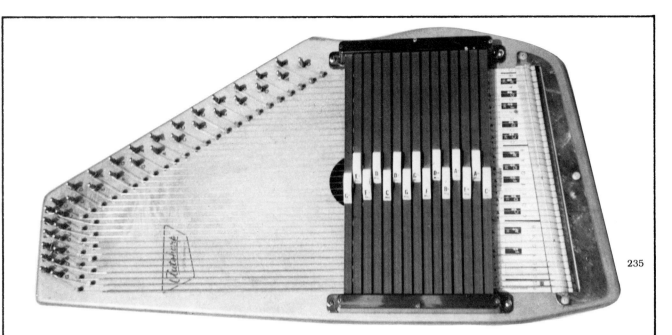

235

This "Berkshire" Model #15EBH shows the soundhole that was reintroduced in 1969. (Chord bars have been rearranged from the standard pattern.)

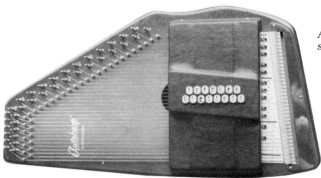

A Model #15C made for the educational market in the late seventies (left).

236

237

In 1978 the Model #15EBH/R was made with an imitation rosewood finish. The "grain" was screened onto the harp, and a label added inside the soundhole.

238

Appalachian
#45B, #45BH

36 strings.
15 chords: C, F, B-flat, G, E, A, D, G7, C7, D7, A7, E7, Am, Gm, Dm.

239

"Appalachian" logo screened onto a 1967 Model #45B.

Logo: Special "Appalachian" logo screened onto the harp.
Label: None.
Music scale: None.
Frame: Laminated pin block.
Soundboard, back and sides: #45B has solid spruce top; #45BH has laminated maple top with spruce veneer. Brown sunburst stain. The Appalachian model has a soundhole.
Special features: No string names by tuning pins. Chord bar assembly is set closer to the end of harp for more playing room. In 1969 the Appalachian model was also offered as an acoustic/electric Model #45BHE.
Size: 23½ inches by 12 inches.
Price: (1967, music dealer) $85.95.
Introduced: 1967.
Discontinued: 1975 with introduction of Model #45C.

Model #45BHE with built-in electric pickup under chord bars.

240

Appalachian
#45C, #45C/R

36 strings.
21 chords: C, F, B-flat, G, D, A, E-flat, A-flat,
G7, C7, D7, A7, E7, B7, F7, B-flat seventh,
Am, Gm, Dm, Cm, Em. (Extra E major
chord bar included.)

*In 1978 Models #45C/R and #45CE/R were introduced. The
sunburst finish was replaced by a natural finish with
brown logo, and a label added inside the soundhole. This
catalog photo claims to be the acoustic/electric Model
#45CE/R, but there is no output jack! Close inspection
reveals that it is the same harp used for the photograph of
the acoustic model (with fake control knobs added), and
the label confirms it to be Model #45C/R.*

Logo: Special "Appalachian" logo screened
onto harp.
Label: None.
Music scale: None.
Frame: Eight-ply laminated pin block.
Soundboard, back and sides: Laminated
soundboard (maple with spruce veneer) with
soundhole. Cherry-colored sunburst stain.
Special features: String names on string
anchor instead of by tuning pins. C-model
harps have the same body as the B-model
harps have. The C-model chord bar assembly is
different, with interchangeable chord bars and
a plastic chord bar cover. (See Chapter 15 for a
closeup of the inside of the C-model chord bar
assembly.) Chord bar assembly is set closer to
end of harp for more playing room. Also
available as acoustic/electric Models #45CE and
#45CE/R.
Size: 23½ inches by 12 inches.
Price: (1975, music dealer) #45C: $119.95.
(1978 music dealer) #45C/R: $140.00. #45CE/R
$160.00.
Introduced: 1975.

*The "Appalachian" Autoharp was changed to twenty-one
chords in 1975, and the model number changed to #45C.*

#21C, #21C/R
Classic, MEG, Educator

36 strings.
21 chords: C, F, B-flat, G, D, A, E-flat, A-flat, G7, C7, D7, A7, E7, B7, F7, B-flat seventh, Am, Gm, Dm, Cm, Em.

243

The "MEG" logo was a decal put on Autoharps that were sold through Music Education Group.

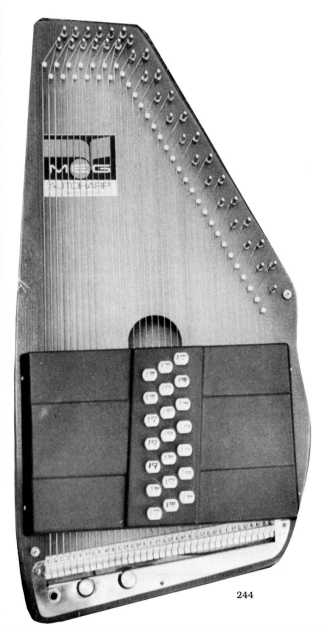

Logo: "MEG" decal.
Label: None.
Music scale: None.
Frame: Eight-ply laminated pin block.
Soundboard, back and sides: Laminated soundboard (maple) with soundhole. Cherry-colored sunburst stain.
Special features: "MEG" harps were made by Oscar Schmidt for Music Education Group. They are the same as the standard models, except for the "MEG" logo. Twenty-one chord harps were also available as acoustic/electric Models #21CE and #21CE/R.
Introduced: 1971.

The first twenty-one chord acoustic harps were MEG harps and available only through Music Education Group dealers. This "Virginian" acoustic/electric model has the string names on the string anchor instead of by the tuning pins. There was also a standard twenty-one chord MEG Autoharp with the string names by the tuning pins and the plastic keyboard music scale below the chord bars. In 1975 MEG Autoharps were renamed "Educator" Autoharps.

244

245

The twenty-one chord C-model harp was made available to the general public in 1975. This 1976 "Classic" Model #21C shows the enlarged Autoharp logo with the trapezoid outline removed. The keyboard music scale does not have the music staff on it. An acoustic/electric Model #21CE was also offered to music retailers in 1975.

In 1978 the imitation rosewood finish was added. A label was put in the soundhole, and the model number changed to #21C/R. The acoustic/electric Model #21CE/R was also available.

246

Cutlass, Lancer
#80

36 strings.
21 chords: C, F, B-flat, G, D,
A, E-flat, A-flat, G7, C7, D7,
A7, E7, B7, F7, B-flat seventh,
Am, Gm, Dm, Cm, Em.

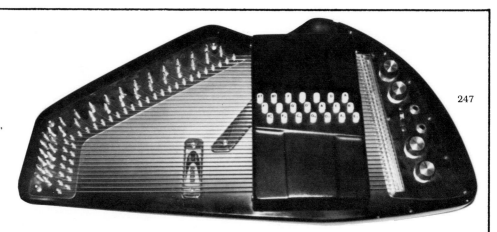

247

The Cutlass with two pickups has "Autoharp Cutlass by Summit" written on the bass pickup.

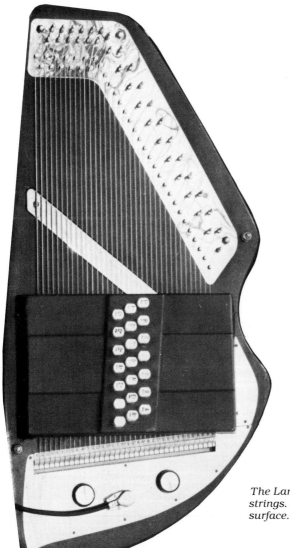

Logo: Special "Cutlass" logo on bass pickup.
None on Lancer (#80).
Label: None.
Music scale: None.
Frame: Laminated pin block, inset into special rout under metal plate.
Soundboard, back and sides: Entire harp is solid wood.
Special features: Solid-body electric model. The Cutlass has two pickups, one bass, one treble. The Lancer has a single pickup.
Price: (ca. 1968, music dealer) Cutlass: $225.00. Lancer: $175.00.
Introduced: 1967.
Discontinued: Cutlass, in the early seventies.

The Lancer has only one pickup placed diagonally across the strings. It is inset into the body of the harp and flush with the surface.

248

Attaché
#30C

36 strings.
21 chords: C, F, B-flat, G, D, A, E-flat,
A-flat, G7, C7, D7, A7, E7, B7, F7,
B-flat seventh, Am, Gm, Dm, Cm, Em.

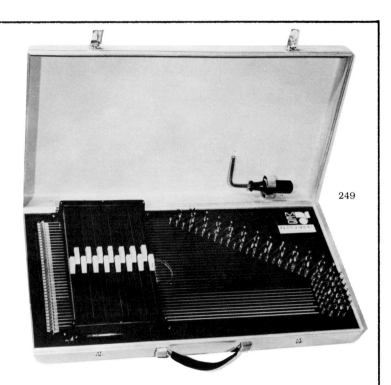

249

Logo: Special "Attaché" logo screened
onto harp.
Label: None.
Music scale: None.
Frame and soundboard: Laminated pin
block. Laminated maple soundboard.
Special features: Designed for desk-top
playing. Built into tan carrying case.
Strings are reversed to eliminate cross-
hand playing. Built-in music rack.
Price: (1978, music dealer) $140.00.
Introduced: 1975. (A fifteen-chord MEG
Attaché model was introduced ca. 1972.)

*The first Attaché Autoharp was made for Music Education
Group. It was a fifteen-chord model with the MEG logo and
available only to the educational market.*

*In 1975 a twenty-one chord Attaché Model #30C was made available to the
general public through music retailers.*

250

Summary: Autoharps 1963 to 1967

Autoharps made by Oscar Schmidt-International, Inc., Jersey City, New Jersey (1963 to 1966) and Union, New Jersey (1966—).

Models: #2¾ (5 chord), #12A, #15A, #15E, #45 (Appalachian), #55 & #55B (Guitaro), Electro-harp. Special "Silvertone" and "Airline" harps were made for Sears and Wards.
Introduced: #2¾ and #12A already in production. #45 (Appalachian), late 1963. #15A, #55 (Guitaro), and Electro-harp, 1964. #15E, #55B (Guitaro), and special Sears and Wards harps, 1965.
Discontinued: #2¾, 1964. Electro-harp, 1966. #12A, #15A, #15E, and #45, 1967. #55 (Guitaro), early 1970s. Silvertone and Airline, 1972.
Logo: 1) Scroll decal. 2) Trapezoid decal. 3) Special logos for special models.
Label: None.
Holders: Model #2¾, wood. Other models bakelite plastic until 1964, then styrene plastic.
Bars: Wood until 1966, then aluminum with a plastic strip inset.
Buttons: Raised, round, white plastic until 1964, then rectangular white plastic with chord name stamped on the button.
Felts: Black.
Bar labels: Oval or rectangular paper labels on bars with round buttons. None on bars with rectangular buttons.
Music scale: 1) Paper decal with Zimmermann figures and standard notation (1963 to 1964). 2) Paper keyboard with standard notation only (1964—).
End cover: Plastic. Extruded until 1964, then molded.
Feet: Wood.
Music stand holes: Two on slanted edge until 1965, then none.
Bridges: Wood. One metal rod inset in upper bridge. Two metal rods at lower bridge.
Tuning pins: Angled backward slightly.
Strings: Loop-end strings wrap around lower end and attach over hitch pins.
Soundboard, back and sides: Painted black, except Appalachian, Guitaro, Electro-harp, Silvertone, and Airline. After mid-1963 soundboards no longer have soundholes (except Appalachian).

Summary: Autoharps 1967 to 1978

Autoharps made by Oscar Schmidt-International, Inc., Union, New Jersey. (Includes harps made by Summit Musical Instruments, Inc.)

Models: #12B, #12BH, #12BH/R, #12C; #15B, #15EB, 15BH, #15EBH, #15C, #15EBH/R; Appalachian: #45B, #45BH, #45BHE, #45C, #45CE, #45C/R, #45CE/R; #21C, #21CE, #21C/R, #21CE/R; Cutlass, Lancer (#80); Attaché. Special "MEG" and "Educator" harps were made for Music Education Group. Silvertone and Airline harps made until 1972 and Guitaro's made until 1978 are included in the section above.
Introduced: B models, Cutlass, and Lancer, late 1967. BH models, 1969. "MEG" harps, 1971. C models, Attaché, and "Educator" harps, 1975. R models, 1978. (#12C and #15C made for the educational market in the mid/late 1970s).
Discontinued: Cutlass and #15BH, ca. 1972-1973. #45BH and "MEG" harps, 1975.
Logo: 1) Trapezoid outline around "Autoharp" name. 2) "Autoharp" name enlarged, outline removed. 3) Special logos for special models.
Label: 1) None. 2) "Oscar Schmidt-International" in gold and black design.
Holders: B models: Styrene plastic. C models (includes Lancer and Attaché): Plastic pegs under chord bar cover.
Bars: B models: Aluminum/plastic. C models: Aluminum.
Buttons: B models: Rectangular white plastic, fused to bar. C models: Moveable, oval white plastic.
Felts: B models: Black. C models: White.
Music scale: Plastic "keyboard" type. In 1975 the music staff was removed and included as a separate strip.
End cover: None.
Feet: Wood or rubber.
Bridges: None. Individual guide posts at top end, aluminum string anchor inset in rout at lower end.
Tuning pins: Perpendicular.
Strings: Ball-end strings hook into slots of string anchor.
Frame: Interlocking frame with laminated pin block on most models. Early B-model harps had four-ply pin blocks. In 1968 they became eight-ply.
Soundboard, back and sides: Natural finish or stained. A few painted. Only the Appalachian model had a soundhole prior to 1969. In 1969 the BH-model harps with soundholes were introduced.

183

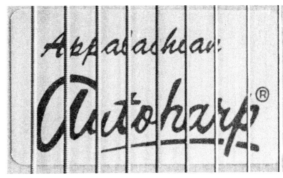

211

First logo (top left): Scroll decal (1963 to 1964).
Second logo (bottom left): Trapezoid-shaped
paper decal (late 1964 to mid-1967).
Appalachian logo (above): Gold decal on
A-model harps (late 1963 to mid-1967).

251

252

Guitaro logo: Screened on plastic (1964—).
Silvertone logo: Screened onto harps made for Sears
(1968 to 1972).
Airline logo: Screened onto harps made for Wards
(1965 to 1972).

221

253

Design changes in the new B-model Autoharps.

Interlocking frame.

Exterior wooden bridge replaced by individual guide posts. Tuning pins are perpendicular to the soundboard.

Laminated pin block. Originally four-ply, but soon changed to eight-ply.

Aluminum chord bars with plastic strip inset. Rectangular buttons are chemically fused to the plastic strip.

Aluminum string anchor replaced lower wooden bridge. Ball-end strings hook into slots in string anchor.

254

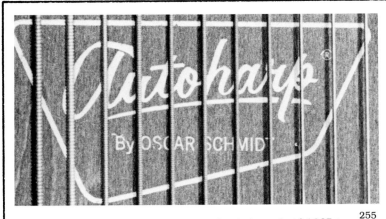

First logo: Trapezoid outline screened onto harp (mid-1967 to 1975).

Second logo: "Autoharp" name enlarged, outline removed (1975—).

256

MEG logo: Autoharps made for Music Education Group (ca. 1971 to 1975).

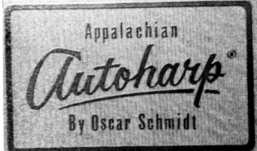

239

Appalachian logo: Brown on B model (mid-1967 to 1975). White on C model (1975 to 1978). Brown on C/R model (1978).

Label: No label until 1978 when a gold and black label was added to the "R" models.

237

Attaché logo: Special logo was made when Attaché model offered to the general public in 1975.

Educator logo: In 1975 all MEG Autoharps were changed to Educator Autoharps (1975—).

243

Rudolf Schlacher

257

Richard Johnstone

258

## CHAPTER 13

OSCAR SCHMIDT-INTERNATIONAL, 1978 to 1983

Bring the family closer together with your music. *Real music* never played this easily. The Autoharp lets you sit down . . . and play . . . the very first time.

Simply pick your favorite song, push the chord button and strum . . . that's all there is to it! Incredibly beautiful music played by *you* . . . or anyone else in the family not in diapers.

Ad in *Woman's Day* magazine, November 24, 1981

In the years since the takeover of Oscar Schmidt-International, Inc., by Fretted Industries, the Autoharp has undergone some of the most significant changes in its hundred-year existence. As soon as the initial difficulties in restarting production were overcome, partners Rudolf Schlacher and Richard Johnstone began to look at ways of redesigning the Autoharp and improving its sound. For the first time, serious attention was paid to the needs of the musicians who were playing the Autoharp.

The rare ability to improve both the musical properties of the instrument and the service relationship between company and musician comes from the unique backgrounds of Schlacher and Johnstone. Schlacher, born in Austria, began a four-year apprenticeship as a muscial instrument builder when he was fourteen years old. Later, he worked for various companies, making and repairing all types of stringed instruments, including violins, guitars, bass fiddles, and zithers. Eventually he ended up in Chicago as manager of a retail music store, specializing in guitar and violin sales and repairs.[1]

Schlacher met Rick Johnstone at the music store, where the latter worked summers while going to school. Johnstone, who had played the guitar for many years with his own trio, the Parkside Singers, gave guitar lessons at the store and was active in sales. The two became friends, and when Schlacher decided he wanted to start his own store in 1970, he asked Johnstone to be his partner. By this time Johnstone was in law school, but he agreed to give it a try, working in the new store during vacations.

The store they opened was the Sound Post, located in nearby Evanston, Illinois. In only one year the store was successful enough for Johnstone to leave law school to devote himself full time to the business. In 1972 a second store was opened in Mount Prospect, Illinois.

With the success of the two stores, Schlacher and Johnstone began to think of manufacturing some type of music product. They decided the product should be for the most popular instrument, the guitar . . . but what should it be? After much discussion and many ideas, Schlacher finally pointed out that violin strings are sold straight in tubes, not curled up in square envelopes as guitar string are, in order to protect the string and prevent damage from coiling. Perhaps guitar strings might benefit from similar packaging.

A test program was developed at Northwestern University that did in fact show a difference in sound between coiled strings and straight strings. As a result of those tests, the new Nashville Straights strings became the first product of Fretted Industries, Inc. (formed February 28, 1975). In less than two years more than a million dollars worth of strings had been sold to retailers throughout the country.

Excited with the manufacturing side of the music business, the two partners began to think of expanding their product line. In early 1977 they purchased the George Washburn Company and began manufacturing guitars, banjos, and mandolins. The two retail stores were put under the management of a third partner, Fritz Tasch, and Schlacher and Johnstone headed the manufacturing business. With Schlacher turning his instrument-building skills toward product development and Johnstone turning his law school background to the business side of the company, Washburn grew to be even more successful than the partners' previous endeavors.

Throughout this time the two retail stores were selling Oscar Schmidt Autoharps. Schlacher and Johnstone became aware of the Schmidt company's problems in mid-1978 when they were no longer able to obtain the product. When Oscar Schmidt-International was put under the control of the court, the factory was allowed to continue producing harps only for Sears-Roebuck, Schmidt's biggest continuous account. No Autoharps were made for retail music stores. Having successfully sold the Autoharp in their stores, Schlacher and Johnstone decided to look into purchasing the financially troubled company. By the end of the year the sale was completed, and by early 1979 Autoharps were once again available to retail stores. The Union, New Jersey, plant was kept as the factory, but the products were now warehoused at Fretted Industries in Northbrook, Illinois.

Most of 1979 was spent in dealing with almost insurmountable problems concerning restarting the business. The factory work force had been reduced to the four men who made the harps for Sears. Great efforts had to be made to rehire the workers who had since taken other jobs. New employees had to be trained to make what is a very labor intensive product. Dealer relationships had to be reestablished and a new company reputation built, a reputation based on good service and a quality product.

259

Mouse made by Becky Farnham as Christmas present for members of the Sweet Betsy from Pike Memorial Autoharp Band.

In the middle of all the initial problems at the factory, Schlacher began to put his efforts into improving the Autoharp. Many prototypes were made and designs rejected until Schlacher was satisfied that the final product had the optimum balance between structural integrity and acoustic quality. The "Centurion" series Autoharps were finally created in mid-1979 and ready for the market by the end of the year. The highest-quality Autoharps produced up until that time, the Centurions featured a new interior bracing system for better acoustics, and a solid spruce soundboard with ash back and sides, edge binding, and a laminated pin block. The Centurions were released to commemorate the one hundredth anniversary of the Oscar Schmidt company, which had been founded by Schmidt in 1879.[2]

The imitation rosewood finish featured on the last of Peterson's harps was discontinued and replaced by a choice of a natural or sunburst finish on the standard models.

178

THE STORY OF THE CENTURION

Information provided by Rudolf Schlacher, President, Oscar Schmidt-International, Inc.

How did the idea for the Centurion originate? Whose idea was it?

Oscar Schmidt wanted to do something unique to celebrate the first one hundred years of the company. Several long-time employees of Oscar Schmidt had many ideas, which were combined by Rick Johnstone, Oscar Schmidt vice president, who has, though his contacts with various autoharpists, a good understanding of their needs.

When was development begun? By whom?

We started with the development of the Centurion Autoharp in January 1979, under the direction of Tom Colonese, Schmidt plant manager at the Union, New Jersey, factory. Since each Centurion harp is hand made, we have only two craftsmen working steadily on these instruments; both have been with the company for many years.

Why was a solid-wood model decided on? What woods were considered and tried?

Through our experience in guitar building, we are well aware of the advantages solid wood can provide. (Solid wood means that there are not several plys of thinner wood glued together.) A variety of exotic woods were considered and experimented with. Woods such as mahogany, rosewood, cherry, walnut, and maple (to mention just a few) were rejected.

What was the final wood selection? Why? Are the woods domestic or imported?

The decision to use ash for the back was reached rather quickly, since other hardwood did not provide the desired tone. Wood such as rosewood sounded rather hard and tinny and did not provide the warm and rich tone we wanted. Using spruce for the top was obvious, since every good stringed instrument from the piano to the violin uses spruce for the sounding board. The structural harp frame is made of matching ash, and the pin block is made of maple. Ash, spruce, and maple are domestic woods and are readily available.

How many prototypes were made? What types of tests were made on them?

Approximately sixty prototypes were produced and supplied to professional harp players for testing and evaluation. We were mainly concerned with the quality of tone, since we knew that the solid wood harp would resonate better and therefore produce a louder tone. Since the Autoharp has to perform under tremendous string tension, our main concern was the solid spruce top. Tests in environmental chambers duplicating the aging of the woods over several years were made with various top bracing systems in order to determine the long term effects of the materials.

How was the new bracing system developed? What changes in sound did it make?

The new bracing system was developed by using Oscar's many years of experience and adapting ideas from other instruments. While maintaining the structural strength of the top, it was our aim to distribute the string vibrations evenly over the entire top surface with the help of the new bracing. The result: more definition between the individual notes and a better balance over the entire tone range.

What type of edge binding is used and how is it applied?

There are two reasons for the binding around the top and back edge of the Centurion Autoharp. The first obvious one is to have a decorative effect. Reason two is to serve as a protective outer edge which prevents the delicate wood from chipping and cracking. We generally use a material called ivoroid which is an imitation of ivory (no longer obtainable) for the outer edge. Celluloid is used for the decorative black and white inner strips along the top.

What type of pin block is used?

The material we use for the pin block is rock maple, which is cross-laminated nine times to provide the best possible pin anchoring. Piano manufacturers, such as Steinway and Baldwin, fashion their pin block the same way, assuring that the instrument maintains its tuning even under the severest conditions.

What type of varnish is used and how is it applied?

The back and sides of each Centurion are usually hand stained and the entire body is sprayed with four coats of nitro-cellulose lacquer to protect the wood.

How is the new felt better? How is "faster chord bar action" achieved?

The improved felt is of the same density and hardness as the black felt used by Oscar Schmidt many years ago. With professional use this felt will show less wear and last considerably longer. On the twelve- and fifteen-chord models, a higher chord bar is used, which brings the damping felt surface closer to the strings, thus reducing the action distance.

The newest Centurion has eleven wound strings instead of nine. Is this a permanent change? Why was it made? Will this change be made in the string set packages?

We added two wound strings (#10 and #11) to overcome the prior tonal weakness of these two strings. We are presently also experimenting if we should change string #12 to a would string. These new strings will be installed on all Autoharps produced by Oscar Schmidt, and they will also be available in the new packaged strings recently introduced by Oscar Schmidt.

How much does the Centurion weigh?

The average weight of a Centurion harp is seven pounds, which is one pound lighter than a regular Autoharp. The refined workmanship and the high quality aged solid woods account for the difference.

When did the Centurion go on the market? Is it a "limited edition"?

The first Centurion Autoharp was introduced to the U.S. market in the fall of 1979. Originally intended as a limited edition, we decided to adopt it as a regular model after receiving overwhelming response from harp players.

What do you recommend for the care of the Centurion?

Since the Centurion is constructed of solid wood, it is to the benefit of the instrument to play it as much as possible. The constant vibration of the wood while playing will reduce the stiffness of the wood fibers, thus allowing the top and back to vibrate more freely. The result? Your already good-sounding Centurion will improve in tone with age and playing.

The biggest enemy of your Centurion harp is the lack of humidity. Therefore, protect your instrument from excessive heat, such as from radiators, hot air ducts, and car trunks in the summer. Extreme temperature changes should also be avoided. Taking this reasonable care of your Centurion Autoharp will provide many years of enjoyment.

Reprinted from **The Autoharpoholic**, *Vol. 1, No. 2 (Summer 1980).*

The Autoharp, in tune with children,

260

Mary Lou Colgin and Friends.

Sckosh Fullerton.

261

262

Hudson Weed.

. . . animals,

Terry and Inga Eriksmoen.

263

Dawn Such.

264

Michael Stokes.

265

Karen Mueller.

266

The Kellett quadruplets.

267

... and the great outdoors!

Ronald Rich.

268

269

The twenty-one-chord model's chord bar cover was streamlined, and the solid-body Lancer redesigned to make the instrument lighter and easier to hold. With the new solid-body design the "Lancer" name was dropped and the new instrument referred to as the "OS-85." In 1980 a special optional "chorus" unit was added to the instrument.

By 1980 the factory was running smoothly under the supervision of plant manager Tom Colonese. Music Education Group, which also had been purchased by Schlacher and Johnstone, was back in business and selling to the educational market. At the Fretted Industries headquarters in Illinois, Autoharp promotion was put in the capable hands of

Yvonne Dickerson, Oscar Schmidt's national sales manager. A slow and steady recovery from the 1978 crisis paid off. A solid foundation had been built, dealers were again stocking the Autoharp, and the consumer was presented with a fine, high-quality musical instrument. On January 4, 1982, Oscar Schmidt-International, Inc., merged with Fretted Industries, Inc.

In early 1981 a special centennial promotion was begun for the Autoharp, celebrating its invention in 1881 and patenting in 1882. The promotion climaxed with Fretted Industries' co-sponsoring the first International Autoharp Championship, held at the Walnut Valley Festival in Winfield, Kansas.

CITY OF PHILADELPHIA

Proclamation

1982 marks the 100th anniversary of the Autoharp, a native Philadelphia musical instrument, for which a patent was issued on May 9, 1882 to Charles F. Zimmermann. He first produced the Autoharp in his shop at 240 North 2nd Street in Philadelphia's Olde City.

The Autoharp, a zither-like musical instrument, is used throughout the Philadelphia School District to introduce students to the pleasures of music and teach them basic chords and harmonies.

The instrument was invented by Zimmermann as a tool to be used with his new style of music notation. In the patent application filed on December 10, 1881, Zimmermann modestly said, "I believe it is the best work which a human being so far has achieved on earth." Despite the slight exaggeration, the Autoharp did become one of the most popular parlor instruments of the late nineteenth century.

THEREFORE . . .

I, William J. Green, Mayor of the City of Philadelphia, do hereby proclaim 1982 as the

YEAR OF THE AUTOHARP

in Philadelphia, with the hope that all citizens will recognize the pleasures of the Autoharp, and honor the 100th anniversary of its birth in our City.

William J. Green
Mayor

Given under my hand and the Seal of the City of Philadelphia, this fifteenth day of January, one thousand, nine hundred and eighty-two.

270

THE AUTOHARP FACTORY TODAY

The Oscar Schmidt-International factory is located in Union, New Jersey, the birthplace of all Autoharps since mid-1966, when the factory was moved from its previous location in Jersey City, New Jersey.

From the outside the factory looks quite unimpressive. It's a plain building at the end of a dead-end street. The calm and quiet of the exterior mask the activities inside where forty-eight employees pass the Autoharps through their various stages around the plant which covers approximately twenty-two-thousand square feet. The plant is run under the watchful eye of general manager Tom Colonese. He makes sure that everything runs smoothly and on schedule for all the products produced at the factory: Autoharps, elementary education instruments (Orff instruments, metallophones, xylophones, bell sets), OSI drums, thumb pianos, hammered dulcimers, and hardshell instrument cases.

Through the front doors and past the outer business office lies the main part of the plant, where it was quite enlightening to see how the manufacturer deals with the tedious tasks of putting on strings and making the chord bars for each of the different chords. Colonese explained each of the stages of production.

The first part of the Autoharp is the frame, with joints that overlap at the corners. With the exception of the solid-body electric models, which are solid wood throughout, all Autoharps begin with this type of frame. The upper part of the frame is, of course, the pin block for the harp. Almost all of the Autoharps now have laminated pin blocks. The pin blocks are put together and shaped prior to being put in as part of the frame. The solid-body harps also have laminated pin blocks, which are inset into a hole routed out of the solid wood.

The frame pieces are glued together with a special radio frequency gluing machine. A vital piece of factory equipment, the R.F. gluer, sets the glue in the frames so that they will not come apart. When the frames have been glued together, they are cut down to an even one-inch thickness. The ribs are actually inset into the sides of the frame for added strength.

Once the frames are ready, the back side and soundboard are added. At this point there is no hole in the soundboard. As the top and bottom are glued onto the frames, they are stacked into a glue box. When the box is full, a board is clamped down on top to press them together firmly until they are dried. This assures that the harps stay flat, and that the parts are securely glued.

When the basic harp box is assembled and trimmed with a band saw, they are ready to be shaped. The shaping machine has an aluminum fixture that is placed on top of the harp box. The shaper follows this piece as a guide so that all the harps are shaped to exactly the same size.

Next the box goes to the machines that rout out the hole for the string anchor and rout out the edge for the models that have binding added to them. A hole cutter then cuts out the soundhole from the top side of the box. The binding is put in place and taped until it is dried.

When the Autoharp is shaped and routed where needed, the finishing is done. Harps are either painted or stained and varnished. They are hung onto drying racks to thoroughly dry before the metal parts are added.

Probably the most-impressive piece of machinery in the factory is the "Zagar," the tool that was the key to the B-model Autoharp. It simultaneously drills seventy-two holes: thirty-six for the tuning pins and thirty-six for the individual bridge pins. The machine insures that the spacing is perfect between the holes, that they are drilled precisely at the proper angle (perpendicular), and that all the holes are drilled to the exact depth required for the type of pin to be installed.

Next the bridge pins are installed. A board of the correct thickness is laid on top of the harp. There are thirty-six holes in the board for the bridge pins, and two pins are tapped into place to hold the board. The other pins are simply dropped into their holes. The harp with the board is then put under a press which is lowered down to press all the pins into the holes. The result is a set of pins exactly the same height.

Throughout these steps considerable precautions are taken to prevent the harp's finish from being scarred. Soft cloths are placed under the harp when the pins are inset, and the harps travel through the factory in special plastic trays to protect them.

A separate area of the factory is set aside to install the electronic parts on the solid-body electric models. The wiring for the tone and volume controls is placed into the string anchor rout, and the magnetic pickup is set into a rout so that it is flush with the surface. The chorus units are also installed in the side of the harp in this part of the factory.

All harps need strings. Putting them on is a task that no player enjoys, but the mind boggles at the thought of the number of strings that must be strung daily at the factory. Again, there are specialized tools that simplify the process as much as possible. First the string is put through the hold in the tuning pin. While the string is held taut, the pin is put into a machine that automatically spins the pin to start the string wrap. Then the ball end is hooked into the anchor and the pin put in its hole. Another tool is used to push the pin into the hole to the proper depth before a third tool is used to bring the string up to tension.

After the pins are in and the strings attached, the chord bars are added, but first the bars need felt. The bars are done in batches, each batch for a different chord. Steel bars of two heights are set into a fixture. The taller bars are where the spaces will be left open for the strings, and the lower bars are where the felts will go. Strips of felt are placed on top of the lower bars in between the taller bars with the pressure-sensitive adhesive side up. The top of the felt is flush with the taller bars. The aluminum chord bars are taped together in one long board and laid on top of the felt. This is then clamped and allowed to set.

When the felt is secured to the bars, the board is removed from the clamps. It looks like a big slab of bacon as it is put into the next machine that slices off each chord bar. The plastic strips are then added to the bars for the standard B-model harps. The C-model harps (twenty-one chords) don't have the plastic strips inset, but both types of bars need buttons.

As might be expected, another clever machine stamps the chord name onto the button. B-model buttons are then glued onto the plastic strips. Then the bars are grouped into sets for the various models. Since the B-model bars have the names of the chords on the glued-on buttons, there is no special problem for them. The C-model bars do not have their buttons attached to them, however, so there is a chart showing all the bars for this model. The person assembling the sets can check the bars against this chart to be sure the correct bars are put into each set.

The last area of the factory is the place where they make the hardshell cases for the Autoharps. First they simply make a box. The box is then cut in two with an angled cut from each of the four sides. The top and bottom are then always a perfect match, and the beveled edge keeps the pieces locked so they can't slide apart.

When the Autoharps are completed and cases lined and latched, everything is shipped off to the warehouse in Northbrook, Illinois. There the harps wait patiently to be adopted by some loving "Autoharpoholic."

Reprinted from **The Autoharpoholic**, *Vol. 3, No. 3 (Summer 1982).*

271

Above: The Oscar Schmidt-International factory, Garden
State Rose, Union, New Jersey.
Below: Frames for a standard Autoharp, a Guitaro, and
an Attaché model.
Autoharp with metal fixture being shaped.
Right: Routing the hole for the string anchor.
The Zagar machine with seventy-two drill bits.
Installing the bridge pins.
Slabs of chord bars with felt.

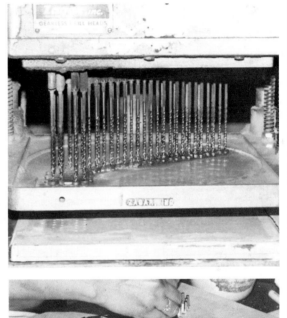

In addition to the contest, the mid-September festival featured an "Autoharp Activity Center" where workshops were sponsored by Fretted Industries and organized and coordinated by *The Autoharpoholic* magazine. The three-day event probably was the biggest gathering of Autoharp players ever. Hundreds of players attended the workshops, a record-breaking thirty-one contestants performed at the competition, and a grand finale had an Autoharp chorus featuring seventy-five harps playing "Will the Circle Be Unbroken."

It was also at the 1981 festival that the seed was planted from which the new three-key diatonic model Autoharps would grow. The basic design of the harp was discussed by Rick Johnstone, Ron Wall, and Becky Blackley in the small trailer at the activity center, and the first handmade prototype returned with Johnstone to the company as a production model. Over the next year the design would be modified and improved by Rudy Schlacher and Tom Colonese. As with the Centurion models, numerous prototypes would be made and rejected until the best design would finally be introduced as the first "Festival" – series Autoharp, named for the event that brought the designers together. By the 1982 Walnut Valley Festival, the two models were ready for the market.

In addition to the diatonic, double-string tuning, each of the two models plays in three keys: one plays in F, C, and G major, the other in G, D, and A major. A set of special lock bars change the open tuning to each of the three diatonic scales. An improved bracing system and enlarged soundhole have brought this acoustic harp to a volume level where it can finally be heard in groups of other instruments.

A later development ultimately added to the Festival harps was the fine-tuning mechanism for each string, in early 1983 becoming a standard feature on the diatonic Festival Autoharps.[3]

Two other new models were introduced in late 1981 and 1982. The Phoenix harp is a fifteen-chord harp with a solid black finish and gold logo on the soundboard. The idea for the Phoenix came from Schmidt's national sales manager, Yvonne Dickerson. Dickerson felt a need to produce an Autoharp with a more traditional look. Many players were very fond of the simple appearance of the old black-body A-model harps, and Dickerson thought that a black-body B-model harp would appeal to many players.

As simple as the concept was, many prototypes were required to develop a marketable instrument. Plant manager Tom Colonese worked on the special problems caused by trying to screen gold over black, and in making a durable black finish. The result is an attractive black gloss applied over a black stain. If the instrument is accidentally dented, the exposed wood will be black and the damage to the instrument thus less noticeable. The gold logo gives a classic finish to the harp.[4]

The other new model was the child-size "Easy Chord" Autoharp, developed in order to make the range of Autoharps accessible to all the members of the family except, perhaps, those in diapers. The full-size Autoharp, of course, has always been popular for family entertainment. In an article in *Crain's Chicago Business* (July 5,

272

City attorney Paul Keller back in his office after attending the first International Autoharp Championship.

273

1982) Rick Johnstone says, "[The Autoharp] is designed for music lovers, not musicians. It's for the ordinary person who can't play anything but the radio." Despite the Autoharp's simplicity, however, its size does limit the age group that can play it; hence the Easy Chord. Johnstone continues: "This instrument appeals to parents who want to introduce their kids to music but in the past have been unable to afford the more expensive band instruments. Because the Autoharp is so simple to play, the child won't become discouraged and toss it into the closet after a few months."

The Easy Chord was introduced onto the market as a solid-body harp late in 1981. In early 1982 the instrument was built with a hollow body and a soundhole. The small size and low price made the harp very popular with teachers, and an instructional program was developed for the schools.

A marketing campaign was designed around a family theme. Music was now something that everyone in the family could

THE DEVELOPMENT OF THE DIATONIC AUTOHARP

Information provided by Yvonne Dickerson, National Sales Manager, Oscar Schmidt-International, Inc.

Everyone's talking about the "new" diatonic tuning. What is diatonic tuning and just now new is it?

Think of a piano keyboard. A chromatic scale will have all the semitones. That is, all the white keys and all the black keys. A diatonic scale is the familiar do-re-mi major scale. For the key of C major, only the white keys on the piano would be used. The standard modern Autoharp has been tuned chromatically, with strings tuned for each of the semitones. On a diatonically-tuned Autoharp, all the strings for notes outside of the do-re-mi scale would be tuned up a half-tone or down a half-tone to one of the notes that is in that particular diatonic scale. The result is two strings in a row tuned to the same note. That's the diatonic Autoharp.

It really isn't new at all. The first Charles F. Zimmermann Model #1 (ca. 1885) was a diatonic Autoharp. Players have been using the tuning on modern Autoharps for about ten years.

If its' been around for almost one hundred years, why hasn't there been a modern diatonic model made until last year?

Oscar Schmidt was aware that folks were experimenting with diatonic tuning. It is a beautiful, full sound. The only problems were in manufacturing. First, was there sufficient demand to warrant production? Second, what key would the harp play? The first diatonic Autoharps only played in one key per harp. Everyone would want a different key, which would require different tunings and different chords. It had all the makings of a late-night horror show featuring Oscar Schmidt.

If it's limited by only one key per harp, why do so many players like it so much?

Everyone was intrigued by its playing potential. Despite its limitations, it offered many advantages. The diatonic Autoharp is louder because several of the strings are double tuned. "Just" or "perfect" tuning can be used instead of equal-tempered tuning. Due to the diatonic tuning, there are no "sour" notes outside of the scale.

Taking advantage of this tuning, Ron Wall [of Mountain View, Arkansas] developed the "open chord" technique of playing. He plays many notes without a chord bar depressed, allowing him to play fiddle tunes at fiddle speed. Wall showed many Autoharp players his ideas at the Walnut Valley Festival in Winfield, Kansas. It opened up so many possibilities for new playing techniques, that many players made the conversion immediately.

Without a factory-made diatonic model, players were left to make the conversion on their own. What happened to make the company decide to try to make a diatonically-tuned production model?

Ron Wall visited Fretted Industries (Oscar Schmidt-International Division) in early 1981. He brought a *three*-key diatonic Autoharp which he had designed. It played in the keys of G, D, and A major because Wall enjoys playing with string bands. The three-key model was a marketable idea, and in March 1981 Rudolf Schlacher [co-owner of Fretted Industries] authorized the production of two test models. One went to Wall, the other to Becky Blackley.

Why did it then take from March 1981 to September 1982 to get the model on the market?

There were a few design problems from a manufacturing point of view which needed to be worked out. Wall's design had chord bars with hooks that muted certain strings when the chord bar was at rest. When the bar was depressed, the hook was lowered with the bar, allowing the string to sound. The hooks didn't work very well. If they were too long, they would hit the soundboard and stop the bar before the pads touched the strings. It was difficult to get them to work precisely right.

From the player's point of view, the design was rather limited. It only had six chords (C, G, D, A, E and Bm), and no key was complete with all the necessary chords. There was only one "open" diatonic scale (for the key of D) for which "open chords" could be played. The other two keys (G and A) could be used only for three-chord songs played with "closed chords."

Becky Blackley got to work on the model given to her. She put a twelve-chord unit on the harp and made ten chords: five major chords and five minor chords to complete each of the three keys (C, G, D, A, E, A minor, E minor, B minor, F-sharp minor, C-sharp minor). She also designed a special "mute bar" which

could take out all the unwanted notes from each scale. Diagrams were sent back to Rudy Schlacher and forwarded on to Oscar Schmidt plant manager, Tom Colonese.

It would be fair to say that at this point the diatonic Autoharp had become everyone's obsession! Blackley's ideas were good and certainly on the right track, but the mute bar didn't work very well either.

As one problem led to another, when did it finally appear that there was a workable basic design?

During the summer 1981 Blackley abandoned the single mute bar idea and made separate bars for each of the three keys. Each bar would lock into a closed position and mute the unwanted notes for the scale of that particular key. Although the design for three separate lock bars was simpler, one chord on the twelve-chord unit had to be eliminated to make room for them. Blackley made two prototypes in her garage: one played in the keys of G, D, and A major, and the other in the keys of F, C, and G major. This design worked quickly, easily, and consistently.

Blackley brought these two harps to the Walnut Valley Festival in Winfield in September 1981. Richard Johnstone [co-owner of Fretted Industries] thought the design very interesting and asked Blackley to show it to Ron Wall. Wall approved of this modification to his design, and Johnstone then asked Wall and Blackley to work out the specifications for a production model.

Judging from the positive reaction to the prototypes at Winfield, this diatonic harp seemed to be a very workable idea. If a working model could be made in a garage, then with proper tooling, the diatonic Autoharp could obviously be made in the factory. One of Blackley's prototypes returned with Johnstone as a design model for Schlacher and Colonese.

When was the first factory prototype made? What design changes have been made since then?

The first prototype came out of the factory at the end of 1981. It was exactly like Blackley's home-made model. It was sent to Bryan Bowers for his reaction.

Bowers wanted more playing room, so Schlacher decided to use C-model bars instead of the wider B-model bars. This did leave more playing room, and the other chord bar that had been removed earlier to make room for the three lock bars could be added back, once again completing all three keys.

Experiments were being done on a new bracing system at this time, and the new fine tuners were also being designed. The wooden chord bar cover was added, too.

The first near-perfect prototype ("P1") was sent to Blackley for the Autoharp's one hundredth birthday party held in May 1982. The lock bars still had some problems. This design had buttons with little collars on them to hold the bars down, but they didn't work all the time. The wooden chord bar cover was there but lacked character.

Finally by July 1982, Schlacher had designed the first production model. The chord bar cover was streamlined and made of either koa or curly maple. The new lock bars worked by levers, and the harp now had a beautiful sound and exquisite look.

The first introduction to the market was in September 1982. The diatonic model Autoharps were named the "Festival" series because the original design was born at the Walnut Valley Festival in Winfield, Kansas. There are two models. The OS-200 plays in the keys of F, C, and G major, and the OS-210 plays in G, D, and A major. One model has the chord bar cover and string anchor cover made out of Hawaiian koa, and the other out of curly maple. Both have custom binding at the edges.

The Festival harps also feature a laminated pin block, an enlarged soundhole, the new bracing system, and the special string anchor with the fine tuners for each string. Each Festival harp is personally signed and numbered by the craftsman.

The lock bars can be used two ways. If no bar is locked down by the lever, then the player has access to all ten chords and plays using the same techniques that would be used for playing a chromatically-tuned Autoharp. If one of the bars is locked in place, the result is a perfect do-re-mi diatonic scale for one of the major keys. The player is now limited to the six chords for that particular key, but "open chords" can also be played, allowing a wide range of playing techniques not otherwise possible.

Reprinted from **The Autoharpoholic**, *Vol. 4, No. 3 (Summer 1983).*

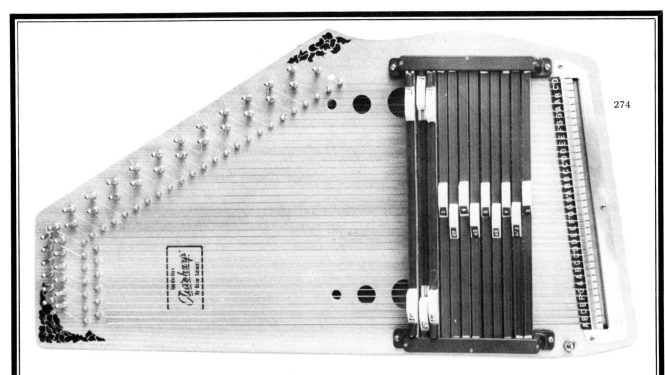

The first three-key diatonic harp with home-made lock bars. The B-model type unit had the lock bars near the pin end of the harp. The center bar is in the "locked" position. The twelve-chord unit necessitated the omission of the C-sharp minor chord.

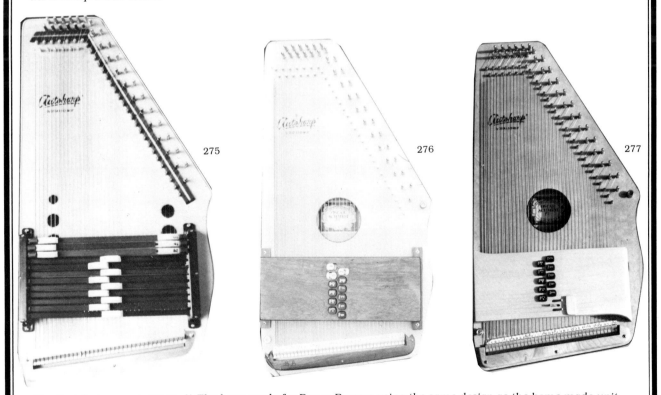

The first factory prototypes: 1) The harp made for Bryan Bowers using the same design as the home-made unit. The strip between the tuning pins and bridge pins marks the original site of the fine tuners. 2) "P1" prototype with the first C-model type wooden cover and lock buttons. Note the harp still had only nine chords. 3) The final design for "P1" with the streamlined cover and brass levers. The tenth chord has been added. The fine tuners which were added to the anchor end of the harp in 1983 are visible in the Festival harp shown on page 176.

enjoy and actively participate in. In the December 2, 1982, issue of the *Pioneer Press*, Johnstone pointed out that the Autoharp's broad appeal is as "a vehicle that 'brings back the basics' by turning off the TV and bringing the family closer together because everyone in the family can play." Retailers were provided with a large poster to display in their music stores during the holiday season. The photograph depicts a cozy family-room scene: mother, father, and three children gathered in front of the fireplace, the television in the background turned off. The mother is playing a standard-size Autoharp to accompany the singing, while the smallest boy plays along on the Easy Chord. It is a warm, traditional holiday "family portrait."

The family theme was further promoted in a large direct-to-the-consumer campaign, organized and promoted by Yvonne Dickerson. A full-page, four-color advertisement appeared in the November 24, 1981, issue of *Woman's Day* magazine. With a discount coupon included in the ad, the promotion was so successful that it was repeated in the 1982 holiday issue (December 14, 1982) and the December 1982 issue of *Frets* magazine: "Turn off the TV! Turn your family on to music with the Autoharp."

The appearance of the ad in *Frets* was significant. *Frets* is a magazine for musicians who play all types of acoustic stringed instruments. The Autoharp promotion had expanded from the retail music dealer, to the schools, to the home front, and now to the serious musician. After a hundred years of development, Charles Zimmermann's invention is finally being perceived as a serious instrument rather than a novelty item and is used by a whole range of players to play virtually every type of music.

The Autoharp now enters its second century, and the outlook is brighter than ever. The revival that began in the 1981–82 centennial year appears to be gaining strength in 1983. Autoharp workshops are being conducted across the country, and most major acoustic music festivals are featuring Autoharp performers. In addition to the International Autoharp Championship held at the Walnut Valley Festival, smaller contests and workshops are being held at many other music events.

Autoharp clubs are forming in areas where players thought they were the only ones interested in the Autoharp. A communications link between those clubs and between individual players has been made through *The Autoharpoholic* magazine. Autoharp classes are being conducted privately by individual teachers, at music schools, and through community colleges. Autoharp players are finally coming out of the closet and into the music world en masse. Throughout its history, the Autoharp has suffered some extremely difficult times, but somehow it has always held on and emerged alive and well again. Novelties soon lose their appeal . . . great inventions survive.

278

Ivan Stiles kicking off the Year of the Autoharp in Philadelphia.

"The Autoharp Song"

Way back in 1881, (it was on December 10),
Applying for a patent was Charles Zimmermann.
He believed it was the greatest work that man had ever made
And ever since that faithful day, the Autoharp's been played.

    So play, play, play the little "auty," little "Autyharp."
    Play, play, play the little "auty," lovely Autoharp.
    Yes, thanks to Charles Zimmermann, I can play it fast and free,
    Or get sounds so golden from the harp I'm holdin' . . .
    Oh, bless you, Charlie Z.!

Then finally on the ninth of May in 1882,
The Autoharp was on its way, now its patent was approved,
To Alfred Dolge to Oscar Schmidt and on to you and me,
But we owe it all to Zimmermann, that brilliant patentee.

Well, Charlie is an angel now, and I respectfully submit,
That all the harps in heaven are now made by Oscar Schmidt.
So if you've never played a single note, can't tell a flat from sharp,
Just take this baby in your arms and play the Autoharp.

    So play, play, play the little "auty," little "Autyharp."
    Play, play, play the little "auty," lovely Autoharp.
    Yeah, play, play, play the little "auty," little "Autyharp."
    Play, play, play the little "auty," lovely Autoharp,
                        lovely Autoharp,
              Yeah, I love my Autoharp!

    by Becky Blackley © 1979

"I'm a Happy 'Harpoholic"

I'm an Autoharpoholic, a former alcoholic
Boozin' and gamblin' was my style, then.
My whiskey, wine, and young men are replaced by my strummin'
Strummin' bluegrass gospel music all the time, now.
I used to be a loner. In the barroom I'm a goner.
I had to quit that lifestyle, don't you know.
I'm an Autoharpoholic, a happy 'harpoholic,
Strummin' bluegrass gospel dearest to my heart.

Meet a lot of friendly people on the road and in the depot
Willin' to pick and strum along with me,
From one town to another, see my sisters and my brothers,
The Good Lord, he's watchin' over me.
Come Sunday mornin' I used to do some groanin'
But now I'm into gospel from the start.
I'm an Autoharpoholic, a happy 'harpoholic,
Strummin' bluegrass gospel dearest to my heart.

If there's a 'Harpoholic Heaven, I intend to be right with 'em.
I'll meet Kilby Snow and Maybelle Carter at the golden gate.
We'll go strummin' on together into eternity forever.
I'll just tell the Ol' Red Devil he'll have to wait.
He really won't need me shovelin' coal, it can't be.
I'll be strummin' bluegrass gospel on my golden harp.
I'm an Autoharpoholic, a happy 'harpoholic,
Strummin' bluegrass gospel dearest to my heart.

    by Onetamae M. Britton © 1982

The autoharp is an instrument on which simple harmony
Is obtained by pressing a chord bar, such as F or G.
Felt dampers thereby deaden the strings that are not needed.
And strumming it makes music, it is generally conceded.

It was invented by Charles F. Zimmermann in 1881,
An event that he compared to the rising of the sun.
"It is," he said, "the very finest work of man on earth."
A statement that was greeted with some mirth.

Music can be played by anyone who hears,
Zimmermann believed, and so did Sears
Which sold thousands of them yonder and hither.
But still it was known as the idiot zither.

Until it was played by Pop Stoneman, a Virginian
Who did his part to change public opinion
By recording many tunes that were fancier and harder
And so did Kilby Snow and Maybelle Carter.

Many musicians otherwise liberal in their views
See an autoharp and ask to be excused.
But they've a surprise coming, in that city bright and fair
They'll find no guitars, only autoharps up there.

    by Garrison Keillor

279

KEY TO THE TAB SYMBOLS

CHORDS AND NOTES:

F   Melody chord. Play *all* the chords shown above the TAB staff for melody picking.

Ⓕ   Rhythm chord. Play only the *circled* chords for rhythm playing. Stay on each chord until the next circled chord appears, then change. When a rhythm chord is followed by an **＊**, change to the circled chord *one note sooner* than indicated.

f   Melody note name. Shown below the TAB staff for melody picking symbols only.

O   "Open chord" (No chord bar depressed).

/   Repeat previous chord (After an "open chord," depress the same chord bar that was released for the "open" note.)

RHYTHM SYMBOLS:

Finger Strokes: (Upward toward the treble end of the harp or downward toward the bass end.)

 Upward/Downward stroke with one finger   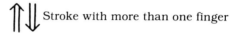 Stroke with more than one finger

 "Scratch" in one *continuous* motion: a *full* upward stroke followed *immediately* by a *short, quick* downward stroke. NOTE: The "scratch" is faster than a full upward stroke followed by a full downward stroke. The downward stroke is almost incidental and is not a full stroke.

 Slow, long stroke across all octaves (usually covers more than one count).

Thumb Strokes: (Upward strokes with the thumb)

 Short stroke in low/bass octave | Long stroke across entire low octave

 Slow, long thumb stroke across all octaves (usually covers more than one count).

MELODY SYMBOLS:

 "Pinch" with the thumb and index or thumb and middle finger simultaneously. Arrows point to the location of the melody note on the staff. Note should be emphasized.

Double top arrow means use two fingers for melody and harmony note.

"Pluck" one string only. Position of the circle on the staff indicates the note.

FINGERS TO USE: (Shown inside "flags" attached to arrows or inside "pluck" circles.)

1: Index finger   2: Middle finger   3: Ring finger   4: Little finger   EX: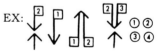

OTHER SYMBOLS:

"Tie" means no action is taken on that count. Previous action continues to sound.

"Stop" symbol means to mute *all* the strings on that count, either by pressing more than one chord simultaneously or by touching the strings with the right hand.

"Rhythm fill" counts as *one* symbol. All actions shown inside must be completed within the time of that count. If the "fill" is empty, fill in any rhythm stroke.

## CHAPTER 14

HOW TO READ THE TAB

The symbols shown in "Key to the Tab Symbols" form the basis of the tablature (TAB) system currently used by *The Autoharpoholic* magazine and in the publications of Oscar Schmidt-International, Inc. The explanation presented here is an overview of the whole system of notation. Step-by-step lessons in learning to read the TAB can be found in *The Autoharpoholic.*

The symbols represent most of the techniques used in playing the Autoharp. Some of them are familiar "standard" symbols, and some are new. They are used to give a general idea of how a given tune *might* be played. Invariably, after a song is learned, the player will make changes. The TAB is just to get started. It is used in combination with standard music notation, the most precise way of representing music in print.

Certainly the player who can read music is at a decided advantage. There is an endless world of music in books which can be adapted to the Autoharp, without having to depend on learning by ear. However, since a lot of musicians read no music, tablatures were created as a form of notation that could be understood both by those who read music and by those who don't. Tablatures can also tell things that standard music notation can't. When there are numerous ways of playing a melody note on a given instrument, the TAB can suggest *how* to play it (e.g., on an Autoharp a note can be played with a "pinch" using two fingers or a "pluck" using one finger). So the standard notation and TAB are used together on a double staff to give the best of both systems. Of course, in the end, the ear is the final

authority, and the music finally *sounds* right when it *is* right.

Following is a brief explanation of the TAB system. Standard notation is discussed only where it is applied to the TAB. Three basic parts to the TAB will be discussed separately: (1) the chords used for either melody playing or rhythm accompaniment (i.e., the left-hand action); (2) the melody line or "tune" of the song, played by the right hand; and (3) the rhythm for both backup accompaniment and for the correct phrasing of the melody.

THE CHORDS The chord bars are generally depressed by the left hand. The names of the chords are written directly above the TAB and below the standard notation. Unless otherwise noted, the chords given are for melody playing (which requires more frequent chord changes). Some of the chords are circled. These are the rhythm chords, and if the player doesn't want to play the melody, only the circled chords need to be played. The same chord continues to be depressed until the next circled chord appears. Then the new chord is played.

THE MELODY There are two common melody symbols, the "pinch" and the "pluck." Other actions can be used for the melody, but they will discussed as they occur. Sometimes a number is added to the symbol to suggest a finger to use.

The melody note is indicated by the location of the symbol on the TAB staff. Here the TAB staff parallels the staff used for standard notation. Since most melodies are written only on the treble staff, the discussion is limited to the treble staff and the TAB staff.

The lines and spaces represent melody notes as shown in Figure 1. That's the range of the harp from the low *a* to the highest *c*. Most sharps (♯) and flats (♭) are indicated at the beginning of the staff in the key signature. Incidental sharps and flats are indicated as they occur.

An easy way to remember the names of the lines and spaces on the treble staff is to know that the letters for the spaces spell out the word *face* and that the letter names for the lines (*e, g, b, d, f*) can be the first letters for the sentence "Every girl/boy does fine."

Even if the player does not read music, however, the melody can still be played from the TAB. A strip of note names for all the strings made from a piece of adhesive tape is placed along the side of the chord bar nearest the pin end of the harp. (On the twenty-one-chord model it is attached to the edge of the chord bar cover.) The letter name of each string is written *directly* over the corresponding string. When holding the harp "Appalachian style" the player can see the name of each string.

The small letters *below* the TAB are the names of the notes in the melody. First the starting note of the melody is located. Then the player follows the line of the melody to pinch or pluck the proper string, playing each TAB symbol as the beats are counted steadily. When the notes go up on the staff, the player goes to the higher strings on the harp.

THE RHYTHM Every song has a time signature given at the beginning of the standard notation. The top number of the fraction is the number of beats in each measure. Measures are enclosed by bar lines.

If the top number is 4 (e.g., 4/4 time), the measure has four beats. The count will be

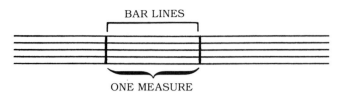

BAR LINES

ONE MEASURE

"one, two, three, four/ one, two, three, four . . .," etc., throughout the song. If the top number is 3 (e.g., 3/4 time), the measure has three beats, and the count is "one, two, three/ one, two, three . . . ." The TAB is designed so that *each word of the count has one symbol*. Each measure has three symbols when counting "one, two, three . . .," four symbols when counting "one, two, three, four . . .," etc. Each action indicated is performed at exactly the same time as the word is said:

COUNT: 1   2   3   4

On the word "one," the melody note is pinched; on "two," two fingers brush upward; on "three," there is a short stroke with the thumb in the low octave; and on "four," there is another upward stroke with the fingers.

For some songs, it is easier to count the "half beats" ("one, and, two, and, three, and, four, and . . .," etc., for 4/4 time; "one, and, two, and, three, and . . .," etc., for 3/4 time). This is indicated at the beginning of each song whenever applicable. Since there are now eight words for 4/4 time, there will be eight symbols per measure (six symbols for 3/4 time).

Figure 1:

a a# b c c# d d# e f f# g g# a a# b c c# d d# e f f# g g# a a# b c

In either case, whether counting the whole beats or the half beats, each word of the count will have one TAB symbol. Anyone who can count steadily can play the correct rhythm.

COUNT: 1 & 2 & 3 & 4 &

If a note *sustains* for more than one word of the count, a "tie" symbol is used.

1   2   3   4

No action is taken on the count of "two." The previous note just continues to sound as the word is said.

In many songs there are "rhythm fill" symbols. The entire "fill" counts as *one* symbol, and all the actions shown inside it must be completed within the time of that *one* count. When two actions are indicated inside the "fill," it usually helps to add an "and" to the count when counting whole beats and an "uh" when counting half beats.

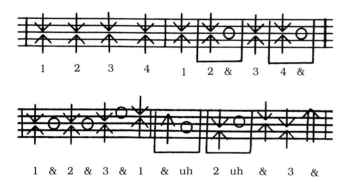

1 2 3 4   1 2 & 3 4 &

1 & 2 & 3 & 1 & uh 2 uh & 3 &

When the "rhythm fill" is empty, the player can add any stroke desired, but some type of rhythm strum should be played.

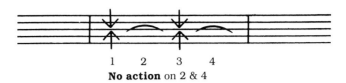

1   2   3   4

No action on 2 & 4

vs.

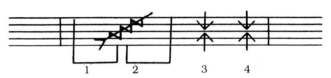

1   2   3   4

Rhythm action on 2 & 4

An action that takes place over more than one word of the count is written as follows (two rhythm fills):

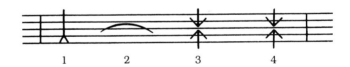

1   2   3   4

The upward thumb stroke is slow, and two words will be said (one, two) as it is played. Compare the above to this:

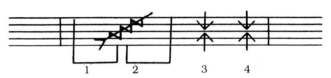

1   2   3   4

Action is *completed* on the first word and then *sustains* for the next word.

Other symbols can, of course, be created for playing techniques other than the common ones used here. However, it is usually easier to use the closest TAB symbol and add a note explaining the variation. Hundreds of variations are possible on these basic techniques, but any TAB system that tried to create a unique symbol for every possible variation would be far too complicated to learn. An explanatory sentence or two with a particular arrangement is usually sufficient to convey the variation.

For a song written in Autoharp tablature, see "A Little Boy for Sale," p. 23.

## CHAPTER 15

AUTOHARPS 1978 to 1983

Autoharps made by Oscar Schmidt-International, Inc., Union, New Jersey (a division of Fretted Industries, Inc., Northbrook, Illinois).

MODELS

#12BH/R	Appalachian (#45C/R)	#85, #85C
#12B	Appalachian (#45C, #45CE)	#200 (Festival)
#15EBH/R	Appalachian (#45B)	#210 (Festival)
#15B, #15BN	#100-12, #100-12E (Centurion)	Guitaro (#55B)
#15BB (Phoenix)	#100-15, #100-15E (Centurion)	Attaché (#30C, #28B)
#21C/R	#100-21, #100-21E (Centurion)	#6 (Easy Chord)
#21C, #21CN	#80	Educator

FEATURES

Logo: One type. "Autoharp by Oscar Schmidt" screened onto soundboard. Special designs for special models.
Label: One type. Black and gold design similar to 1978 label, with "International" removed and the dates "1879" and "1979" added. Label also gives model number, handwritten or printed.
Holders: B-model type: Styrene plastic. C-model type: Plastic pegs under chord bar cover.
Bars: B-model type: Aluminum/plastic. C-model type: Aluminum.
Buttons: B-model type: Rectangular white plastic, fused to bar. C-model type: Moveable, oval white plastic.
Music scale: Plastic keyboard type, without music staff or none.
Feet: Rubber. Standard models have large rubber feet attached with inset screws. Centurion and Festival harps have small rubber-topped nailheads.
Bridges: None. Individual guide posts at top end, aluminum string anchor inset in rout at lower end.
Tuning pins: Perpendicular.
Strings: Ball-end strings hook into slots of string anchor.
Frame: Interlocking frame with eight-ply laminated pin block.
Soundboard, back and sides: Natural finish, stained, or painted. All have soundholes, except solid-body harps.
Prices: August 1982 company price list unless specified otherwise.

#12BH/R, #12B
Monterey

36 strings.
12 chords: C, F, B-flat, G, G7, C7, D7, A7,
E7, Am, Gm, Dm.

280

*The new label designed in 1979
was similar to the 1978 label, except the word "International" was
removed and the dates "1879"
and "1979" added for the company centennial. Each label has
the model number, either handwritten (as this #100-21E label) or
printed.*

Music scale: Plastic keyboard.
Soundboard, back and sides: Sunburst
stain. Laminated maple soundboard.
Decorations: Double white line screened
around soundhole.
Size: 23½ inches by 12 inches.
Price: (1982) $155.00.

281

*Standard twelve-chord Model #12B from 1982 catalog. The sun-
burst stain replaced the previous solid-stain (and occasional
imitation rosewood finish) of the earlier Model #12BH/R.*

#15EBH/R, #15B, #15BN

Berkshire

36 strings.
15 chords: C, F, B-flat, G, D, E-flat, G7, C7, D7, A7, E7, F7, Am, Gm, Dm.

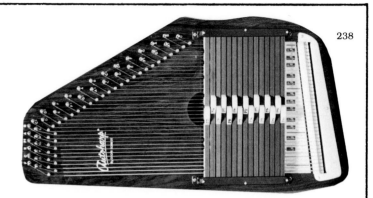

The Model #15EBH/R with the imitation rosewood finish was discontinued in 1979, replaced by a choice of a sunburst stain or natural finish with edge binding.

A standard Model #15B with sunburst finish.

Music scale: Plastic keyboard.
Soundboard, back and sides: Sunburst stain (#15B). Also available in natural maple finish (#15BN). Laminated maple soundboard.
Binding: Model #15BN has imitation tortoise-shell edge binding.
Decorations: Double white line screened around soundhole.
Size: 23½ inches by 12 inches.
Price: (1982) #15B: $180.00. #15BN: $200.00.

#15BB

Phoenix

36 strings.
15 chords: C, F, B-flat, G, D, E-flat, G7, C7, D7, A7, E7, F7, Am, Gm, Dm.

Music scale: Plastic keyboard.
Soundboard, back and sides: Black gloss finish over maple.
Decorations: Logo, string names and double lines around soundhole are screened in gold.
Special features: Also available with twenty-one chords.
Size: 23½ inches by 12 inches.
Price: (1982) $200.00.
Introduced: 1982. (21-chord option, 1983.)

The "Phoenix" Model #15BB is made with a traditional black finish.

283

#21C/R,
#21C,
#21CN

Classic

36 strings.
21 chords: C, F, B-flat, G, D,
A, E-flat, A-flat, G7, C7, D7,
A7, E7, B7, F7, B-flat seventh,
Am, Gm, Dm, Cm, Em.

*The imitation rosewood finish on Model #21C/R was discontinued in
1979.*

246

Music scale: Plastic keyboard.
Soundboard, back and sides: Sunburst stain
(#21C). Also available in natural maple finish
(#21CN). Laminated maple soundboard.
Binding: Model #21CN has imitation tortoise-
shell edge binding.
Decorations: Double white line screened
around soundhole.
Size: 23½ inches by 12 inches.
Price: (1982) #21C: $195.00. #21CN: $215.00.

A standard Model #21C with a sunburst finish.

284

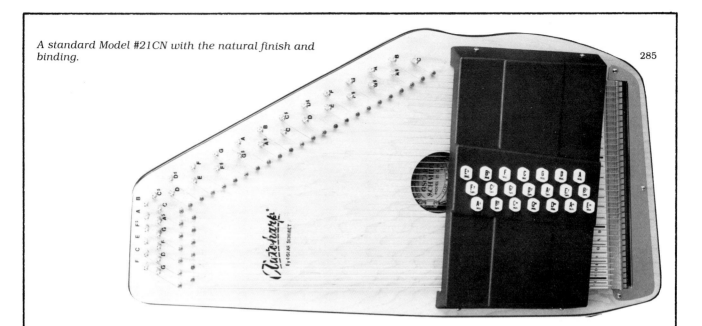

A standard Model #21CN with the natural finish and binding.

285

A closeup view of a C-model Autoharp with the chord bar cover removed. The aluminum bars hook over the pegs on the plastic chord bar holders. (One end of the chord bar holder has a hole, the other, a notch.) There is a spring over each peg. The metal brackets under the holders are to hold the chord bar cover in place. The chord bar button sets in the groove in the top of the bar and can be moved into any of the three positions shown. This is an acoustic/electric model, and the magnetic pickup is visible under the strings, below the chord bars. The output jack and tone and volume controls are attached to the string anchor cover.

286

Appalachian
#45C/R, #45C, #45B

36 strings.
21 chords: C, F, B-flat, G, D, A, E-flat, A-flat, G7, C7, D7, A7, E7, B7, F7, B-flat seventh, Am, Gm, Dm, Cm, Em. (Extra E major chord bar included.)

The special "Appalachian" logo is screened onto the soundboard in brown ink.

Logo: Special "Appalachian" logo.
Music scale: None.
Soundboard, back and sides: Natural finish. Back and sides stained dark brown. Laminated spruce top. Maple back and sides.
Decorations: Double line screened around soundhole.
Special features: Chord bar assembly is set closer to end of harp for more playing room. Also available as an acoustic/electric model (#45CE) or a fifteen-chord model (#45B).
Size: 23½ inches by 12 inches.
Price: (1982) #45B: $210.00. #45C: $215.00. #45CE: $260.00.
Introduced: Model #45B reintroduced in 1982.

The Appalachian Model #45C is the same as the earlier #45C/R. This Appalachian acoustic/electric Model #45CE/R is the same as the newer Model #45CE.

287

Centurion Series
#100-12, #100-15, #100-21

36 strings.
12 chords (#100-12): C, F, B-flat, G, G7, C7, D7, A7, E7, Am, Gm, Dm.
15 chords (#100-15): C, F, B-flat, G, D, E-flat, G7, C7, D7, A7, E7, F7, Am, Gm, Dm.
21 chords (#100-21): C, F, B-flat, G, D, A, E-flat, A-flat, G7, C7, D7, A7, E7, B7, F7, B-flat seventh, Am, Gm, Dm, Cm, Em.

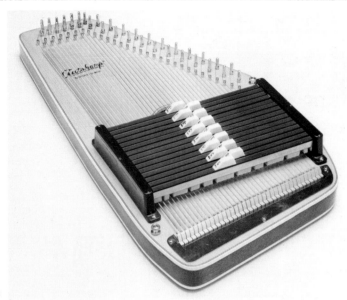

288

Centurion Model #100-15.

Centurion Model #100-21.

Music scale: None.
Soundboard, back and sides: Natural finish solid spruce top. Stained hardwood (most commonly ash) back and sides.
Binding: Ivoroid on sides. Celluloid along top edge.
Special features: All models also available as acoustic/electric models (#100-12E, #100-15E, #100-21E).
Size: 23½ inches by 12 inches.
Price: (1982) #100-12: $270.00. #100-15: $280.00. #100-21: $290.00. #100-21E: $340.00.
Introduced: 1979.

See the "Story of the Centurion" in Chapter 13 for more on the Centurion Series Autoharps.

The ivoroid edge binding on the side of the harp gives the impression that the harp is thinner than the standard models. The laminated pin block interlocks with the ash side piece.

289   290

#80, #85, #85C

Lancer

36 strings.
21 chords: C, F, B-flat, G, D, A, E-flat, A-flat, G7, C7, D7, A7, E7, B7, F7, B-flat seventh, Am, Gm, Dm, Cm, Em.

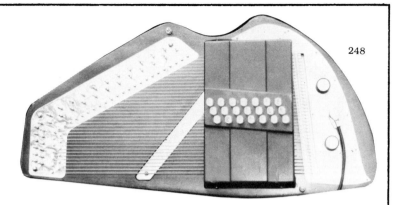

248

The solid-body harps made in 1979 were the same style as those made in 1978.

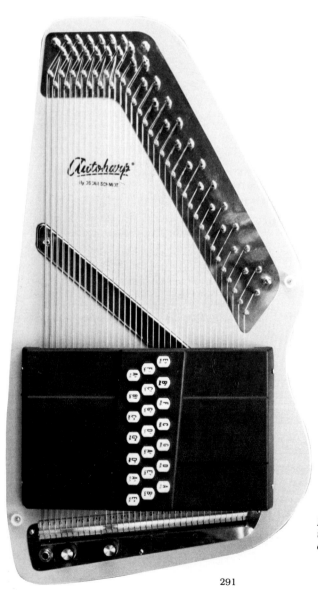

Label: None.
Music scale: None.
Frame: Laminated pin block inset into special rout under metal plate.
Soundboard, back and sides: Entire harp is solid wood (poplar).
Special features: Solid-body electric model. Magnetic pickup, placed diagonally across the strings, is inset in rout and flush with the surface. In 1980 an optional "chorus" unit was offered on the Model #85C.
Sunburst stain or painted. (Early #85 models were offered in red, yellow, and ivory; in 1983 color choices are ivory or black.)
Size: 24½ inches by 13½ inches.
Price: (1982) #85: $260.00. #85C: $350.00.
Introduced: #85C in 1980.

In 1980 the shape of the Lancer was streamlined to make it lighter and easier to hold. This Model #85 is bright canary yellow with ivoroid binding at the edges.

291

The chorus unit was offered on the #85C in 1980. The first models had the chorus unit placed in the side of the harp next to the chord bar unit. The chorus unit has adjustable speed and depth controls and can be switched on and off.

292

In 1981 the chorus unit was moved up higher on the side of the harp and the large bolts on the metal plate over the pin block were replaced by screws.

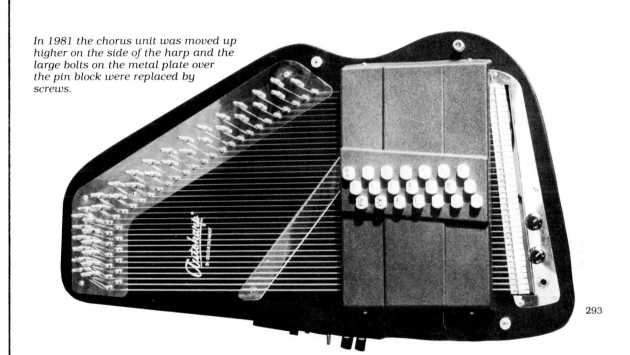

293

294

The new placement of the chorus unit (since 1981) is on the side of the harp between the chord bar unit and the magnetic pickup. This allows the player's right arm to reach around the harp without hitting the control knobs.

Festival Series
#200, #210

36 strings.
13 bars.
10 chords: #200: B-flat, F, C, G, D, Gm, Dm, Am, Em, Bm. #210: C, G, D, A, E, Am, Em, Bm, F-sharp minor, C-sharp minor.

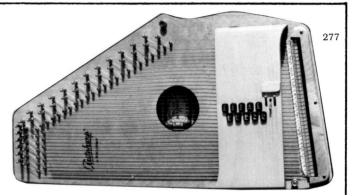

The first prototype (#P1) for Model #210. This harp plays in the keys of G, D, and A major.

Music scale: None.
Tuning pins: Fine-tuning system added to string anchor in 1983. (See harp held by Rudolf Schlacher on page 176.)
Strings: #200: f, g, c, d, e, f, f-sharp, g, a, a-sharp, b, c, d, d, e, e, f, f-sharp, g, g, a, a-sharp, b, c, d, d, e, e, f, f-sharp, g, a, a, a-sharp, b, c.
#210: f-sharp, g, c, c-sharp, d, e, f-sharp, g, g-sharp, a, b, c, c-sharp, d, e, e, f-sharp, f-sharp, g, g-sharp, a, a, b, c, c-sharp, d, e, e, f, f-sharp, g, a, a, a-sharp, b, c.
Frame: Narrowed at lower end (string anchor end).
Soundboard, back and sides: Natural finish solid spruce top. Back and sides are koa (#200) or curly maple (#210). Each harp is signed and numbered by the craftsman.
Binding: Ivoroid on sides. Celluloid along top edge.
Special features: Matching koa or curly maple chord bar cover and string anchor cover. No note names by tuning pins. Three brass levers operate special lock bars, one for each key.
Size: 23 inches by 12 inches.
Price: (1983) $450.00.
Introduced: 1982.

See "The Development of the Diatonic Autoharp" in Chapter 13 for more on the Festival Series Autoharps.

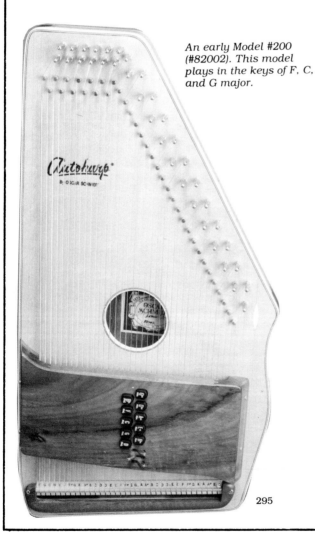

An early Model #200 (#82002). This model plays in the keys of F, C, and G major.

A closeup of the three brass levers inside the chord bar cover. Each lever locks a bar down to mute the two notes not in the diatonic scale for that key. With a pure diatonic scale "open" chords can be played.

Guitaro #55B

297

24 strings.
15 chords: C, F, B-flat, G, D, G7, C7, D7, A7, E7, B7, Am, Gm, Dm, Em.

298

Logo: Special "Guitaro" logo on plastic.
Bars and buttons: Two-part bars. Buttons centered. (Closeup.)
Music scale: None.
Soundboard, back and sides: Sunburst finish.
Decorations: Double white line screened around soundhole.
Special features: A-model type construction.
Size: 29 inches by 12 inches.
Price: (1981) $180.00.
Discontinued: 1982.

Attaché #30C

36 strings.
21 chords: C, F, B-flat, G, D, A, E-flat, A-flat, G7, C7, D7, A7, E7, B7, F7, B-flat seventh, Am, Gm, Dm, Cm, Em.

Logo: Special "Attaché" logo.
Music scale: None.
Decorations: Double white line screened around soundhole.
Special features: Built into carrying case (tan until 1979, then brown). Fifteen-chord model (#28B) reintroduced in 1983.
Price: (1982) $240.00.

299

Attaché
Autoharp°
By OSCAR SCHMIDT

#6

Easy Chord

18 strings.
6 chords: C, F, B-flat, G, C7, D7.

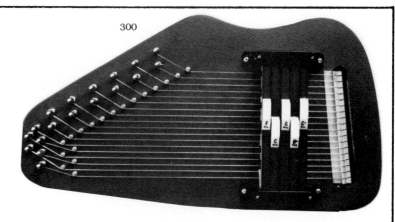

300

Label: None.
Holders: Styrene plastic. Screws attaching holders to soundboard are inside the holders and not visible.
Music scale: None.
Soundboard, back and sides: Natural finish or stained (candy apple red or golden oak).
Special features: Child-size harp plays in keys of C, F, and G.
Size: 15 inches by 8 inches.
Price: (1982) $59.95.
Introduced: 1981.

An early prototype for the Easy Chord has only five chords. The solid-body harp is red. The first model to go on the market had six chords and the solid-body harp was offered in red, black, ivory, yellow, or natural finish.

In 1982 the Easy Chord Model #6 was redesigned for hollow body construction. It was offered in red, yellow, golden oak, or natural finish. In late 1982 the yellow stain was discontinued. This 1982 catalog photo shows (left to right) the golden oak, natural, and red stained harps.

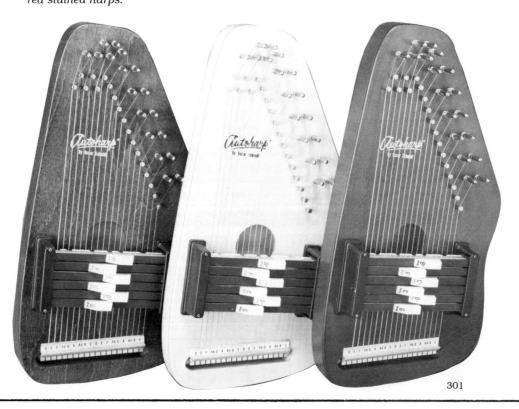

301

Summary: Autoharps 1978 to 1983

Autoharps made by Oscar Schmidt-International, Inc., Union, New Jersey (a division of Fretted Industries, Inc., Northbrook, Illinois).

Models: #12BH/R, #12B; #15EBH/R, #15B, #15BN, #15BB (Phoenix); #21C/R, #21C, #21CN; Appalachian: #45C/R, #45C, #45CE, #45B; Centurion series: #100-12, #100-12E, #100-15, #100-15C, #100-21, #100-21E; #80 (Lancer), #85, #85C; Festival series: #200, #210; #55B (Guitaro); #30C, #28B (Attaché); #6 (Easy Chord). "Educator" models are made for Music Education Group, but are the same as the standard models.
Introduced: #12BH/R, #15EBH/R, #21C/R, #45C/R, #80, #55B, #30C, and "Educator" harps already in production. #12B, #15B, #15BN, #21C, #45C, #45CE, and Centurion series, 1979. #85 and #85C, 1980. #6, 1981. #15BB, #45B, and Festival series, 1982. #28B, 1983.
Discontinued: #80, 1980. #55B, 1982.
Logo: "Autoharp by Oscar Schmidt" screened onto soundboard. Special logos for special models.
Label: Black and gold design with dates "1879" and "1979" at top. Label gives the model number, either handwritten or printed. No labels on solid-body models.
Holders: B-model type: Styrene plastic. C-model type: Plastic pegs under chord bar cover.
Bars: B-model type: Aluminum/plastic. C-model type: Aluminum.
Buttons: B-model type: Rectangular white plastic, fused to bar. C-model type: Moveable, oval white plastic.
Felts: White or black.
Music scale: Plastic keyboard type, without music staff. Many models have no music scale.
Feet: Rubber. Standard models have large rubber feet attached with inset screws. Centurion, Festival, and Easy Chord harps have small rubber-topped nailheads.
Bridges: None. Individual guide posts at top end, aluminum string anchor inset in rout at lower end.
Tuning pins: Perpendicular.
Strings: Ball-end strings hook into slots of string anchor.
Frame: Interlocking frame with eight-ply laminated pin block.
Soundboard, back and sides: Natural finish, stained, or painted. All have soundholes, except solid-body harps.

By OSCAR SCHMIDT

Logo (left): Used on all standard models (1978—).
Label (below left): Used on all models (1979—).
Special logos (below, center and right): used on special models (1978—).

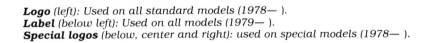

302

303

304

305

Top:
Maybelle Carter
Kilby Snow
Pop Stoneman
Center:
Mike Seeger
Bryan Bowers
Bottom:
Jean Ritchie
John Sebastian
Bill Clifton

306

307

308

309

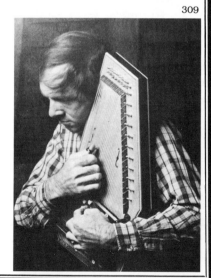

THE AUTOHARP PEOPLE

Throughout its one hundred years, the Autoharp has been used to play virtually every type of music. The first "Autoharp virtuoso" was Aldis J. Gery, who in the late nineteenth century played the Autoharp with the popular Gilmore's Band (led by Victor Herbert). Unfortunately, we will never be able to fully appreciate his playing style, because his music wasn't recorded; but thanks to the invention of the phonograph, we can listen to the music of the many Autoharp players of the twentieth century.

One of the areas in which the Autoharp became very popular in the early twentieth century was the rural mountain areas of the United States. Music was often the main form of entertainment in these regions, and the Autoharp allowed most anyone to join in the music-making. It was used in the home, on the front porch, in the church, and in the schools, so that anyone growing up in those areas was bound to run across the Autoharp at some time or place.

One of the first musicians to bring the sound of the Autoharp back out from the hills was Ernest "Pop" Stoneman, who had played the Autoharp since he was eight years old (beginning with "Molly Hare"). Eventually Stoneman became the first person to make a record with the Autoharp when, on September 6, 1924, he recorded "The Titanic" and "The Face That Never Returned" for Okeh Records. This record with Autoharp and harmonica was Stoneman's first recording of any type of music. Stoneman recalled, "That's how come I got on. If I'd took a guitar up there he

wouldn't have wanted it, cuz he had guitar pickers . . . plenty of them. But I had something he didn't have, something different. He never had [heard the Autoharp], never had seen one before."[1]

A multi-instrumentalist, Stoneman went on to make many recordings of "hillbilly music," both solo and with other artists. His Autoharp can be heard on the 1957 recording of *The Stoneman Family: Old-time Tunes of the South*, which contains the first recorded instrumental tune played on the Autoharp, Stoneman's own composition "Stoney's Waltz." All thirteen of his children played instruments, and several generations of the Stoneman family have carried on the musical tradition. Patsy Stoneman plays Autoharp on the more recent *First Family of Country Music*.

"I feel that the Autoharp is part of our heritage, and since Dad passed away in 1968, I have continued that tradition and have hopes that one of the grandchildren will feel as I do about it, so that the sound of the Autoharp will never leave our music.

"Daddy built his first Autoharp himself when he was in his early teens using old parts from a piano, since he had no money to order one from the catalog. He used an Autoharp that had been in the family for years as a pattern. In 1914 he used that Autoharp to make a recording on someone's recorder. I guess that the sound it produced must have pleased him, and he went on to record better than two hundred recordings from 1924 until about 1931–32, using an Autoharp on most of them. I guess you can

Ernest V. "Pop" Stoneman.

310

tell that I am proud of the heritage left us by our parents."[2]

Stoneman played with the Autoharp on his lap, usually on top of a special case that he made to give the harp more resonance. He also frequently used an electric pickup for added volume. His style for melody playing was the standard "pinch" with the thumb and index finger. Stoneman played below the chord bar assembly, and filled in the rhythm with an upward stroke made by the back of the index finger. He had to make a special type of pick from spring wire in order to make this "backward" motion of the index finger.[3] The best collections of his Autoharp music are on *Mountain Music Played on the Autoharp*, recorded by Mike Seeger in 1957 and 1961, and *Ernest V. "Pop" Stoneman, 1893–1968*, produced by his family from tapes found eleven years after his death.

The Stoneman Family.   311

Although Stoneman was the first to introduce the Autoharp as a solo melody instrument, it was the original Carter Family who established the Autoharp as a standard rhythm instrument for old-time and traditional music. The original Carter Family was made up of Alvin Pleasant ("A.P.") Carter, his wife, Sara Dougherty Carter, and Sara's first cousin, Maybelle Addington Carter. Maybelle had married A.P.'s brother, Ezra J. Carter, making the two women both cousins and sisters-in-law by marriage. The trio, formed when Maybelle moved to Maces Springs, Virginia, began recording together in July 1927 and continued to gain popularity until they disbanded in 1943. During those sixteen years, the original Carter Family became one of the most important influences on American traditional music, an influence still apparent in bluegrass, country, and folk-revival music today.[4]

The favorite choice of instruments for the Carter Family was guitar and Autoharp. It should be noted (since it is often reported incorrectly) that Sara, not Maybelle, played the Autoharp with the original trio. Although Sara Carter used the harp just for a rhythmic accompaniment for the group, the

sound of the Autoharp was so fundamental to their music that Sara switched to the guitar only when her Autoharp lacked the proper chords. Like Stoneman (and virtually all others at that time), Sara played with the harp either on her lap or on a table and strummed below the chord bar assembly.

Maybelle Carter began to play the Autoharp publicly when she performed with her daughters, Helen, June, and Anita (all of whom play the Autoharp, too). She preferred the sound of strumming the strings above the chord bars, but still laid the harp on a table and crossed her hands to play. She had been playing both rhythm and melody on the Autoharp when a technical problem led her to develop the distinctive "Appalachian-style" of playing with the harp held upright in her arms:

"When I first started, I held [the Autoharp] on my lap or sitting flat on a table, but I had so many problems finding a table or a chair to sit down in. When I started working with my girls I'd feature the harp on maybe one or two tunes on our show dates and sometimes I'd have a table or something to set it on, and sometimes I wouldn't. So I thought, well, there's got to be a way . . . I've got to figure out some way to hold this thing without having to have something to sit it on. So I thought I'll try holding it up in my arms. It was a problem. I like to broke my arm trying to play it like that, but I finally got to where I could do pretty good."[5]

Holding the harp upright in the arms made it easier to play above the chord bars and also made it easy for Maybelle to approach the microphone when it was time for an Autoharp break. When Mother Maybelle and the Carter Sisters finally reached the Grand Ole Opry, Maybelle's new style quickly became the "standard" for Autoharp players everywhere. So popular was Maybelle's Autoharp playing that she played on records with the Wilburn Brothers and for Flatt and Scruggs. She aroused such interest in the Autoharp that it wasn't long before one of the Wilburn Brothers and Earl Scruggs had bought their own Autoharps and were learning to play themselves!

Scruggs recently stated, "The Autoharp has always been a very important instrument for me. I've played one a little, and it was the first instrument my son Randy learned to play. Lester [Flatt] and I also did an album using one when we recorded *Songs of the Famous Carter Family*. Mother Maybelle [Carter] played the Autoharp all the way through on that one. Of course, I'm so partial to anything the Carter Family has ever done, that I can't help but have high regards for the Autoharp, and I think the instrument played a big part in their type of music."[6] Today, Maybelle's style is still used by her daughters, while Janette Carter (daughter of A. P. and Sara) is continuing in the rhythmic style used in the original Carter Family.

Not all accomplished Autoharp players got to walk onto the stage of the Grand Ole Opry. Many of them were still in their mountain homes, sharing their music with their families and nearby neighbors. Much of this music and these musicians would never have been known to the world at large if it weren't for Mike Seeger, who in 1957 began recording the Autoharp music of Pop Stoneman, Kilby Snow, and the father-and-son team of Neriah and Kenneth Benfield. He did more recording in late 1961, and the ultimate result was *Mountain Music Played on the Autoharp*. Seeger's unique background made him more than qualified to produce this album. As a multi-instrumentalist who played the Autoharp (both solo and with the New Lost City Ramblers), he knew and loved the old-time music he was collecting. As a scholar, he paid close attention to detail and carefully documented the intricacies of each musician's style. The liner notes of this album alone are worth the price of the record. After more than fifteen years, the record itself stands as the classic collection of traditional Autoharp music.

Neriah McCubbins ("Mr. Cub") Benfield was from North Carolina. He played with his son, Kenneth Lee Benfield, and both used the Autoharp for instrumental music only. They usually played one Autoharp and one guitar, trading instruments between them, but the Autoharp played the lead while the

Kilby and Jim Snow.   312

guitar played backup! Like Stoneman, they, too, played below the chord bars with the harps flat on their laps. They used thumb picks, but generally used no fingerpicks. They played melody notes with the back of the nail, in an upward motion, similar to frailing on a banjo. Occasionally Neriah Benfield would use one fingerpick, but he wore the pick on the nail side of his finger to make this type of stroke. Additional melody notes were played with a downward motion of the index finger while the thumb filled in the rhythm. The Benfields appeared together at the 1964 Newport Folk Festival.[7]

Perhaps the most unique Autoharp player on the *Mountain Music* album is John Kilby Snow. Snow was left-handed and developed a distinctive style of playing "drag notes." He would begin by pressing a chord bar and strumming (below the chord bars) upward toward the treble end across the strings with his finger. Just before reaching the note to be slurred, he would release the chord bar, sounding a couple of notes not normally in the chord. When he struck the desired note, he again depressed the chord bar, and continued the strum across the remaining strings. In order to easily strum up the scale with his index finger, Snow would turn the harp around "backwards" on his lap. Being left-handed, he could of course play quite comfortably in this position. Indeed, he had

Peggy Seeger and Neill MacColl.

313

turned what could have been a considerable disadvantage into a technique for which being left-handed was a tremendous asset![8]

After the *Mountain Music* album, Seeger also recorded a solo album of Kilby Snow's music, *Kilby Snow: Country Songs and Tunes with Autoharp.* Says Seeger, "Kilby Snow was more close to bluegrass with his playing. He used it as a fiddle. He'd play his tunes, but he also accompanied himself more like an old-time banjo player or guitar player would, in that he played the tune while he was singing."[9] A two-reel film of Snow and Seeger is available for rent from Traditional Arts Services in Portland, Oregon. (See "Services" in Appendix C for the address.)

Seeger is not only an important folklorist, but a talented Autoharp player. According to Autoharp historian A. Doyle Moore, "Seeger has an interest and performing skill so infectious that following each of his concerts a new crop of potential and often productive players is born."[10] Seeger found that the Autoharp fit in perfectly with his old-time and traditional style of music: "It belongs real nice with lyric ballads like 'Lord Thomas' and 'Fair Ellender.' Maybelle [Carter], Pop [Stoneman], and Kilby [Snow] are the most important ones for me with the Autoharp. In my own playing I tend to be closer to Maybelle's chording behind my voice, although I've started doing something a little more like Kilby recently. I've taken fiddle tunes and a couple of guitar tunes like 'Victory Rag' and done them on the Autoharp, but more than that I play songs that I'm singing."[11] In addition to recording with the New Lost City Ramblers, Seeger has recorded with his sister Peggy, who also plays Autoharp. Among Seeger's many recordings, *Old-time Country Music* contains some of his best Autoharp music.

While Seeger was pursuing the music of the Autoharp, Doyle Moore was tracing the history of the instrument itself. Moore had become interested in the history of the Autoharp through the music. His fine old-time Autoharp can be heard on the 1962 recording of the *Philo Glee and Mandoline Society* (out of print). However, Moore's main contribution to the Autoharp world remains his 1963 article on the history of the Autoharp, "The Autoharp: Its Origin and Development from a Popular to a Folk Instrument." It was probably inevitable that Seeger and Moore would meet and combine their talents. Moore, who is by profession a graphic arts teacher, designed the cover for the *Mountain Music* album.

314

A. Doyle Moore with the Philo Glee and Mandoline Society.

The interest in the Autoharp generated by Seeger, Moore, and Mother Maybelle in the early sixties led to numerous other recordings with Autoharp on them. A far too short example of Arnold Watson (Doc Watson's brother) can be heard on *The Doc Watson Family* album. Tex Isley, who played with the Charlie Monroe band, did some good Autoharp work on *Clarence Tom Ashley and Tex Isley Play and Sing American Folk Music*. Jean Ritchie began to use the Autoharp on her recordings, although it wasn't a new instrument for her: "I can't really remember the first time I was introduced to the Autoharp," she says. "They've just been around me all my life. Missionary ladies in church would put them on their laps and go 'br-r-r-r-ing!' and make harpy sounds on them and sing hymns. I thought that's all there was to an Autoharp

for a long time. Then I heard the Carter Family and saw Mother Maybelle play. I realized that one could make a nice sound with the Autoharp, a sound that I wanted to use on certain songs: that sort of full, fruity sound that you want when you sing an old-time or old gospel song. It's just perfect."[12]

An entire side of Andy Boarman's *Mountain State Music* album is devoted to the Autoharp. Although this album was not recorded until 1976, Boarman had been playing his autoharp for many years near his home in West Virginia. His style is as unique and distinctive as the playing of his contemporaries on the *Mountain Music* album. "He plays the instrument while it rests on a table or bench. His strum is directed to the area to the right of the chord bars because of the stronger string tension. Frequently while playing on stage he rests the Autoharp on a barrel perforated with sound holes to enhance the tone of the instrument. (Rumors abound that Andy equipped his barrel with a tone ring, but he will neither confirm nor deny this.)"[13]

315

Cecil Null and Annette.

216

Lindsay Haisley.

316

Bill Clifton has used the Autoharp on many of his records and in 1982 released his *Autoharp Centennial Celebration!* album of all instrumental tunes. Clifton says, "[I] first began to use the autoharp on my early morning radio programs in Charlottesville, Virginia, about 1949 . . . but it never found its way onto any of my commercial recordings until 1960. Over the years concert and festival audiences have shown a lot of interest in the autoharp . . . most especially the instrumental tunes. The autoharp is at once a joyful and melodious musical instrument that never fails to capture the attention and warm affection of its listener. A hundred years has done little to detract from its novelty, but much to add to the instrument's musical diversity and depth . . . winning new friends and proponents from all schools of musical persuasion."[14]

By the mid-sixties the Autoharp was gaining the attention of musicians in different fields of music. Nashville recording artist Cecil Null was one of the most unique players of the sixties. He played his unusual,

custom-made Autoharps on his recording of orginal country tunes, *New Sounds in Folk Music.* The old-time family singing group known as the Phipps Family appeared at the 1964 Newport Folk Festival, demonstrating a style based on the Carter Family. Canadian performers Ian and Sylvia Tyson included Autoharp on most of their early recordings, and Mimi Farina often played Autoharp while her husband, Richard, played the mountain dulcimer. Arlo Guthrie, son of Woody Guthrie, used the Autoharp in his stage shows to play folk and country music. A report in the Chicago *Sun-Times* (February 27, 1966) says that Guthrie "exhibited a good deal of talent on both the guitar and Autoharp."

The Autoharp even entered the realm of rock music when John Sebastian played it regularly with his group, The Lovin' Spoonful. John's playing inspired the development of the first electric model Autoharps, and the unique sound of the electric harps can be heard today in the playing of Gove Scrivenor (on *Shady Gove* and *Coconut Gove*), Michael Stanwood (on *Cowtowns and Other Planets*), and Lindsay Haisley (on *Christmas on the Autoharp*). Sebastian, too, still plays the Autoharp and his electric harp can be heard on Randy Vanwarmer's *Warmer* album.

317

John McCutcheon with Wrystraw.

Lindsay Haisley is a contemporary-style player with a traditional background. His first album, *Live at the Kerrville Folk Festival*, is a blend of the traditional and the new. Among the songs written by Haisley, "The Isleboro March" is exceptional, and Haisley claims "the credit for this song should go to the Autoharp. No one ever taught me much about playing the Autoharp, but the Autoharp has taught me a lot about playing music. My Autoharp actually wrote this song, and every time I let my guard down, the harp slips in a few more licks so that like a rosebush, I have to prune it back occasionally."[15]

Haisley's second album is an all-Autoharp recording entitled *Christmas on the Autoharp*, and despite its seasonal appeal, the album is clearly destined to become one of the classic recordings in any collection of Autoharp music. Haisley's style is distinguished by the frequent use of diminished chords and the pure tones that he gets from the electric harp. Says Haisley, "The low notes of the harp are brought out really well on the electric harp. In the work that I've done, in recording, the low tones on the harp sound just like the pedal tones on the organ. I really like the full spectrum of sound that you get from the electric harp when you can get way down to the low notes."[16]

The Autoharp, of course, continues to thrive in the mountain and rural regions which became its adopted home early in this century. The multitalented John McCutcheon lives in Gate City, Virginia, a short distance from his friend and musical inspiration, Janette Carter. McCutcheon is both a musician and a traditional/old-time music preservationist. He invariably includes the Autoharp in his performances and annotates each song with historical notes. He has several albums to his credit, both solo and with his former group, Wrystraw, and feels an obligation to pass this music on to the next generation. "The highlight of my entire musical career was a tour I did with Janette Carter. All my performing career I've been very conscious of the many traditional musicians who shared their music with me, so I really wanted people to hear Janette because I love Carter Family music and Janette is just a wonderful person to be around. She's been a neighbor and friend of mine for about ten years, and we'd talked for awhile about doing a tour together. It was wonderful. There were very large crowds, and to me it was one of the most exciting musical experiences I ever had because here I was repaying a very great debt that I only in part repaid for all the generosity that Janette and many, many other people had been kind enough to give me. It was really exciting seeing six hundred young people singing 'Will the Circle Be Unbroken' led by one of the Carter Family."[17]

318

Jean Simmons.

218

Many other outstanding old-time and traditional Autoharp players come from these southern rural areas. Betty Waldron of Floyd County, Virginia, has won several Autoharp contests, and she teamed up with her son, Mark, on her *Parlour Picking* album. Jean Schilling of Cosby, Tennessee, has recorded two albums of traditional music, playing Autoharp while her husband, Lee, joins in on hammered dulcimer. *Porches of the Poor* and *Keep on the Sunny Side* both feature the Autoharp. Mountain View, Arkansas, is the home of Jean Simmons, whose Autoharp can be heard on the National Geographic recording *Music of the Ozarks* and on several albums by The Simmons Family. Marsha Jones plays Autoharp on many of the records made by the Grandpa Jones Family, also of Mountain View.

Evo Bluestein. 319

The Autoharp's popularity has crossed the country too. One of the best old-time family groups is the Bluestein Family of Fresno, California. The Bluesteins have three albums to their credit and can be heard backing up such noted musicians as Jean Ritchie. Both Gene Bluestein, the father, and his son Evo play the Autoharp, and any performance of the family will certainly include some great old-time Autoharp. Evo Bluestein also has one solo album of old-time music, *Deep Shady Grove.*

Cathy Barton. 320

A good place to hear many of these Autoharp players from either coast is right in the middle of the United States, Winfield, Kansas. The Walnut Valley Festival which takes place in Winfield every September has featured some of the finest bluegrass, old-time, and traditional musicians and groups in its eleven-year history. For the past several years there has been a sharp increase in the number of Autoharps seen at the festival. Cathy Barton, a multi-instrumentalist from Columbia, Missouri, is a frequent performer at the Walnut Valley Festival, and her Autoharp can be heard on *Reflections on the Carter Family*, by Ron Penix, Barton, Dave Para, and Jay Round. Says Barton, "On this recording we have not attempted to duplicate the Carter sound, but rather have utilized some new instrumentation such as the hammered dulcimer, bass, and five- and six-string banjos along with the guitar and Autoharp characteristic of the Carter's music. Although in most cases we

The original Carter Family: Maybelle, Sara, and A.P. Maces Springs, Virginia, ca. 1927. 321

The entire family in Texas, 1939. 322

The Carter Family

Maybelle and daughters June, Anita, and Helen, early 1950s. 323

A.P. and Sara with children Janette and Joe, early 1950s. 324

Janette, 1982.

June, 1981.

Anita and Helen, 1982.

325

326 327

Ron Penix.

328

plays solo, his Autoharp sounds like a full orchestra. The influence of traditional music on Wall's playing is clearly evident, and he in turn has influenced many other players. His unique style comes from a diatonically tuned harp and the use of "open" chords (strings plucked without a chord bar depressed). His ability to do this cleanly and accurately allows him to catch sixteenth notes easily and keep pace with any fiddler. Wall has taught his "open" chord technique to many Autoharp players, and the style is becoming increasingly popular.

have tried to adhere to the original Carter vocal arrangements, we have taken occasional liberties even here to sing these songs in our own individual manner. We hope the result will be satisfactory to old and new Carter Family enthusiasts."[18]

Barton and Round also backed up Ron Penix on his earlier album, *Hammered Dulcimer Reunion*. Despite the deceptive title, this is an important Autoharp album. All three musicians play Autoharp, and these two albums demonstrate the skills that Penix put to use to place third in the 1981 International Autoharp Championship held at the Walnut Valley Festival.

Another frequent performer at the Winfield festival is the extraordinary Autoharp virtuoso Ron Wall from Mountain View, Arkansas. Wall is also a regular performer at the Ozark Folk Center in Mountain View. Anyone who has ever heard Wall play an up-to-tempo fiddle tune on his Autoharp will forever be in awe of this young man's talents. Wall can be heard on a cassette tape recorded at the Ozark Folk Center entitled *Autoharp Melodies*, and although Wall

Ron Wall.

329

221

Also known for the diatonically tuned Autoharp is Bryan Bowers. Although Bowers now makes his home in Seattle, Washington, he can be heard in concert in most any part of the country when he is on tour and on his two albums, *The View from Home* and *Home, Home on the Road*. Bowers, too, has been greatly influenced by traditional music, and says, "I think the music I enjoy the most is bluegrass, country, folk, and occasionally blues. I'm a big fan of Kilby Snow, of Mother Maybelle and the Carter Family style of playing, and I like Pop Stoneman a lot. Mike Seeger plays some real fine stuff on the Autoharp. And there's this fellow, Ron Wall. He plays an open tuning, only he doesn't push the chord bars down all the time. He just kind of flows through the chord changes. I like his stuff a lot."[19]

diatonically, she, too, has been influenced by the earlier Autoharp players: "I taught myself to play Autoharp by listening to the *Mountain Music Played on the Autoharp* album and learning those tunes. I was influenced most by Kilby Snow's techniques and then later by Bryan Bower's diatonic tuning method. As I began experimenting and developing my own techniques, I was inspired by banjo, mandolin, and guitar players."[20]

Stevie Beck.

331

One of the most widely heard Autoharp players is Stevie Beck, who can be heard across the country performing on the popular radio show "A Prairie Home Companion." Host Garrison Keillor introduces her as "Miss Stevie Beck, Queen of the Autoharp." Like Wall, Bowers, and Phipps, Beck tunes her harp diatonically, but her music is quite eclectic, drawing from a variety of styles: "I love old-time music: the

Bonnie Phipps.

330

Another excellent Autoharp player is Bonnie Phipps, from Denver, Colorado. Phipps won first place at the 1982 International Autoharp Championship and that same year released her first album, *Autoharpin'*. Although she tunes her instrument

Carter Family, Gid Tanner, etc. I'm also very fond of Cajun, some bluegrass, some country-western, and late fifties rock and roll. I suppose that every musician I have ever heard has influenced me in some way. Some musicians are very clean players, some very emotional, some humorous. I glean what I can from each and try to apply the characteristics I enjoy to my own music."[21]

Woody Padgett.

332

Woody Padgett's diatonic Autoharp can be heard on the two recordings by the Mill Run Dulcimer Band, *Sunday at the Mill* and *Chickens in the Yard.* This five-member group based in the Washington, D.C. area prefers the instrumentation of two dulcimers, guitar, Autoharp, and bass, and has developed a sound that is traditionally based, but uniquely their own.

Patrick Couton.

333

The Autoharp has even crossed the Atlantic Ocean where French Autoharp virtuoso Patrick Couton is becoming internationally known. His extraordinary Autoharp arrangements for the standard chromatic harp can best be heard on *Autoharp Ce Soir,* which he recorded with his mandolin-playing partner, Georges Fischer.

Many of the musicians mentioned here are no longer with us, but they are still here through their music. They have left us with a wealth of styles upon which we can build our music, and our new styles will in turn be left for others. Individuals pass on, but the music remains. Kilby Snow left us with this thought: "I do hope that we will all meet up yonder in the end. We'd play a golden harp up there. What a wonderful sound it would be, for truly I do believe there will be music in heaven!"[22]

334

335

336

337

Top:
**Nathalie Forrest with
a Chromaharp.
Mr. Wright with his own harp.
John McCutcheon with a
Mike Autorino harp.**
Middle:
**Mike Seeger with a Bob
Welland harp.
Mary Morgan with a Morgan
Company harp.**
Bottom:
**Keith Young with his own
harp.
Ron Wall with his own harp.
Cecil Null with his own harp.**

338

339

340

341

CHAPTER 17

AUTOHARP RELATIVES

If imitation is the greatest form of flattery, then Charles Zimmermann's Autoharp has been receiving compliments from the time it was first introduced. The following pages show chorded zithers other than the "Autoharp" brand. Some are old, some are new, but despite variations in their designs, they all function by the same principle as the Autoharp: bars with pads mute certain strings to produce chords.

Harp by Bob Welland, 627 Library Place, Evanston, IL 60201. (312) 869-4534.

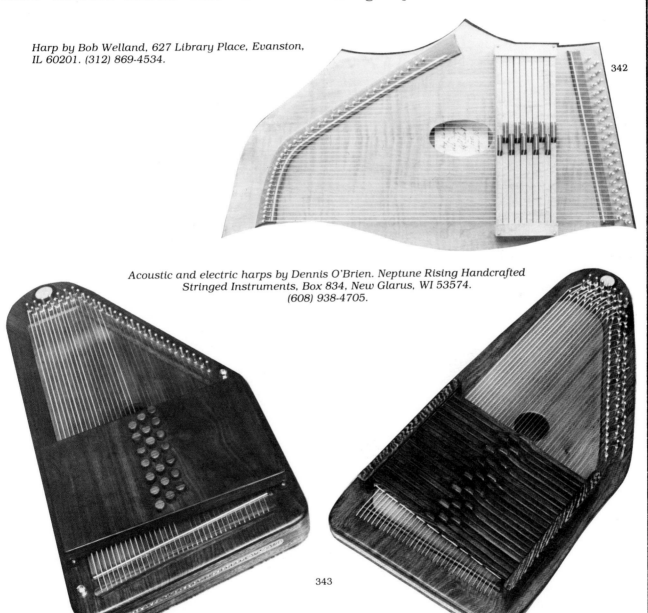

342

Acoustic and electric harps by Dennis O'Brien. Neptune Rising Handcrafted Stringed Instruments, Box 834, New Glarus, WI 53574. (608) 938-4705.

343

Thirty-chord harp with koa resonator (left) by Mike McClellan, 22283 Cass Avenue, Woodland Hills, CA 91364.

344

345

Chromaharp (above) by Rhythm Band, Inc., P.O. Box 126, Fort Worth, TX 76101. (817) 335-2561.

Seventeen-chord harp with fast release chord bar holders (below) by Keith Young, 3815 Kendale Road, Annandale, VA 22003. (703) 941-1071.

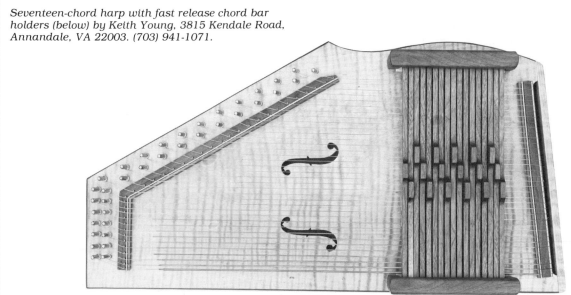

346

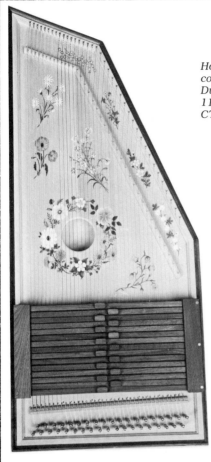

Harp by Carl Dudash also comes as a kit. Carl Dudash Harpsichords, 11 Jewel Street, Enfield, CT 06082. (203) 749-6800.

347

Harp by the Morgan Company, Route 3, Box 204, Dayton, TN 37321. (615) 775-2996 or 775-2897.

348

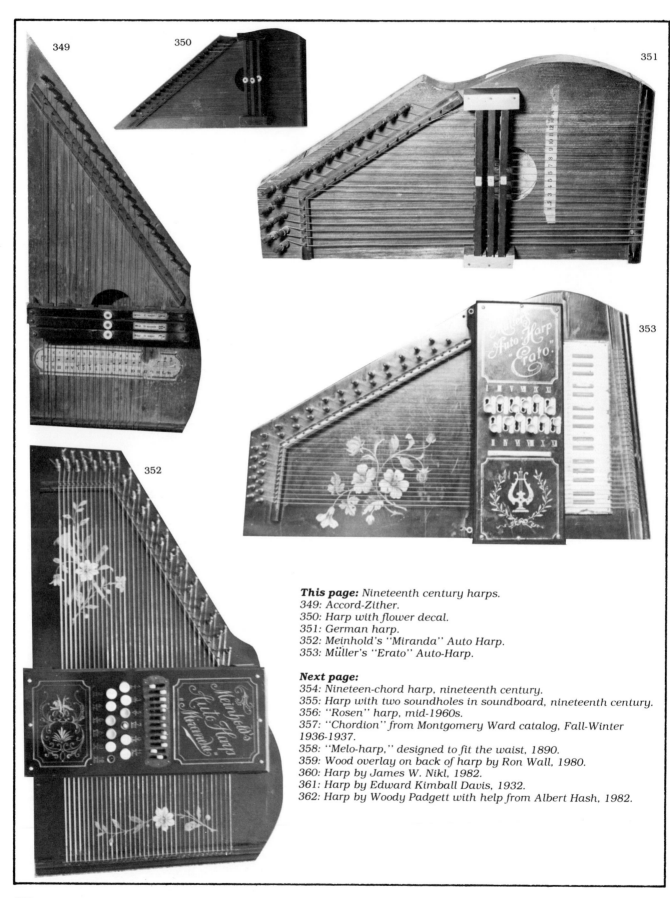

This page: *Nineteenth century harps.*
349: Accord-Zither.
350: Harp with flower decal.
351: German harp.
352: Meinhold's "Miranda" Auto Harp.
353: Müller's "Erato" Auto-Harp.

Next page:
354: Nineteen-chord harp, nineteenth century.
355: Harp with two soundholes in soundboard, nineteenth century.
356: "Rosen" harp, mid-1960s.
357: "Chordion" from Montgomery Ward catalog, Fall-Winter 1936-1937.
358: "Melo-harp," designed to fit the waist, 1890.
359: Wood overlay on back of harp by Ron Wall, 1980.
360: Harp by James W. Nikl, 1982.
361: Harp by Edward Kimball Davis, 1932.
362: Harp by Woody Padgett with help from Albert Hash, 1982.

354

355

356

357

358

359

360

361

362

Decals

Left: Decal from Model #2¾ (#1001) made for the American Autoharp Company.

Right: Decal from Model #2¾ (#2155 and #6693) was later used by the C. F. Zimmermann Company on its own Model #72⅞.

363

364

The most common decal on the Dolgeville Model #72⅞ is the griffin.

365

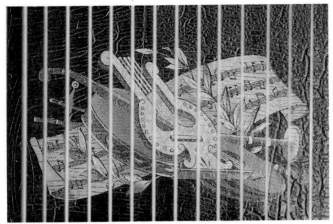

366

Above: The last decal used on the Dolgeville Model #72⅞ was used again by the Phonoharp Company on its Models #72⅞ and #73, and by Oscar Schmidt-International on its Model #73 made in 1936 (#0686).

367

Above: The decal used on the Dolgeville Model #73 and possibly on the Phonoharp Model #6.

368

Above: Decal from Oscar Schmidt-International Model #73 (#0589).

Right: Decal from Oscar Schmidt-International Model #73 (#0757).

369

The Gift of Music

Left: Golden Autoharp given to Ron Penix by Maybelle Carter.

Right: Autoharp with gold lamé chord bar cover and marble finish given to Rick Johnstone by Rudy Schlacher.

370

371

372

Above: Marquetry on Dolgeville Model #72, ca. 1894.

Something Special

Right: Toasted almond stain and gold logo on Smithsonian Catalog Autoharp, 1982.

373

374

375

Booklet cover, 1895.

Advertisement, 1979.

Advertisement, 1895.

G. Willikers Catalog, 1982.

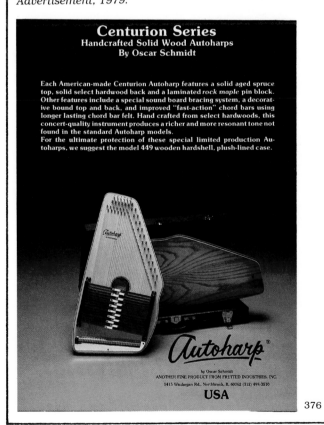

376

377

233

ACCESSORIES

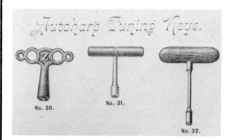

1893.

1896.

1893.

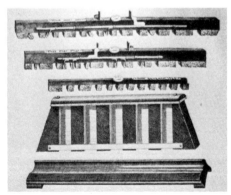

1896.

1896.

1893.

1893.

1896.

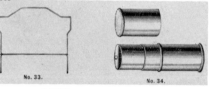

SHOWING HOW THE PICKS ARE USED IN PLAYING THE AUTOHARP.

1896.

AUTOHARP CHORD-STRIKER

1893.

1896.

From company catalogs.

Zimmermann strings, 1896.

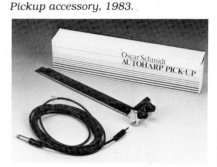

(MARCA CAMPANA)

Bell Brand strings were made through the 1970s. 378

Oscar Schmidt
AUTOHARP.
STRINGS

Model B

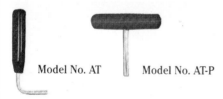

36 C

Oscar Schmidt strings, 1983.

Pickup accessory, 1983.

Accessories packet, 1982. 379

Model No. AT   Model No. AT-P

Tuning wrenches, 1983.

Parts kit, 1983.

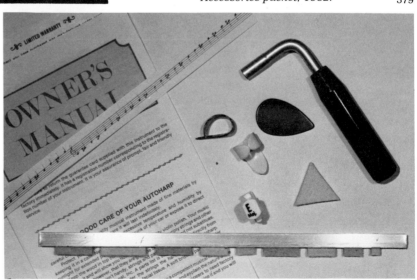

Cases.

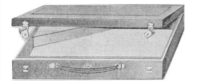

Cloth-covered case, 1893.

Ebonized wood case, 1893.

Ebonized wood case with lock, 1893.

Ebonized wood case with Model #5, ca. 1891.

380

Canvas bag, 1893.

Cashmere bag, rubber coated, 1896.

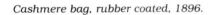

Leather-board case, 1896.

381

Case for Phonoharp opens at the end, ca. 1917.

Seal leather case for Parlor Grand, 1896.

From company catalogs.

Chipboard case, ca. 1944.

Chipboard case, ca. 1956.

Guitaro chipboard case, 1978.

Fibreboard case, ca. 1959.

Styrofoam case, 1969.

Padded bag, 1983.

Molded plastic case, 1978.

Hardshell case, 1983.

Chipboard case, 1983.

TRADEMARK AND PATENTS

UNITED STATES PATENT OFFICE.

CHARLES F. ZIMMERMANN, OF PHILADELPHIA, PENNSYLVANIA.

TRADE-MARK FOR STRING INSTRUMENTS

STATEMENT and DECLARATION of Trade-Mark No. 22,339, registered January 17, 1893.

Application filed December 22, 1892.

STATEMENT.

To all whom it may concern:

Be it known that I, CHARLES F. ZIMMERMANN, a citizen of the United States, residing at Philadelphia, Pennsylvania, and doing 5 business at No. 240 Second street, in said city, have adopted for my use a Trade-Mark for a String Instrument, of which the following is, a full, clear, and exact specification.

My trademark consists of the word symbol 10 "Autoharp." This has generally been arranged as shown in the accompanying fac simile which shows the word "Autoharp" in ornamental letters, but the style of lettering is unimportant and other words, characters or 15 designs may be added to the word "Autoharp" without materially affecting the character of my trademark, the essential feature of which is the word "AUTOHARP."

This trademark I have used continuously in my business since the 9th day of May 1882. 20

The class of merchandise to which this trademark is appropriated is musical instruments and the particular description of goods comprised in said class upon which I use it is string instruments. 25

It is my practice to apply my trademark to the instruments by means of suitable labels on which it is printed or embossed in color as above described. I may also print or emboss my trademark upon the body or 30 case of the instrument.

CHARLES F. ZIMMERMANN.

Witnesses:
HENRY SCHAEFER,
H. S. CALLAWAY.

Trademark registrations:

C. F. Zimmermann	January 17, 1893
Alfred Dolge	March 2, 1893
C. F. Zimmermann Company	February 7, 1894
Theodore Roth	Details unknown
Phonoharp Company	March 9, 1911 (California)
International Musical Corporation	May 17, 1927
Oscar Schmidt-International	May 17, 1947
	Renewed 1967

United States Patent Office.

CARL FRIEDRICH ZIMMERMANN, OF PHILADELPHIA, PENNSYLVANIA.

Letters Patent No. 110,719, dated January 3, 1871.

IMPROVEMENT IN MUSICAL NOTATIONS FOR ACCORDEONS.

The Schedule referred to in these Letters Patent and making part of the same.

To all whom it may concern:

Be it known that I, CARL FRIEDRICH ZIMMERMANN, of the city and county of Philadelphia and State of Pennsylvania, have invented a new System of Self-Instruction for Accordeons; and I do hereby declare that the following is a full, clear, and exact description of the same, reference being had to the accompanying drawing and to the letters of reference marked thereon.

My invention consists of a system of lines and figures which can be played in the same time as notes; and also of a method whereby the said system of lines and and figures can be applied to the various German accordeons.

On reference to the accompanying drawing making part of this specification—

Figure 1 indicates the motion of the bellows of the German and French accordeons;

Figure 2 shows the figures and rests in their various divisions of time; and

Figure 3 represents the key-board of an accordeon, and shows the method whereby the system of lines and figures can be applied to all kinds of German accordeons.

By my new system the keys of an accordeon are numbered as shown at fig. 3. The keys produce two different notes, one in drawing, and one in pressing. When to draw and when to press is shown in fig. 1. The division between the air and tenor figures and the bass is either a heavy line, A, or two parallel lines, B. They indicate the motion of the bellows, that is, whether to draw or press. The heavy line A indicates to press the German accordeon, and the parallel lines B to draw the same. In the French accordeon the heavy line A indicates to draw and the parallel lines B to press. The motion of the air or tenor and the bass remains invariably the same.

In this new-line system, the duration of sound and of all the rests, O, fig. 2, each one, precisely up to the next following, is indicated by an exact division of the space.

To accomplish this, every piece of music is divided as nearly as possible into equal spaces, x y, fig. 2, by heavy vertical bars or lines, a, and subdivided by light lines, b, for quarter time; for instance, a whole note requires four spaces, f g k k; one-half note requires two spaces, l m; one-quarter note requires one space, n; one-eighth note requires one-half space o; and one-sixteenth note requires one-quarter space, p; in the substitution of figures for notes the figures correspond with the keys of the accordeon, which are

numbered, and also with the notes in the music; for instance, in the quarter notes figure 6 corresponds with e in the quarter time, with d, with e, and again with d.

The relation of the German accordeon to my system of lines and figures is a matter of paramount importance, but not with regard to the French accordeon or flutina, all the varieties of which are founded on the same principle, and arranged according to one and the same scale. It is only among German manufacturers of accordeons that there are three different ways of selecting the starting-point of a piece of music for the first key; for instance, some start with the fifth note in their scale on the first key, which is numbered one; some are started with the third note in their scale on the first key, which is numbered one; and others are started with the first note in their scale on the first key, which is also numbered one. My system of lines and figures is designed for the first above-described accordeon, (that which is started with the fifth note in its scale and numbered one.) To make it applicable to the second kind of accordeon, (that which is started with the third note in its scale on the first key, numbered one,) it will be necessary to arrange the lower row of the supplemental drawing marked supplemental view No. 1 of the accompanying drawing, over the keys of the accordeon, shown at fig. 3, placing O of the row over 1 of the keys.

To make my system applicable to the third description of German accordeons, (or that which is started with the first note in the scale on the first key, numbered one,) arrange the upper row marked supplemental view No. 2, placing O O, over key 1 of the accordeon.

What I claim as my invention, and desire to secure by Letters Patent, is—

1. The system of musical notation, consisting of the three-lined staff, fig. 1, and adaptable to either French or German accordeons, as shown and described.

2. In connection with the above staff, the measure divided by equal space-marks x y, fig. 2, between which the key-numbers are indicated, substantially as described.

In testimony whereof I hereunto sign my name to this specification in presence of two subscribing witnesses.

CARL FRIEDRICH ZIMMERMANN.

Witnesses:
C. G. ZIMMERMANN,
FRANCIS D. PASTORIUS.

UNITED STATES PATENT OFFICE.

CHARLES F. ZIMMERMANN, OF PHILADELPHIA, PENNSYLVANIA.

HARP.

SPECIFICATION forming part of Letters Patent No. 257,808, dated May 9, 1882.

Application filed December 10, 1881. (No model.)

To all whom it may concern:

Be it known that I, CHARLES F. ZIMMERMANN, a citizen of the United States, resident of the city and county of Philadelphia, in the State of Pennsylvania, have invented certain new and useful Improvements in Harps, of which the following is a specification, reference being had to the accompanying drawings, wherein—

Figure 1 is a plan of a harp with my improvements shown as applied thereto. Fig. 2 is an elevation on line 1 1, Fig. 1. Fig. 3 is an enlarged vertical section on line 2 2, Fig. 1. Fig. 4 is a similar view on line 3 3, Fig. 1; and Fig. 5 is a broken plan, partly in section, of the appliances constituting my invention, and shown as drawn to an enlarged scale.

My invention has relation to harps, and has for its object to provide a harp with appliances designed and adapted to be operated to come into contact with certain determined strings of such instrument to reduce them to silence and render them incapable of vibrating to give a musical tone during such contact. Such appliances I call "trigger-bars," and they are arranged transversely with the strings of the harp. A harp so provided has the size of a zither, and which I term an "autoharp," and the manner in which the instrument is played is entirely new. The player glides with the thumb of his right hand over all the sounding-strings of the instrument to the tone of the melody, while the different trigger-bars render those strings silent which do not belong to the respective chord, such trigger-bars simply doing the work of the performer, who does not now need his left hand for the accompaniment, the tones of the different chords being given by the various trigger-bars. Each one of the latter renders certain strings of the autoharp silent, so that the remaining strings compose a certain chord. The more strings and trigger-bars applied to such instrument the more perfect the latter will be. The instrument may be used for accompaniment to the voice or another musical instrument, or the melody may be played at the same time with the accompaniment, as on any other harp.

My invention has for its further object to provide the autoharp with trigger-bar arranged to simultaneously contact with or touch all the strings of the instrument in the middle of their length, thus temporarily shortening such strings and raising their tone, thereby providing means whereby a melody may be played upon harps in the different octaves. Such trigger-bar I call the "flageolet" trigger-bar, because by its contact with the harp-strings the latter then give the flageolet or falsetto tones when struck. Such trigger must always touch the middle of the strings. This requirement rendered it necessary to change the shape of the common zither to that shown in the drawings, so that such bar can be placed immediately across the middle of each string of the harp.

My invention accordingly consists of a harp shaped as shown in the drawings, and which is provided with two sets of trigger-bars, each such bar being provided with depending fingers located and arranged thereon, so that when the bar is moved said fingers will come in contact with the strings of the instrument for the purpose above set forth.

Referring to the accompanying drawings, A represents my autoharp of the required shape, as shown—*i. e.,* wider in the middle than at its ends, the latter being correspondingly configured. *a a* represent the strings thereof tuned to the natural scale or key. The sides *a¹ a²* of such harp are provided with receptacles or boxes B B¹, having partitions or dividing-strips *b b¹* for forming a series of chambers or bearings in such receptacles. The latter are centrally located upon the harp, as shown, and are adapted for and designed to receive the ends of a series of bars, C C¹, extending across the harp-strings a slight distance above the same, as indicated in Figs. 3 and 4. Such bars or push-rods, or, as I shall hereinafter term them, "triggers," are provided with push-buttons *c c* and springs *c¹ c¹*, as shown, so that when manual pressure is applied to said buttons said triggers are pushed in their determined paths of movement, the reaction of springs *c¹ c¹* reversely moving such triggers when such pressure is released from said buttons.

The triggers C C¹ are provided on their under sides with a series of depending fingers, *c² c²,* located between the harp-strings, as shown in Figs. 3 and 4, and are of such length that they will engage or contact with the strings when the triggers are moved.

The triggers C C represent the chord-triggers, and are more plainly shown in Fig. 4—that is, each said trigger has its depending fingers *c² c²* so arranged that when pushed in the direction indicated by arrow *x* it will reduce to silence or cut out of the natural scale certain strings of the harp or autoharp which do not belong to the chords wanted.

The instrument may have a diatonic scale of fifteen strings or a chromatic scale of thirty or more strings, and accordingly two to seven or more trigger-bars, C. Each of these trigger-bars may render it possible to select two, or even three and four, chords by working such bar one way or the other, it resting between two springs, *c¹ c¹,* one at each end, which keep the fingers or teeth of the bar between the strings when not in use.

To provide for convenient and ready ascertainment of the required trigger to be pushed for any of the chords, a series of numbers or other characters representing the chords may be placed upon the side *a¹,* directly in front or in line with the ends of such triggers, as shown at D, Fig. 2. Such trigger-bars C themselves select the accompaniment—*i. e.,* the different tones of the various chords—so that the performer, by simply gliding over all the strings and changing the trigger-bars, can perform as many arpeggio chords as are provided for in the trigger bars, the number of which is not limited and may embrace the harmonies of all scales.

The trigger C¹ represents the flageolet or octave trigger, and is adapted and designed to be pushed in the direction indicated by arrow *y,* or the reverse of that in which triggers C are moved. Such arrangement is merely for

the convenience of the harpist, and is not therefore a necessary one, as all of said triggers may, if desired, be moved in the same direction. When such flageolet-trigger is moved as described all of its depending fingers come into contact with all of the strings of the harp, respectively, as illustrated in Fig. 3, such contacting of all of the strings of the instrument having the effect of temporarily shortening them. Consequently when they are then vibrated they give a note in a higher key, and a melody then played thereon will be rendered in one of the octaves. It is for this reason that I term such trigger the "flageolet" or "octave" trigger.

It will be noticed that bar C¹ is arranged transversely over the middle of all the strings of the instrument and so adjusted that when moved its triggers touch them lightly at such point, thereby producing the falsetto or flageolet tone.

If desired, the strings of the harp may be numbered and such numbers placed upon the triggers, as shown at *c,* Fig. 1. Such method of so numbering the strings upon the triggers may be that copyrighted to me January 3, 1871; or any other suitable or desired notification of such strings may be employed. Such figures or numbers are used instead of notes. When the strings are so noted or characterized the harp may then be mechanically played or performed upon in all the various scales and chords by a person unfamiliar with the harp, provided such person be furnished with numbered or characterized music corresponding to the notification placed upon the triggers. For this reason I denominate a harp provided with the said described triggers and numbered strings or scale marked thereon an "autoharp." When the triggers are not in use the springs *c¹ c¹* keep their depending fingers out of contact with the harp-strings, so that, if desired, the latter may be manipulated in the usual or customary manner.

It is evident that my invention is entirely different from the pedals of a harp, or devices to take the place of such pedals, which merely change the vibration, length, and tone of the strings without rendering any of them silent, while my trigger-bars are employed to do the work heretofore done by the performer with the left hand. The latter in my instrument does not need to be used for the accompaniment, the tones of the different chords being given by the different trigger-bars.

What I claim as my invention is as follows:

1. The combination, with a harp of the form substantially as shown and described, of a series of bars, C C, arranged transversely across the strings thereof, and provided with depending teeth or fingers designed and adapted to come into contact with and silence or "cut out" certain strings when said bars are moved, substantially as set forth.

2. In a harp of the form substantially as shown and described, the combination of trigger-bars C and C¹, the latter being placed transversely across the middle of the strings of the harp, substantially as shown, and for the purpose set forth.

3. In combination with harp A, the transversely-arranged triggers C C¹, provided with depending fingers or teeth *c²,* resting at one end against springs *c¹ c¹,* substantially as shown, and for the purpose set forth.

4. The combination, with a harp of the form shown and described, of a series of trigger-bars arranged transversely across the strings of said harp, and constructed, substantially as shown and described, for silencing certain strings thereof, substantially as and for the purpose set forth.

In testimony that I claim the foregoing I have hereunto set my hand this 9th day of December, 1881.

CHARLES F. ZIMMERMANN.

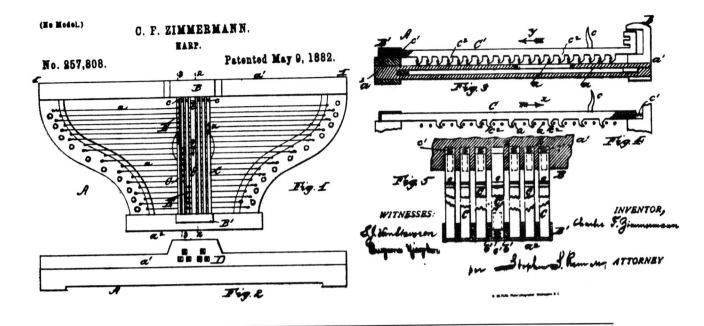

The following patents pertain to the Autoharp. Those marked * are known to have been owned by the Autoharp manufacturer.

Number	Date	Owner	Subject
#110,719	1/3/1871	C. F. Zimmermann	Notation System
*#257,808	5/9/1882	C. F. Zimmermann	Original Autoharp Patent
*#445,978	2/10/1891	J. L. DeGood	Autoharp
*#490,407	1/24/1893	C. H. Eisenbrandt	Hammer for Autoharp
*#493,099	3/7/1893	W. Leiner	Attachment
*#510,857	12/12/1893	I. Hammerl	Autoharp
*#511,970	1/2/1894	I.A. Salmon	Autoharp
*#518,512	4/17/1894	W. J. Richie	Autoharp
*#521,109	6/5/1894	A. J. Gery & R. Dolge	Concert Autoharp
*#522,870	7/10/1894	H. Ackermann	Stringed Instrument
*#530,369	12/4/1894	L. Utt	Attachment
*#540,988	6/11/1895	J. J. Joyce	Autoharp
*#542,533	7/9/1895	W. B. Owen & J. H. Crowell	Stringed Instrument
#541,352	6/18/1895	A. Govan & J. Worton, Jr.	Autoharp
#557,290	3/31/1896	C. Sucker	Autoharp
*#557,509	3/31/1896	T. H. Roth, R. Dolge, & L. Melcher	Autoharp
*#558,797	4/21/1896	A. J. Gery & R. Dolge	Plectrum for Autoharp
#559,124	4/28/1896	G. B. Durkee	Autoharp
#559,764	5/5/1896	J. S. Back	Autoharp
#566,388	8/25/1896	W. Eschemann	Autoharp
*#574,307	12/29/1896	R. Dolge	Autoharp
*#574,308	12/29/1896	R. Dolge	Autoharp
*#574,309	12/29/1896	R. Dolge	Autoharp
*#575,638	1/19/1897	R. Dolge	Autoharp
#575,707	1/26/1897	E. V. Dexter	Autoharp
*#583,162	5/25/1897	C. F. Zimmermann	Autoharp
*#593,102	11/2/1897	J. J. Joyce	Autoharp
#588,366	8/17/1897	J. A. Taylor & W. Eschemann	Autoharp
#591,729	10/12/1897	W. B. Behnke	Autoharp
*#593,126	11/2/1897	T. H. Roth & J. J. Joyce	Autoharp
*#593,701	11/16/1897	S. G. Stuart	Autoharp
*#596,906	1/4/1898	F. G. McPherson	Autoharp
#604,914	5/31/1898	J. E. Eckert	Autoharp
#975,865	11/15/1910	W. S. Holloway	Autoharp
*#1,097,048	5/19/1914	G. L. Reynolds & F. M. Nickerson	Autoharp
#1,171,484	2/15/1916	J. W. Van Hoy	Stringed Instrument
*#1,799,172	4/7/1931	J. H. Large	Autoharp
#2,473,442	6/14/1949	C. B. Page	Stringed Instrument
#2,975,666	3/21/1961	C. O. Musser	Guitaro
*#3,237,503	3/1/1966	G. R. Peterson, Jr. et al	B-model Chord Bar
*#3,401,586	9/17/1968	G. R. Peterson, Jr.	Cutlass (Solid-body)
*#3,499,357	3/10/1970	G. R. Peterson, Jr.	Magnetic Pickup
*#3,548,067	12/15/1970	G. R. Peterson, Jr.	Styrofoam Case
*#3,596,754	8/3/1971	G. R. Peterson, Jr.	

Copies of patents may be purchased for $1.00 each from the Commissioner of Patents and Trademarks, Washington, DC 20231.

SOURCES

1. ARTICLES

"Alfred Dolge and Son and the Autoharp." *Music Trades,* December 21, 1895.

"Alfred Dolge Sued." *Press,* December 3, 1892.

Arndt, W.W. "And Bring Your Autoharp." *Harvest Years,* November 1971, pp. 44-46.

"The Autoharp." *Freund's Musical Weekly,* November 20, 1895.

"The Autoharp." *Music Trade Review,* December 28, 1895.

"The Autoharp." *Musical Courier,* February 8, 1893.

"Autoharp Advances." *Music Trade Review,* ca. 1895, p. 49.

"The Autoharp and Santa Claus." *Indicator,* January 5, 1895.

"The Autoharp in Chicago." *Indicator,* December 7, 1895.

"The Autoharp: Its Successful Use with Gilmore's Band." *Freund's Musical Weekly,* May 15, 1895.

"The Autoharp on Sumter." *Music Trade Review,* September 14, 1895, p. 10.

"Autoharp Progress: How Alfred Dolge & Son Have Improved the Autoharp Until Zimmerman [sic], Its Inventor, Scarcely Knew It." *Music Trade Review,* August 3, 1895.

"The Autoharp Resounds Through Pike's Peak." *Music Trade Review,* ca. March, 1896, p. 13. [Reprinted from the *New York World,* March 8, 1896.]

"The Autoharp Room." *Presto,* May 23, 1895, p. 19.

"Autoharp Survey." *Mugwumps,* Vol. 3, No. 6, pp. 16-17.

"Autoharp Survey Report." *Mugwumps,* Vol. 5, No. 2, p. 13 +.

Benson, Peter. "No More Grooves!" *The Autoharpoholic,* Fall 1980, pp. 11-12.

Blackley, Becky. "Autoharp × 2 = Versatility." *Frets,* March 1982, pp. 36-38.

_____. "The Autoharp—History & Place in Bluegrass." *Bluegrass Breakdown,* January/February 1983, pp. 6-16.

_____. "C.F. Zimmermann's System of Musical Notation." *The Autoharpoholic,* Winter 1983, pp. 10-13.

_____. "The Concert Harp." *The Autoharpoholic,* Winter 1982, pp. 18-20.

_____. "Custom Chording for Your Autoharp." *Frets,* November 1980, pp. 36-37.

_____. "How to Build a Chorded Zither." *The Autoharpoholic,* Fall 1982, pp. 16-20.

_____. "How to Convert Your Harp to the Diatonic Scale." *The Autoharpoholic,* Winter 1981, pp. 21-22.

_____. "How to Make a Strap." *The Autoharpoholic,* Summer 1980, p. 6.

_____. "How to Play the Diatonic Autoharp." *The Autoharpoholic,* Spring 1981, p. 20.

_____. "How to Read the TAB." *The Autoharpoholic,* Fall 1981, pp. 15-16.

_____. "How to Tighten the Playing Action." *The Autoharpoholic,* Fall 1980, p. 21.

_____. "The Oscar Schmidt International, Inc., Factory, Union, New Jersey." *The Autoharpoholic,* Summer 1982, pp. 16-21.

_____. "Strings, Springs, and Other Things: Getting Your Act Together (and Keeping It That Way)." *The Autoharpoholic,* Spring 1980, p. 2.

_____. "View from the Top: Bryan Bowers." *The Autoharpoholic,* Winter 1981, pp. 8-11.

_____. "View from the Top: John B. Sebastian." *The Autoharpoholic,* Fall 1980, pp. 16-20.

_____. "View from the Top: Lindsay Haisley." *The Autoharpoholic,* Spring 1983, pp. 8-12.

_____. "View from the Top: Mike Seeger." *The Autoharpoholic,* Summer 1981, pp. 16-20.

_____. "View from the Top: Patrick Couton." *The Autoharpoholic,* Spring 1982, pp. 16-20.

_____. "View from the Top: Stevie Beck." *The Autoharpoholic,* Winter 1983, pp. 18-21.

Bluestein, Evo. "View from the Top: Jean Ritchie." *The Autoharpoholic,* Fall 1981, pp. 6-10.

Bowers, Bryan. "Teach-in: Tuning the Autoharp." *Sing Out!,* March-April 1975, pp. 13-14. [Reprinted in *The Autoharpoholic,* Spring 1981, pp. 10-11.]

_____. Columns in *Frets,* May 1981, June 1981, July 1981, August 1981, September 1981, November 1981, June 1982, October 1982.

Burton, B. "Use an Autoharp on the Playground." *Recreation,* June 1955, pp. 279-280.

"Can It Be Done?" *Music Trades,* January 26, 1895.

"Cavalli and the Cats at the Dolgeville Reunion." *Freund's Musical Weekly,* ca. February 1895, p. 15. [Also in the *Presto,* February 7, 1895.]

"Chord Bar Arrangements." *The Autoharpoholic,* Spring 1982, pp. 22-25.

Cleator, M. "Making Use of the Autoharp." *Music Educators Journal,* Vol. 47 (1960), p. 102 +.

"A Dolgeville Social." *Presto,* November 28, 1895.

"Dolgeville." *Little Falls (N.Y.) Journal and Courier,* December 6, 1892.

"Dolgeville." *Little Falls (N.Y.) Journal and Courier,* Industrial Edition, December 1895.

"The Garcia Benefit," *Presto,* December 5, 1895, p. 10.

Goff, Paula. " 'Gadget' Manages to Survive 100 Years." *Reporter,* January 15, 1982.

Gorak, David A. "Sweet Sales Music Promised by Firm's Easy-Play Autoharp." *Crain's Chicago Business,* July 5, 1982.

Haltin, H. "Study and Teaching: An Orchestra of Autoharps." *Music Educators Journal,* March 1973, pp. 61-63.

"An Interview with Mr. Aldis J. Gery, Concert Autoharpist." *Presto,* January 3, 1895, p. 19. [Reprinted in *The Autoharpoholic,* Winter 1982, pp. 23-24.]

"John Kilby Snow, 1905-1980." *The Autoharpoholic,* Fall 1980, pp. 8-9.

Kalb, E. C. "The Autoharp Solved a Problem." *School Musician,* June 1951, p. 15 +.

King, Michael. "On Tuning." *The Autoharpoholic*, Summer 1980, p. 8. [Reprinted in Henry Rasof's *The Folk, Country, & Bluegrass Musician's Catalogue*, pp. 139-140.]

Larsen, Chris Nyholm. "The Autoharp." *Seattle Folklore Society Journal*, June 1978 (1979), pp. 2-13.

Mehlman, Elaine. "Playing the Night Away: Easy Chord Autoharp Can Make Playing Instruments Easy, Cheap." *Pioneer Press*, December 2, 1982.

Mirken, Margie. "Autoharp Adjustments." *Frets*, April 1983, p. 9.

――――――. "Autoharp Hotrodding." *Frets*, May 1983, p. 8.

――――――. "Troubleshooting Autoharps." *Frets*, February 1983, p. 9.

Moore, A. Doyle. "The Autoharp: Its Origin and Development from a Popular to a Folk Instrument." *New York Folklore Quarterly*, December 1963, pp. 216-274. [Reprinted in *Mugwumps*, January 1973, pp. 1-14. Also reprinted in Harry Taussig's *Folkstyle Autoharp*, pp. 10-20.]

Morgan, Tom and Morgan, Mary. "The Autoharp As We See It." *Bluegrass Unlimited*, September 1979, pp. 34-37.

"Not Yet." *Herkimer County* (N.Y.) *News*, December 9, 1892.

Padgett, Woody. "Diatonic Just Tuning." *The Autoharpoholic*, Winter 1981, pp. 18-19.

――――――. "Understanding Autoharp Strings." *The Autoharpoholic*, Fall 1982, pp. 8-9.

Paglia, Gwen. "City Attorney a Picker and Strummer at Heart." *Park Ridge* (Ill.) *Herald*, October 1, 1981.

Phipps, Bonnie. "Autoharp Styles." *Frets*, April 1981, pp. 34-36.

――――――. "Experimental Autoharp." *Frets*, March 1983, pp. 38-40.

"Progress of the Autoharp." *Musical Courier*, March 27, 1895.

Sallis, James. "The Autoharp." *Frets*, June 1979, pp. 17-19.

Seeger, Mike. "Mountain Music Played on the Autoharp." Folkways Records, 1965. [Liner notes from album of the same name.]

Seeger, Peter. "The Autoharp Played Stoneman Style." *Sing Out!*, December-January 1961-62, pp. 16-17.

Snow, Kilby. Autobiography in "Country Songs and Tunes Played on the Autoharp." Folkways Records, 1969.

Taussig, Harry A. "Teach-in: Autoharp." *Sing Out!*, February-March 1966, pp. 38-39.

"Tesla's Marvelous Achievement: Earth Electricity to Kill Monopoly." *Musical Age*, ca. March 1896. [Reprinted from the *New York World*, March 8, 1896.]

Tipton, G. "The Autoharp Is Anybody's Instrument." *School Musician*, May 1952, pp. 12-13 and February 1953, p. 8 + .

Traum, Artie. "A Short and Wild History of the Concertina (and a Coda on the Autoharp)." *Oak Music Report*, Spring 1981, pp. 14-17.

"W. S. B. Matthews on the Autoharp." *Music Trade Review*, September 21, 1895.

Waldrop, Evelyn B. "Happy Harmonizing." *Music Journal*, September 1952, p. 36 + .

Wolfe, I. "Enjoy Playing the Autoharp." *Music Ministry*, June 1972, pp. 32-33.

Zimmermann, C. F. Unpublished autobiography. Written in German and translated by Gisela Swanson, Urbana, Illinois, ca. 1963, and Rudolf Schlacher, Northbrook, Illinois, 1983.

Untitled items regarding the Autoharp appeared in the following publications:

American Art Journal, January 5, 12, and 26, 1895.

Dolgeville Herald, November 30 and December 28, 1892.

Herkimer County (N.Y.) *News*, December 9, 1892.

Indicator, January 12, 26, and November 16, 1895.

Little Falls (N.Y.) *Journal and Courier*, December 6, 1892.

Little Falls (N.Y.) *Evening Times*, December 1, 1892.

Music Trades, February 6, 9, and September 28, 1895.

Musical Courier, February 8, 1893; October 16 and December 25, 1895; January 29, 1896.

New York Recorder, January 27, 1895.

Presto, February 7, May 23, November 21, December 5, 12, 19, and 26, 1895.

Saturday Globe, December 3, 1892.

Utica (N.Y.) *Morning Herald*, December 1, 1892.

2. PERIODICALS

Autoharp Teachers' Digest. 5194 Driftwood, Kalamazoo, MI 49009 (616) 375-6729. [Two mimeographed pages monthly. Ideas for teaching the Autoharp.]

The Autoharpoholic. P.O. Box 504, Brisbane, CA 94005. (415) 467-1700. [Quarterly magazine for Autoharp enthusiasts.]

Bluegrass Unlimited. P.O. Box 111, Broad Run, VA 22014. (703) 361-8992. [Monthly magazine of general interest to harpers.]

Frets. 20605 Lazaneo, Cupertino, CA 95014. (408) 446-1105. [Monthly magazine with some articles of interest to harpers.]

JEMF Quarterly. John Edwards Memorial Foundation Collection, Wilson Library,, University of North Carolina, Chapel Hill, NC 27514. [JEMF is a non-profit archive and research center to study and preserve music.]

Mugwumps: The Magazine of Folk Instruments. 15 Arnold Place, New Bedford, MA 02740. (617) 993-0156. [Good for collectors.]

Sing Out! Magazine. P.O. Box 1071, Easton, PA 18042. [General interest.]

3. REFERENCE BOOKS

Blackley, Becky. *The Autoharp Book.* Brisbane, Cal.: i.a.d. Publications, 1983. [Available from i.a.d. publications, P.O. Box 504, Brisbane, CA 94005.]

――――――, ed. *The Care and Feeding of the Autoharp, Vol. 1.* Brisbane, Cal.: i.a.d. Publications, 1981. [Reprints from *The Autoharpoholic* Magazine, 1980-1981. Also available from the address above.]

The C. F. Zimmermann Company catalog. Dolgeville, N.Y.: Alfred Dolge & Son, September 1896. [A copy is included in the collection of the John Edwards Memorial Foundation at the University of North Carolina.]

Franz, Eleanor. *Dolge*. Herkimer, N.Y.: Herkimer County Historical Society, 1980. [Copies may be ordered for $11 plus $2 postage from the Herkimer County Historical Society, 400 North Main Street, Herkimer, NY 13350.]

Montgomery Ward Company catalogs. Chicago: Montgomery Ward Company, Inc., 1917-1920, 1922, 1923, 1926, 1934, 1935, 1939-1968, 1971-1974. [Catalog set examined at the California Historical Society, San Francisco, was not complete. Autoharps may have appeared in catalogs other than those listed.]

Phonoharp Company catalog. Boston: The Phonoharp Company, n.d. (ca. 1912). [A copy is in the John Edwards Memorial Foundation Collection.]

Rasof, Henry. *The Folk, Country, & Bluegrass Musician's Catalogue*. New York: St. Martin's Press, 1982. [Has chapter on the Autoharp.]

Sandberg, Larry, and Weissman, Dick. *The Folk Music Sourcebook*. New York: Alfred A. Knopf, 1976. [A bit out of date, but good general source.]

Sears, Roebuck Company catalogs. Chicago: Sears, Roebuck Company, Inc., 1894-1924, 1955-present. [Microfilms of these catalogs are available in many public libraries.]

Zimmermann, C. F. *The Autoharp*. Philadelphia, January 1893. [The last catalog of the Philadelphia models. A copy is in the New York Public Library.]

Zimmermann, C. F. *Simplified Harmony Teacher and Short-hand Writing of Chords, In English and German—Also—New Method of Music by Figures*. Philadelphia: C. F. Zimmermann, ca. 1889. [Copies are in the Boston Public Library and the John Edwards Memorial Foundation Collection.]

4. INSTRUCTION BOOKS AND SONGBOOKS

Adams-Jeremiah, Dorothy. *The Autoharp: A Guide for Use in Accompaniment*. South Croydon, Surrey, England: Alfred Lengnick, 1966.

Allee, Ernie. *Hymns and Gospel Songs for Autoharp*. Kansas City, Mo.: Lillenas Publishing Co., 1972.

Autoharp Gems: A Grand Collection of Standard Melodies Arranged for the Autoharp by Herman Hermanson and Aldis J. Gery. (Series 1-6). Dolgeville, N.Y.: The C. F. Zimmermann Co., 1896.

Autoharp Pocketbook. Pacific, Mo.: Mel Bay Publications, 1980.

The Autoharp: A Most Useful Instrument for the Elementary School Music Program. Jersey City, N.J.: Oscar Schmidt-International, Inc., n.d. (ca. 1960).

Bair, Edna Mae. *How to Teach Your Class to Play Autoharp Accompaniments For Songs in Our Singing World*. Boston: Ginn & Co., 1955.

Bayless, Kathleen M. *A Practical Approach in Learning to Play the Autoharp*. Kent, Ohio: Kathleen M. Bayless, 1968.

Blackley, Becky. *Canon in D* [by] *Johann Pachelbel*. Brisbane, Cal.: i.a.d. Publications, 1981. [Adapted and arranged for the diatonic Autoharp.] Distributed by *The Autoharpoholic*.

——————. *Harp! The Herald Angels Sing!* Northbrook, Ill.: Oscar Schmidt-International, Inc., 1981. [Christmas songs arranged for the Autoharp.]

——————. ed. *The Bryan Bowers Songbook*. Northbrook, Ill.: Oscar-Schmidt-International, Inc., 1983. [Forthcoming.]

Blair, Elizabeth. *Autoharp Accompaniments to Old Favorite Songs*. Evanston, Ill.: Birchard Publishing Co., 1958.

Bock, Fred. *Autoharp Songs for Sunday School*. Kansas City, Mo.: Lillenas Publishing Co., 1972.

Brimhall, John. *Americana for Autoharp*. n.p.: California Music Press, Inc., 1976.

Carlyle, J. J. *Carlyle's Simple Method of Accompaniment for the Auto Harp*. Leicester, England: T. H. Crumbie, 1895.

Colgin, Mary Lou. *Chords and Starts for Guitar and Autoharp, A Collection of Children's Songs*. n.p.: Mary Lou Colgin, 1979.

Creutz, George M. *The Autoharp Self-Instructor*. n.p.: George M. Creutz, 1895.

Diers, Ann. *Twenty-one Songs Arranged for Autoharp, Guitar, and Zither*. Boston: Boston Music Co., 1964. Distributed by Frank Music.

Dykema, Peter William. *Autoharp Accompaniment by Lillian Mohr Fox to Songs from Sing Out!* Boston: C. C. Birchard and Co., 1953.

Fox, Lillian Mohr. *Autoharp Accompaniments to Old Favorite Songs: Manual of Instructions*. Boston: C. C. Birchard and Co., 1947.

Fun with the Autoharp. Pacific, Mo.: Mel Bay Publications, 1971.

Grand Collections of Popular Music. Dolgeville, N.Y.: C. F. Zimmermann Co., ca. 1896. [Series #1 and #2.]

Haase, H. D. *H. D. Haase's Improved Method of Figure Music for the Autoharp*. Greene, Iowa: H. D. Haase, 1897.

Hall, Frances. *Christmas Songs for the Autoharp and How to Play Them*. Boston: Boston Music Co., 1956.

——————. *Favorite Folksongs, Ballads, and Spirituals for Autoharp*. Boston: Boston Music Co., 1965. Distributed by Frank Music.

——————. *Frances Hall's How to Play the Autoharp, Including Thirty-one Favorite Songs with Autoharp Accompaniment*. Boston: Boston Music Co., 1956.

Harmonette Instructor. Dolgeville, N.Y.: C. F. Zimmermann Co., ca. 1896.

Have Fun with Music on the Autoharp. Jersey City, N.J.: Oscar Schmidt-International, Inc., 1959. [For Model #73.]

Holm, Ann. *Picking Styles for the Autoharp*. Rockford, Ill.: Charlotte's Web School of Folk Music, n.d.

Instant Picture Chord Autoharp No. 1. n.p.: Remick Music Corp., 1967. [Arranged by Dan Fox.]

Instant Picture Chord Autoharp No. 2, Bob Dylan. New York: M. Whitmark & Sons, 1967. [Arranged by Dan Fox.]

Instructor for Autoharp, with Choice Collection of Popular Figure Music. Toronto, Canada: Whaley, Royce, and Co., n.d. (ca. 1896).

Instructor for Autoharp. Dolgeville, N.Y.: C. F. Zimmermann Co., ca. 1896. [For Styles #1, #2¾, #3, #4, #5, #6, Parlor Grand, and Concert Grand.]

Instructor for the Autoharp, Style No. 73. Jersey City, N.J.: Oscar Schmidt-International, Inc., 1948. [Also for Style No. 2¾.]

Instructor for the Zimmerman [sic] *Autoharp, Style No. 73*. Jersey City, N.J.: Oscar Schmidt-International, Inc., 1947.

Jones, Clayton S., and Koehler, Barbara McClintock. *Traditional Autoharp*. Pacific, Mo.: Mel Bay Publications, 1978.

Krone, Beatrice Perham. *Harmony Fun with the Autoharp.* Chicago: Neil A. Kjos Music Co., 1952.

Ludwig, Alice Jeanne, and Ludwig, Louis I. *Colors and Chords for the Autoharp and Other Chording Instruments.* Brooklyn, N.Y.: Carl Van Roy Co., 1957.

The Many Ways to Play the Autoharp: A Modern Step by Step Instruction Book of Basic Techniques, Vol. 1. Union, N.J.: Oscar Schmidt-International, Inc., 1966.

The Many Ways to Play the Autoharp: Advanced Techniques, Vol. 2. Union, N.J.: Oscar Schmidt-International, Inc., 1966.

McLaughlin, Roberta Grogan, and Dawley, Muriel. *Make Music with the Autoharp.* Brooklyn, N.Y.: Carl Van Roy Co., 1958.

McLaughlin, Roberta Grogan, and Dawley, Muriel. *Sing and Play with the Autoharp.* n.p., 1954.

Music for Everyone on the Autoharp. Jersey City, N.J.: Oscar Schmidt-International, Inc., 1964.

Null, Cecil. *Autoharp Instruction Book.* n.p.: Cedarwood, 1969. Distributed by Hansen.

_____. *Pickin' Style for Autoharp.* Nashville, Tenn.: Robert B. Ferguson Music, 1963. Distributed by Charles Hansen.

Nye, Robert, and Peterson, Meg. *Teaching Music with the Autoharp.* Union, N.J.: Music Education Group, 1973.

Okun, Milton, ed. *The Beatles' Greatest Hits.* Greenwich, Conn.: Cherry Lane Music Co., 1980.

_____, ed. *John Denver's Greatest Hits: Melody and Travis Picking.* Greenwich, Conn.: Cherry Lane Music Co., 1977.

_____, ed. *John Denver's Greatest Hits: Mountain and Arpeggio Strums.* Greenwich, Conn.: Cherry Lane Music Co., 1977.

_____, ed. *Kenny Rogers' Greatest Hits for Autoharp.* Port Chester, N.Y.: Cherry Lane Music, Co., 1982.

Oliver, Lord. *Funway How to Play the Autoharp.* n.p.: California Music Press, n.d. Distributed by Charles Hansen.

One Hundred-One Songs for Autoharp and Recorder. New Westminster, B.C., Canada: Empire Music Publishers, 1965.

Peterson, Meg. *Autoharp Anthology: Nostalgia.* Melville, N.Y.: MCA/Mills, n.d.

_____. *Autoharp Anthology: Pop Classics.* Melville, N.Y.: MCA/Mills, n.d.

_____. *Autoharp Parade: 100 Favorite Songs for Young People.* Union, N.J.: Oscar Schmidt-International, Inc., 1967.

_____. *Autoharp Parade: 100 Folk and Familiar Favorites.* Union, N.J.: Oscar Schmidt-International, Inc., 1967.

_____. *Autoharp Parade: 100 Hymns and Spirituals.* Union, N.J.: Oscar Schmidt-International, Inc., 1967.

_____. *Autoharp Songbook.* Pacific, Mo.: Mel Bay Publications, 1981.

_____. *The Complete Method for Autoharp and Chromaharp.* Pacific, Mo.: Mel Bay Publications, 1979.

_____. *Hymns for Autoharp.* Pacific, Mo.: Mel Bay Publications, 1978.

_____. *Let's Play the Autoharp.* Pacific, Mo.: Mel Bay Publications, 1981.

_____. *Make Wonderful Music with the Guitaro.* Union, N.J.: Oscar Schmidt-International, Inc., 1964.

_____. *More Songs for Autoharp.* Pacific, Mo.: Mel Bay Publications, 1981.

Peterson, Meg, and Fox, Dan. *Songs of Christmas for Autoharp.* Pacific, Mo.: Mel Bay Publications, 1980.

Peterson, Meg, and Olofson, Cary. *Play Along with the Easy Chord Autoharp.* Northbrook, Ill.: Oscar Schmidt-International, Inc., 1983.

Phipps, Bonnie. *Beginning Autoharp.* Sherman Oaks, Cal.: Alfred Publishing Co., Inc., 1983.

Pierce, Charles F. *Pierce's New Method for the Autoharp.* Bassett, Neb.: Charles F. Pierce, 1895.

Popular German Music, Vocal and Instrumental. Dolgeville, N.Y.: C. F. Zimmermann Co., ca. 1896.

Practical Instructor and Selection of Popular Melodies for the Autoharp Ne Plus Ultra. n.p., n.d. (ca. 1895).

Pratt, G. B. *Pratt's Easy Method for Playing the Autoharp.* Elgin, Ill.: Wilson Press, 1896.

Rightmire, Richard W. *The Virtuoso Autoharp: A No-note Method Leading to Solo and Accompaniment Playing.* New York: Clef Music Publishing Corp., 1967.

Rogers, Lucretia. *Let's Play the Autoharp.* Minneapolis: Schmidtt Foundation, 1961.

Royal Collections of Operatic Airs. Dolgeville, N.Y.: C. F. Zimmermann Co., ca. 1896.

The Salvation Army Autoharp Tutor. London, England: Salvation Army Publishing Department, 1893.

Scelsa, Greg, and Millang, Steve. *The Youngheart Autoharp Songbook.* Northbrook, Ill.: Oscar Schmidt-International, Inc., 1982.

Sesame Street: Autoharp. New York: Warner Brothers Publications, Inc., n.d. (ca. 1973).

Shealy, Alexander. *The Autoharp: Complete Method and Music (with 150 Selections).* Carlstadt, N.J.: Lewis Publishing Co., 1970.

Snyder, Alice M. *Sing and Strum.* Melville, N.Y.: Belwin/Mills, 1957.

Spaeth, Sigmund Gottfried. *Golden Autoharp Harmonies.* Des Moines, Iowa: National Autoharp Sales Co., 1953.

Standard Collections of Dance Music. Dolgeville, N.Y.: C. F. Zimmermann Co., ca. 1896.

Standard Sacred Selections. Dolgeville, N.Y.: C. F. Zimmermann Co., ca. 1896.

Swanson, Bessie R., and Sannerud, David. *Music Fundamentals through Folk Song.* Belmont, Cal.: Wadsworth Publishing Co., 1977.

Taussig, Harry A. *Folk Style Autoharp: An Instruction Method for Playing the Autoharp and Accompanying Folk Songs.* New York: Oak Publications, 1967.

Taylor, Lyman. *Advanced Autoharp Notation & Technique.* Greenville, N.Y.: Lyman Taylor, 1976.

Tracy, R. S. *Autoharp Music Books, Series #1-#13.* Facts of publication unknown. Included on Oscar Schmidt-International, Inc. price list, ca. 1936. [Includes hymns, patriotic airs, college songs, favorite songs, popular songs, concert solos, waltzes, marches, and dance music.]

_____. *Zimmermann Autoharp Instructor, Model 73.* n.p., n.d. (ca. 1925) [Also for models 2¾ and 72⅞.]

Waldrop, Evelyn Brock. *Sing N' Strum Autoharp Song Folio.* New York: William J. Smith Music Co., 1953.

Watters, Lorrain E. *A Teacher's Guide for the Golden Autoharp.* Des Moines, Iowa: National Autoharp Sales Co., 1955.

Welsch, H. *Welsch's New Method for the Autoharp.* n.p.: H. Welsch, 1894.

Yoder, Roselyn. *Quick Fun with the Autoharp.* New York: Shattinger International Music Corp., 1976. Distributed by Hansen House.

_____. *U-2 Can Be a Fake Autoharp Player.* n.p.: California Music Press, 1971. Distributed by Charles Hansen.

Zimmermann, C. F. *Choice Collection of Popular Figure Music for the Autoharp.* n.p., n.d. (ca. 1891) [For Styles #1, #2, #2¾, #3, #4, #5, and #6.]

_____. *Collection of Popular Figure Music for C. F. Zimmermann's Miniatur [sic] Autoharp.* n.p., n.d. (ca. 1885).

_____. *Instructor for Autoharp.* Facts of publication unknown. Listed in 1893 catalog. [For Styles #1, #2, #2¾, #3, #4, #5, and #6.]

_____. *Popular Songs for the Autoharp.* Philadelphia: C. F. Zimmermann, date unknown (ca. 1890).

5. DISCOGRAPHY [Albums and cassette tapes.] (*selected discography.)

Allwright, Graeme. *Graeme Allwright.* Mercury Records: 125.509 MDL. [Richard Borofsky on harp.]

_____. *Graeme Allwright.* Disques Mouloudji: EM 13506S. [Richard Borofsky on harp.]

_____. *Le Jour De Claite.*

Alsop, Peter. *Uniforms.* Flying Fish: FF 256.

The Amazing Rhythm Aces. *Too Stuffed to Jump.* ABC Records: ABLD 940.

The Annual Folk Festival of the Smokies, Vol. 1 & 2. Traditional: FFS-528 & FFS-529.

Anthology of American Folk Music. Folkways: FA 251, FA 252, FA 253. [Harp playing by the Carter Family, Floyd Ming, and "Pop" Stoneman with Eck Dunford.]

Arthur, Dino. *Open Boat.* Biscuit City: BC 1311. [Michael Stanwood on harp.]

Ashley, Clarence Tom, and Tex Isley. *Clarence Tom Ashley and Tex Isley Play and Sing American Folk Music.* Folkways: FA 2350.

The Band. *Stage Fright.* Capitol: SW-425.

Beamer, Evelyn. *Songs God Gave Me.* Mountain Records.

Blackmon, Richard. *Self-Song.* Unicorn Sound.

*Bluestein, Evo. *Deep Shady Grove.* Swallow: 2002.

*The Bluestein Family. *A Horse Named Bill and Other Children's Songs.* Greenhays: GR 709.

*_____. *Let the Dove Come In.* Philo/Fretless: FR 156.

*_____. *Sowin' on the Mountain.* Philo/Fretless: FR 141.

_____. *Travelin' Blues.* Swallow: 2003.

*Boarman, Andy. *Mountain State Music.* June Appal: JA 025.

*Bowers, Bryan. *Home, Home on the Road.* Flying Fish: FF 091.

*_____. *The View from Home.* Flying Fish: FF 037.

Breeding, Brooke. *Tying the Leaves.* Ozark Folk Center.

Breeding, Brooke, and Larry Poff. *God and Love.* Ozark Folk Center.

Brennan, Jo. *Strawberry Wine.* Niknak Productions.

Buddies. Kapp: 3445. [Maybelle Carter on harp.]

Carol, Bonnie. *Fingerdances for Dulcimer.* Kicking Mule: KM 220. [Bonnie Phipps on harp.]

The Carter Family. *All Time Favorites.* Acme: LP #1.

_____. *All-Night Sing.* Camden: CAL 767.

*_____. *The Best of the Carter Family.* Columbia: CS-9119/CL-2319.

_____. *The Carter Family Album.* Liberty: LRP-3230/LST-7230.

_____. *The Carter Family Sings the Country Album.* Columbia: CS-9417/CL-2617.

_____. *A Collection of Favorites by the Carter Family.* Decca: DL 4404.

_____. *Country and Western Classics.* Time-Life Records: TLCW-06.

_____. *Country's First Family.* Columbia: KC-34266.

_____. *The Famous Carter Family.* Harmony: HL 7280.

_____. *Great Original Recordings by the Carter Family.* Harmony: HL 7300.

_____. *Happiest Days of All.* RCA/Camden: ACL-1-0501.

_____. *Keep on the Sunny Side.* Acme: LP #2.

_____. *Keep on the Sunny Side.* Columbia: CS-8952/CL-2152.

_____. *Lonesome Pine Special.* RCA/Camden.

_____. *Mid the Green Fields of Virginia.* Victor: LPM 2772.

_____. *More Golden Gems from the Original Carter Family.* RCA/Camden.

_____. *My Old Cottage Home.* RCA/Camden: ACL-1-0047.

_____. *On Border Radio.* JEMF: 101.

_____. *The Original and Great Carter Family.* Camden: CAL 586.

_____. *The Original Carter Family in Texas, Vol. 1-7.* Old Homestead: 111, 112, 116, 117, 130, 136, 139.

_____. *Original Carter Family from 1936 Radio Transcripts.* Old Homestead: OHS 90045.

_____. *Songs of the Carters.* Columbia.

_____. *Travelin' Minstrel Band.* Columbia: KC-31454.

*Carter, Janette. *Howdayado!* Traditional: JC-573.

Carter, Joe, and Janette Carter. *Joe and Janette Carter.* County: CO-706.

*Carter, Maybelle. *Mother Maybelle Carter and Her Autoharp Play Famous Songs with the Stephen Scott Singers.* Smash: 27025/67025.

_____. *Mother Maybelle Carter.* Briar: 101.

_____. *Mother Maybelle Carter.* Pickwick Records: JS-6172.

*_____. *Mother Maybelle Carter.* Columbia: CG-32436.

_____. *Mother Maybelle Carter Sings Favorites of the Carter Family.* Cumberland: SRC-69524.

_____. *Mother Maybelle Carter . . . Pickin' and Singin'.* Smash: MGS-27041.

_____. *Mother Maybelle Carter: A Living Legend.* Columbia: CS-9275/CL-2475.

Carter, Sara, and Maybelle Carter. *An Historic Reunion . . . Sara and Maybelle.* Columbia: CS-9361/CL-2561.

*Clifton, Bill. *Autoharp Centennial Celebration!* Elf Records: ELF 101.

_____. *Blue Ridge Mountain Blues.* County: CO 740. [Mike Seeger on harp.]

_____. *Bluegrass in the American Tradition.* Nashville: NLP 2018. [Mike Seeger on harp.]

_____. *Carter Family Memorial Album.* Starday: SLP 146. [Mike Seeger on harp.]

_____. *Clifton and Company.* County: CO 765.

_____. *Code of the Mountains.* Starday: 271. [Mike Seeger on harp.]

_____. *Come by the Hills.* County: CO 751.

_____. *Happy Days.* Golden Guinea: GSGL.

_____. *Mountain Folk Songs.* Starday: 111.

_____. *Mountain Ramblings.* London: HAU 8325. [Mike Seeger on harp.]

_____. *Soldier, Sing Me a Song.* Starday: SLP 213. [Mike Seeger on harp.]

_____. *Wanderin'.* Hillbilly: HRS 001.

Clifton, Bill, and Red Rector. *Another Happy Day.* County: CO 758.

Clifton, Bill, and Red Rector. *Are You from Dixie?* Bear Family: BF 15013.

Clifton, Bill, and the Hamilton County Bluegrass Band. *Two Shades of Bluegrass.* Kiwi: SLC 93.

Colburn, David, and Deborah Stuart. *Colburn and Stuart Never Really Grew Up.* Macy Coffey Productions.

Cook, Russell. *Red Haired Boy.* Sword and Shield Recording Co.: LPS 9201.

The Country Gentlemen. Folkways: FA 2409.

Country Ham. *The Old Country Church.* Vetco: 519.

_____. *The Old Paint Mare.* Vetco: 517.

_____. *Old Time Mountain Music.* Vetco: 510.

_____. *Where the Laurel Blooms.* Vetco: 515.

*Couton, Patrick, and Georges Fischer. *Autoharp Ce Soir.* Iris: TR 1012.

Couton, Patrick. *Patrick Couton.* Discovale/Iris: WM 30.

Cranberry Lake. *Lowdown Symphony.* Swallowtail: ST-10.

The Debusk-Weaver Family. *Meeting in the Air.* Folkways: FTS 32431.

_____. *Rest at the End of the Road.* Lasting Sounds: LSS-778106-T.

Dickens, Hazel, and Alice Gerrard. *Hazel and Alice.* Rounder: 0027.

Dusty, Slim. *The Man Who Steadies the Lead.* EMI Australia: SCXO-8040.

Echoes of the Ozarks, Vol. 1-3. County: 518, 519, 520.

Farina, Mimi, and Richard Farina. *Celebrations for a Gray Day.* Vanguard: VSD-79174.

Faye, Rita. *Rita Faye's Autoharp.* Capital: T-1606.

Flatt, Lester, and Earl Scruggs. *A Boy Named Sue.* Columbia: C32244.

Flatt, Lester, and Earl Scruggs. *Country and Western Classics.* Time-Life Records: TLCW-04. [Maybelle Carter on harp.]

Flatt, Lester, and Earl Scruggs. *Songs of the Famous Carter Family.* Columbia: CL 1664/CS 8464. [Maybelle Carter on harp.]

Folk Festival at Newport, 1959, Vol. 2. Vanguard: 9063. [Mike Seeger on harp.]

The Folktellers. *Tales to Grow On.* Weston Woods: WW 711.

Frummox. *Frummox II.* Felicity: FR-003. [Lindsay Haisley on harp.]

Garrett, C. E. *Goosepimple Junction.* Private Release: 35265.

Gatlin, Larry, and the Gatlin Brothers Band. *Not Guilty.* Columbia: FC 37464.

Gerber, Tillie. *Tillie Gerber.* Private Release.

Gillihan, Robert, and Mary Gillihan. *Robert and Mary Gillihan.* Ozark Folk Center: 010069.

The Goins Brothers. *Take This Hammer.* Rebel: 1568.

Golden Ring and New Golden Ring, Vol. 1 & 2. Folk Legacy Records.

The Grandpa Jones Family. *Family Gathering.* CMH Records: CMH 9026.

_____. *Grandpa Jones Family Album.* CMH Records: CMH 9015.

Grooms, Don. *Walk Proud My Son.* You'ni Records. [Martin Schuman on harp.]

*Haisley, Lindsay. *Christmas on the Autoharp.* Armadillo: ARLP 82-1.

* _____. *Lindsay Haisley Live at the Kerrville Folk Festival.* Gazebo: BE 502.

Hamilton, Dana, and David Lindsey and the Sweet Song String Band. *Cold Frosty Morn.* Private Release: SSSB-001.

Harris, Emmylou. *Light of the Stable.* Warner Brothers: BSK 3484. [Bryan Bowers on harp.]

_____. *Roses in the Snow.* Warner Brothers: BSK 3422. [Bryan Bowers on harp.]

Hellman, Neal. *Appalachian Dulcimer Duets.* Kicking Mule: KM 222.

Hill, Paul, and Jack Moose, Clyde Robinson, and Morris Herbert. *Too Near to Turn Back Now.* Old Homestead: OHS 70031.

The Hollow Rock String Band. Rounder: 0024. [Jim Watson on harp.]

The Hotmud Family. *Till We Meet Here Again.* Vetco: 501.

Isley, Tex, and Gary Craig, and the New North Carolina Ramblers. *North Carolina Boys.* Leader: LEA 4040.

Johnian, Paul, and Mona Johnian. *How Great Is God.* Prestige: PP77-131.

Johnian, Paul, and Mona Johnian. *Paul and Mona Proclaim Hosanna in the Highest.* Reignbow: ES 8010313.

*Jones, Clay. *Traditional Autoharp.* Sunny Mountain: EB 1006.

Kahn, Si. *New Wood.* June Appal: 002.

Koch, Fred, and Friends. *This Little Cow.* Red Rover Records: RRR-111.

Lambert, Curley. *Blue Grass Evergreen.* Old Homestead: 90072.

The Malcolm Price Trio. *Country Session.* Decca: LK 4627.

Maphis, Rose Lee, and Joe Maphis. *Rose Lee and Joe Maphis.* Capitol: T 1778.

Marcus, Youra, and Christi Gibbons. *Sans Titre . . .* Arfolk: SB 373(Y).

A Martin County Hornpipe. Warren Nelson Records. [Michael Stanwood on harp.]

McCutcheon, John. *Barefoot Boy with Boots On.* Front Hall: FHR 021.

_____. *How Can I Keep from Singing?* June Appal: 003.

Metheny, Pat, and Lyle Mays. *American Garage.* ECM: 1115.

_____. *As Falls Wichita, So Falls Wichita Falls.* ECM Productions.

_____. *The Pat Metheny Group.* ECM: 1114.

Michaelangelo. *One Voice Many.* Columbia.

*The Mill Run Dulcimer Band. *Chickens in the Yard.* A Major Recording Company: MRLP 4042.

*_____. *Sunday at the Mill.* Lark: LRLP 3094.

Mitchell, Howie. *Howie Mitchell.* Folk Legacy: FSI 2.

Moore, Charlie. *Country Music Memories, Vol. 2:* Old Homestead: OHS 90135.

Morgan, Tom, and the Good Old Boys. *Maple on the Hill.* Folkways: FTS-31072.

The Morgans. *Music from Morgan Springs.* Davis Unlimited: 33035.

Music of the Ozarks. National Geographic Society: 703.

The New Deal String Band. *Down in the Willow.* Argo: ZFB 69 [Tom Paley and Janet Kerr on harp.]

The New Lost City Ramblers. *American Moonshine and Prohibition.* Folkways: FH 5263.

_____. *Earth is Earth.* Folkways: FF 869/FF 369.

_____. *Gone to the Country.* Folkways: FA 2491.

_____. *Modern Times.* Folkways: FTS 31027.

_____. *The New Lost City Ramblers.* Folkways: EPC 602.

*_____. *The New Lost City Ramblers, Vol. 1-5.* Folkways: FA 2395-2399.

_____. *The New Lost City Ramblers with Cousin Emmy.* Folkways: FTS 31015.

_____. *The Newport Folk Festival, 1960, Vol. 1.* Vanguard: 9083.

_____. *Old-Timey Songs for Children.* Folkways: FC 7064.

_____. *On the Great Divide.* Folkways: FTS 31041.

_____. *Radio Special #1.* Folkways: EPC 603.

_____. *Remembrance of Things to Come.* Folkways: FTS 31035.

_____. *Rural Free Delivery, No. 1.* Folkways: 2496.

_____. *Songs from the Depression.* Folkways: FC 5264.

_____. *String Band Instrumentals.* Folkways: FA 2492.

_____. *Tom Paley, John Cohen & Mike Seeger Sing Songs of the New Lost City Ramblers.* Folkways: FA 2494.

_____. *Twentieth Anniversary Concert, Carnegie Hall.* Flying Fish: FF 090.

_____. *Twenty Years/Concert Performances.* Flying Fish: FF 102.

The New Vinton County Frogwhompers. *We Always Wanted to Be a Big Name Band.* A Big Name Label: MG1-1001.

*The Nitty Gritty Dirt Band, and others: *Will the Circle Be Unbroken.* United Artists: UAS-9801.

*Null, Cecil. *New Sounds in Folk Music.* Briar International: Briar M-107.

Old Kentucky String Band. *Twilight is Stealing.* Old Homestead: 80008.

Oliver, Bill. *Texas Oasis.* Live Oak Records. [Lindsay Haisley on harp.]

The Original Bluegrass (& Country Swing) Spectacular. CMH Records: CMH 5902.

The Original Bogtrotters, 1937-1942. Biograph Records: RC 6003.

The Original Orchard Grass Band. *Walking in My Sleep.* Orchard Grass Music: STLP-100-Vol. 1. [Betty Waldron on harp.]

*Penix, Ron, Cathy Barton, and Jay Round. *Hammered Dulcimer Reunion.* Take Two Productions: T2P-001.

*Penix, Ron, Cathy Barton, Dave Para, and Jay Round. *Reflections on the Carter Family.* Take Two Productions: T2P-002.

*Philo Glee and Mandoline Society. *PG & MS.* Campus Folksong Club Recording: CFC 101. [A. Doyle Moore on harp.]

The Phipps Family. *Echoes of the Carter Family.* Starday: SLP 248.

_____. *The Most Requested Songs of the Carter Family.* Starday.

_____. *Old Time Mountain Pickin' and Singin'.* Starday.

_____. *The Phipps Family.* Folkways: FA 2375.

*Phipps, Bonnie. *Autoharpin'.* Kicking Mule: KM 228.

Prima Convention Italiana di Musica Old Time & Bluegrass. Ponderosa Records: PR-1001. [Ezio Guaitamacchi on harp.]

The Rackensack, Vol. 1 & Vol. 2. Ozark Folk Center: LP 278, LP 279.

Raw Honey. *Ragweed.* Private Release: RH-105.

The Red Clay Ramblers. *Stolen Love.* Flying Fish: FF 009.

_____. *The Red Clay Ramblers.* Folkways: FTS 31039.

Redbow, Buddy. *BRB.* First American Records: FA 7745. [Michael Stanwood on harp.]

Redpath, Jean, and Lisa Newstadt and the Angel Band. *Angels Hovering 'Round.* Philo/Fretless: FR 138.

Rhoads, Mary Faith, and the Dobbs Brothers. *Take Care of Yourself.*

Ritchie, Jean. *High Hills and Mountains.* Greenhays: GR 701. [Evo Bluestein on harp.]

_____. *Jean Ritchie at Home.* Pacific Cascade: LPL 7026.

_____. *None But One.* Greenhays: GR 708.

_____. *Precious Memories.* Folkways: FA 2427.

_____. *Sweet Rivers.* June Appal: FA 037. [John McCutcheon on harp.]

The Rosehip String Band. Flying Fish: FF 013.

Round the Heart of Old Galax, Vol. 1 & Vol. 2. County: CO 533, CO 534.

Rowan, Peter. *Peter Rowan.* Flying Fish: FF-071.

Saperstone, Debby, and George Wilson. *Kissing is a Crime.* Front Hall: FHR 019.

Schilling, Jean, and Lee Schilling. *Porches of the Poor.* Traditional: JLS-617.

*_____. *Keep on the Sunny Side.* Traditional: TR 021.

Scrivenor, Gove. *Coconut Gove.* Flying Fish: FF 084.

_____. *Shady Gove.* Flying Fish: FF 048.

Seckler, Curley, and the Nashville Grass. *Take a Little Time.* CMH Records: CMH-6241.

Seeger, Mike. *Mike Seeger.* Vanguard: VSD 79150.

_____. *Music from True Vine.* Mercury: SRM 1-627.

*_____. *Oldtime Country Music.* Folkways: FA 2325.

_____. *Second Annual Farewell Reunion.* Mercury: SRM 1-685.

_____. *Tipple, Loom & Rail: Songs of the Industrialization of the South.* Folkways: FH 5273.

Seeger, Mike, and Alice Gerrard. *Alice Gerrard and Mike Seeger.* Greenhays: GR 704.

Seeger, Mike, and Alice Gerrard. *Mike and Alice Seeger in Concert.* King (Japan): SKK 662.

Seeger, Mike, and Alice Gerrard. *Strange Creek Singers.* Arhoolie: 4004.

Seeger, Mike, and Peggy Seeger. *American Folksongs for Children.* Rounder: 8001-3.

Seeger, Mike, and Peggy Seeger. *Mike and Peggy Seeger.* Argo: DA 80.

Seeger, Peggy. *A Song for You and Me.* Prestige International: INT 1358.

_____. *No Tyme Lyke the Present.* EMI: 2556.

_____. *Peggy Alone.* Argo: ZDA 81.

_____. *Penelope Isn't Waiting Anymore.* Rounder: 4011.

Seeger, Peggy, and Ewan MacColl. *Blood and Roses, Vol. 2 & Vol. 3.* Blackthorne: ESB 80, ESB 81.

Seeger, Peggy, and Ewan MacColl. *Cold Snap.* Folkways: 8765.

Seeger, Peggy, and Ewan MacColl. *Contemporary Songs.* Folkways: 8736.

Seeger, Peggy, and Ewan MacColl. *Freeborn Man.* Blackthorne: BR 1065.

Seeger, Peggy, and Ewan MacColl. *From Where I Stand.* Folkways: 8563.

Seeger, Peggy, and Ewan MacColl. *Saturday Night at the Bull and Mouth.* Folkways: 8731.

Seeger, Peggy, and Ewan MacColl. *The New Britton Gazette, Vol. 2.* Folkways: 8734.

Seeger, Peggy, and Ewan MacColl. *Two-Way Trip.* Folkways: 8755.

The Seegers. *American Folksongs, Sung by the Seegers.* Folkways: FA 2005. [Mike, Peggy, Barbara, and Penny Seeger.]

The Shelor and Kimble Families. *Music from Patrick and Carroll Counties, Virginia.* Heritage: XXII.

The Simmons Family. *Neighbors.* Dancing Doll: CO 829.

_____. *Portraits of Life.* Dancing Doll: LP 412.

*_____. *Wandering through the Rackensack.* Traditional: V-3053.

Smith, Betty. *For My Friends of Song.* June Appal: JA 018.

Smith, Carl. *Sunday Down South.* Columbia: CL-959. [Maybelle Carter on harp.]

*Snow, Kilby. *Kilby Snow: Country Songs and Tunes with Autoharp.* Folkways: FA 3902.

Sop'n Up the Gravy. Log Cabin: 8001.

Sprung, Roger, Hal Wylie, and the Progressive Bluegrassers. *Irish Grass.* Showcase: S-6. [Drew Smith on harp.]

Sprung, Roger, Hal Wylie, and the Progressive Bluegrassers. *Irish Bluegrass Connection.* Showcase: S-7. [Drew Smith on harp.]

Sprung, Roger, Hal Wylie, and the Progressive Bluegrassers. *Southwest Winds.* Showcase: S-8. [Drew Smith on harp.]

*Staber, Dick. *Listen to My Song.* Fretless: FR 149.

*Stanwood, Michael, and Bruce Bowers with Fingers Akimbo. *Cowtowns and Other Planets.* Biscuit City: BC 1319.

Starcher, Buddy. *Buddy Starcher and His Mountain Guitar.* Starday: SLP 211.

Stoneman, Ernest V. "Pop." *Ernest V. Stoneman and the Stoneman Family.* Starday: SLP 200.

*_____. *Ernest V. "Pop" Stoneman, 1893-1968.* Stone House Records: NR 10817.

_____. *Pop Stoneman Memorial Album.* MGM: SC 4588.

_____. *The Stoneman Family and Old-Time Southern Music.* Folkways: FA 2315.

*Stoneman, Ernest, Kilby Snow, and Neriah and Kenneth Benfield. *Mountain Music Played on the Autoharp.* Folkways: FA 2365.

The Stonemans. *Country Hospitality.* Recording Productions of America: RPA-LP-1019.

_____. *Cuttin' the Grass.* CMH Records: CMH 6210.

_____. *The First Family of Country Music.* CMH Records: CMH 9029.

_____. *On the Road.* CMH Records: CMH 6219.

Sundell, Jon. *The Eagle and the Sparrow.* June Appal: JA 008.

Sunnyside. *Something Good.* Old Homestead: 70018.

Sunrise and Jessica. *Alive at Peirre's.* Lucky Mud: LMR 1001.

A Survey of Rural Music of the Southeast United States. Private issue. [1977 field collection recorded and edited by Mike Seeger.]

The Tex-i-an Boys. *Songs of Texas.* Folkways: 5328.

Thomas, Frank, and Anne Thomas. *Cracker Nights.* Olustee Records. [Martin Schuman on harp.]

Tyson, Ian, and Sylvia Tyson. *Early Morning Rain.* Vanguard: VSD-79175.

Tyson, Ian, and Sylvia Tyson. *Lovin' Sound.* MGM: SE-4388.

Tyson, Ian, and Sylvia Tyson. *Northern Journey.* Vanguard: VSD-79154.

Tyson, Ian, and Sylvia Tyson. *So Much for Dreaming.* Vanguard: VSD-79241.

Unity Bluegrass Band. *Getting around Tuit.* UB-101-77.

Van Denburg, AAltje. *Somebody's Tall and Handsome.* Van-Ayr Recording: VA 33-101A.

Van Ronk, Dave. *Inside/Dave Van Ronk.* Stateside: SL 10153.

Vanwarmer, Randy. *Warmer.* Bearsville Records: BRK 6988. [John Sebastian on harp.]

Vaughn, Palani, and the King's Own. *E Ka La Helu'eha, Vol. 1-4.* Nakahili Productions.

Wakefield, Frank. *Frank Wakefield.* Rounder: 0007.

*Waldron, Betty, and Mark Waldron. *Parlor Picking.* Outlet Records: STLP 1028.

*Wall, Ron. *Autoharp Melodies.* Private Release, recorded at the Ozark Folk Center.

Watson, Doc. *The Doc Watson Family.* Folkways: FTS 31021/2366.

The West Orrtanna String Band. *Orrtanna Home Companion.* Renovah: RS-932.

West, Hedy, and Bill Clifton. *Getting Folk Out of the Country.* Folk Variety: FV 12008.

The Wilburn Brothers. *Carefree Moments.* Vocalion: VL-3691.

Williamson, George, and Mary Williamson. *Old Time Country Duets.* Old Homestead: OHS-80010.

Wiseman, Mac. *New Traditions, Vol. 2.* Vetco: 509.

The Woods Band. Mulligan Music Ltd.: LUN 015.

Wrystraw. *From Earth to Heaven.* June Appal: JA 028.

Wylie, Hal, and Roger Sprung. *Bluegrass Gold.* Showcase: S-4. [Ginny Laengle and Roger Sprung on harp.]

6. EVENTS

Clark College Bluegrass Festival, Clark College Activities Office, 1800 E. McLoughlin Blvd., Vancouver, WA 98663 (Autoharp workshops)

Cosby Dulcimer Convention, Jean & Lee Schilling, Box 8 Highway 32, Cosby, TN 37722 (615) 587-5543 (Autoharp workshops)

Kerrville Folk Festival, P.O. Box 1466, Kerrville, TX 78028 (512) 476-1239 (Autoharp workshop)

Libertyville School of Folk and Old Time Music, 1700 N. Milwaukee Ave., Libertyville, IL 60048 (312) 362-0707 (Autoharp Classes and workshops)

Old Fiddlers Convention, Oscar Hall, 328A Kenbrook Dr., Galax, VA 24333 (703) 236-6355 (Autoharp contest)

Old Time Country Music Contest and Pioneer Exposition, Bob Everhart, 106 Navajo, Council Bluffs, IA 51501 (712) 366-1136 (Autoharp workshop and contest)

Old Town School of Folk Music, 909 W. Armitage, Chicago, IL 60614 (312) 525-7472 (Autoharp classes and workshops)

Ozark Folk Center, Mountain View, AR 72560 (501) 269-3851 (Autoharp weekend with workshops and contest)

Pickin' & Grinnin' Workshops, Innovative Arts, Inc., 4222 Milwaukee St., Madison, WI 53714 (Autoharp workshops)

San Francisco Folk Music Club Festival, 885 Clayton, San Francisco, CA 94117 (415) 661-2217 (Autoharp workshop)

Summer Folk Institute, Gene Bluestein, English Department, California State University, Fresno, CA 93740 (One week all-day course on folk instruments, including Autoharp)

Traditional Music and Summer Solstice Festival, Elaine and Clark Weissman, 4401 Trancas Place, Tarzana, CA 91356 (213) 342-7664 (Autoharp workshops)

Tumwater Bluegrass Festival, Jan Jackson, 220 E. Union, Olympia, WA 98501 (206) 456-2343 (Autoharp workshops)

Village School of Folk Music, 645 Osterman Ave., Deerfield, IL 60015 (312) 945-5321 (Autoharp classes)

Walnut Valley Festival, P.O. Box 245, Winfield, KS 67156 (316) 221-3250 (Three days ongoing Autoharp workshops and International Autoharp Championship)

Winnipeg Folk Festival, Rosalie Goldstein, 8-222 Osborne St., S., Winnipeg, Manitoba, Canada R3L 1Z3 (204) 453-2985 (Autoharp workshop)

Zimmermann Autoharp Club Meetings. For the club chapter nearest you, send a self-addressed stamped envelope to: *The Autoharpoholic,* P.O. Box 504, Brisbane, CA 94005 (415) 467-1700 (Get-togethers with workshops and jams)

7. PLACES

Archive of Folk Culture, Library of Congress, Washington, D.C. 20540 (Extensive materials on folk music)

The Bennington Museum, Bennington, VT 05201 (302) 442-2180 (Has one Dolgeville Autoharp)

Carter Family Memorial Music Center, P.O. Box 111, Hilton's, VA 24258 (703) 386-9480 (Festival and museum with Carter Family memorabilia)

Country Music Hall of Fame and Museum, 4 Music Square East, Nashville, TN 37203 (615) 244-2522 (Has Autoharps owned by Sara Carter and Pop Stoneman)

Fretted Industries, 1415 Waukegan Rd., Northbrook, IL 60062 (312) 498-3510 (Collection of old Autoharps. Call for appointment.)

Gryphon Stringed Instruments, 211 Lambert Ave., Palo Alto, CA 94306 (415) 493-2131 (Has 1895 Concert Model Autoharp . . . see it!)

Historical Museum of the Wabash, 1411 South 6th St., Terre Haute, IN 47802 (Has one Dolgeville Autoharp)

House of Cash Museum, Johnny Cash Parkway, Hendersonville, TN 37075 (615) 824-5110 (Has Autoharps and memorabilia of Maybelle Carter and the Carter sisters)

John Edwards Memorial Foundation Collection, Wilson Library, University of North Carolina, Chapel Hill, NC 27514 (Has much of the original material from the research of A. Doyle Moore and Becky Blackley)

Musical Museum, Deansboro, NY 13328 (315) 841-8774 (Has several old Autoharps and many other unusual instruments)

Oscar Schmidt-International, Inc., 1079 Garden State Road, Union, NJ 07083 (201) 964-1075 (The Autoharp factory. Call for an appointment.)

Washington State Historical Society Museum, 315 N. Stadium Way, Tacoma, WA 98403 (Has one Dolgeville Autoharp)

8. SERVICES

The Autoharpoholic Magazine, Published by i.a.d., P.O. Box 504, Brisbane, CA 94005 (415) 467-1700 (Provides subscribers with names of other players in their area, teachers, Autoharp clubs, information on coming events, and a mail-order service for parts, accessories, records, etc.)

Jacalyn Post, 5193 Driftwood, Kalamazoo, MI 49009 (616) 375-6729 (Individualized Autoharp lessons by mail)

Traditional Arts Services, 2518 S.E. 17th Ave., Portland, OR 97202 (503) 231-6050 (Has two-reel film of Kilby Snow with Mike Seeger)

FOOTNOTES

FOOTNOTES, Chapter 1

1. The original Zimmermann autobiography, written in German, was found in the papers of Rudolf Dolge (son of Alfred Dolge) at the Dolgeville public library. A. Doyle Moore had it translated by Gisela Swanson of Urbana, Illinois. Copies of the German original and the English translation are in the archives of the John Edwards Memorial Foundation. (See the bibliography in the Appendix C for the address under the *JEMF Quarterly*.)

   A second translation was made by Rudolf Schlacher in January 1983 to clear up some points in the extremely disjointed text. The confusion is the result of the wording in the original German manuscript, which is awkward and poorly punctuated. Every effort has been made to accurately describe the events in Zimmermann's life from this autobiography. Schlacher is the present president of Oscar Schmidt-International, Inc., the current manufacturer of the Autoharp.

2. The Historical Society of Pennsylvania and the Philadelphia Historical Commission provided the following information:

   Gopsill's *Philadelphia Directory* (1880) lists under "Music Stores": Zimmermann, Charles F., 238 N. Second.

   Boyd's *Philadelphia Business Directory* (1882) lists the same name and address under "Musical Instruments, Makers of."

   Boyd's 1884 listing changes the address to 240 N. Second. This is also repeated in directories from 1887 and 1891.

   The 1885 date as the beginning of Autoharp manufacture comes from "The Autoharp: Its Origin and Development from a Popular to a Folk Instrument," by A. Doyle Moore (*New York Folklore Quarterly*, Vol. 19, No. 4, December 1963, p. 216-274). No source is cited, but due to the many changes in design that took place after the original 1882 patent, it seems likely that several years passed before the Autoharp was ready for the market. *C.F. Zimmermann's Simplified Harmony Teacher and Shorthand Writing of Chords* says that the Autoharp was introduced "three years ago." There is no publication date on this booklet, but it contains a quote from January 1889. That would place the Autoharp's introduction in early 1886, but publications, exhibitions, and awards show that the Autoharp was on the market by mid-1885. It is unlikely that it could have been much earlier than that, however.

3. *C.F. Zimmermann's Simplified Harmony Teacher and Short-hand Writing of Chords* (ca. 1889), p. 19.

4. *Dolgeville Herald*, November 30, 1892.

5. A Philadelphia catalog (undated, but containing a quote from 1889) announces an Autoharp #7: "This Autoharp is still in course of construction and will soon be on the market." No tentative price is given, but the description of the harp is interesting: three-and-a-half chromatic octaves, ten bars producing forty-two chords (ten major chords, ten minor chords, ten seventh chords, and all twelve diminished chords), and one flageolet bar. This is the only mention of the "flageolet" bar other than in the original patent. The catalog dated January 1893 has no mention of a model #7, and none have appeared in the course of this research. It's unlikely that this model ever passed the prototype stage.

6. Details of Dolge's purchase of the Autoharp company can be found in the following publications: *Utica Morning Herald*, December 1, 1892; *Dolgeville Herald*, November 30, 1892; *Saturday Globe*, December 3, 1892; *Little Falls Journal and Courier*, December 6, 1892; *Little Falls Evening Times*, December 1, 1892. The account given here is based on these articles, which were read into a tape recorder by A. Doyle Moore at the Dolgeville Public Library on July 16, 1962.

7. A. Doyle Moore, "The Autoharp: Its Origin and Development from a Popular to a Folk Instrument," *New York Folklore Quarterly*, Vol. 19, No. 4 (December 1963), pp. 216-274.

8. Moore states in his article: "On December 23, 1892, Alfred Dolge purchased the controlling stock in the Company . . . ." However, the office of the Secretary of the Commonwealth at the Department of State of the Commonwealth of Pennsylvania stated in a letter dated November 18, 1982, that their office failed "to disclose . . . a corporation either Foreign or Domestic" for a company bearing the name of C.F. Zimmermann or the Autoharp. Since this wasn't a corporation, there wouldn't have been any stock to purchase. The December 23, 1892, date must simply have been the date of the final closing of the sale of the company.

9. In a phone conversation on April 11, 1983, a spokesperson at the U.S. Patent and Trademark Office stated that a search for the date of the transfer of Patent #257,808 failed to turn up any transfer of that patent to anyone. The patent remained registered in the name of C.F. Zimmermann until its expiration.

10. Information on Zimmermann's death came from Phyllis Zimmermann, the great-grandaughter of Charles F. Zimmermann. Her grandparents, C. Gustav Zimmermann (August 15, 1853, to May 12, 1905) and Matilda K. Zimmermann (January 6, 1859, to January 21, 1934) are also buried in the family plot in Mt. Vernon Cemetery in Philadelphia. Her father, Charles G. Zimmermann, made the bronze plaques that are on his parents' graves.

FOOTNOTES, Chapter 4

1. Details of Dolge's early life can be found in Eleanor Franz's sensitive account of Dolge's life, *Dolge*, published by the Herkimer County Historical Society in 1980. It is available from the society (400 N. Main Street, Herkimer, New York 13350) for $11.00 plus $2.00 postage.

   A brief biography can also be found in the December 1895 Industrial Edition of the *Little Falls Journal and Courier*. Much of the biographical information on Alfred Dolge contained here is based on these two accounts.

2. *Musical Courier*, December 28, 1892.

3. "The Autoharp and Harpists," *Dolgeville Herald*, January 11, 1893.

4. Ibid.

5. "The Autoharp Company," *Saturday Globe*, January 14, 1893.

6. Ibid.

7. *Saturday Globe*, January 21, 1893.

8. *London and Provincial Music Trades Review*, October 15, 1893.

9. Eleanor Franz, *Dolge* (Herkimer, N.Y.: Herkimer County Historical Society, 1980), pp. 69-70.

10. Ibid, p. 72.

11. "The Autoharp: Its Successful Use with Gilmore's Band," *Freund's Musical Weekly*, May 15, 1895.

12. "Progress of the Autoharp," *Musical Courier*, March 27, 1895.

13. "The Autoharp Room," *The Presto*, May 23, 1895, p. 19.

14. *Musical Courier*, October 16, 1895.

15. "Alfred Dolge and Son and the Autoharp," *Music Trades*, December 21, 1895.

16. *Musical Courier*, January 29, 1896.

17. Franz, p. 72.

18. "Industries of the Past that Have Gone Forever," *Little Falls Evening Times*, October 26, 1938; and an interview with Mr. E. Stone by A. Doyle Moore, July 15, 1962.

19. Franz, pp. 73-80.

20. Ibid, p. 74.

21. Ibid, pp. 74-78.

22. *Little Falls Evening Times*, October 26, 1938.

23. Franz, pp. 85-87.

24. Ibid, pp. 87-89. The office of the secretary of state of the state of California shows no incorporated city of Dolgeville, California, in its records. Dolgeville was apparently made part of Alhambra prior to that city's incorporation. Alhambra City Hall confirms that one of the oldest tracts in that city is "Dolgeville."

25. "Alfred Dolge Laid at Rest," *Musical Courier Extra*, July 8, 1922.

26. Franz, p. 89.

27. Ibid, pp. 89 and 100.

28. Ibid.

FOOTNOTES, Chapter 7

1. It's also possible that Autoharps were available through Montgomery Ward catalogs during this time. At the time of this research, the Ward catalogs were not yet available on microfilm, and the collection at the California Historical Society in San Francisco begins with the 1916 catalog, which unfortunately is missing the musical instrument section. The Autoharp was included in the 1917 Ward catalog, making it quite likely that it had been included in catalogs from previous years.

2. A. Doyle Moore, "The Autoharp: Its Origin and Development from a Popular to a Folk Instrument," *New York Folklore Quarterly*, Vol. 19, No. 4 (December 1963). Moore says that Phonoharp acquired the patents and the rights to manufacture the Autoharp about 1910. Most of the Autoharp patents would have already expired from their seventeen-year term, but the 1910 manufacturing date is very likely. Although Moore does not cite his source for this information, the Phonoharp Company is known to have registered the Autoharp trademark in March 1911. Since a trademark must be used in commerce before it can be registered, Phonoharp probably began to market the Autoharp by late 1910, and certainly prior to March 1911.

3. A. Doyle Moore, Interview with Mr. Ernest Stone, July 15, 1962, Dolgeville, N.Y. Moore made his personal notes from that interview available to the author.

4. Letter from Eleanor Franz dated March 20, 1983.

5. The Phonoharp Company acquired many of the items from Dolgeville: logo designs, decals, and some original metal plates with cuts of Dolgeville Autoharp models and the Dolgeville logo. The plates are in the collection of Oscar Schmidt-International, Inc., today. Someone must have brought these items from Dolgeville to the Phonoharp Company in Boston. Roth, being in an important position in the C.F. Zimmermann Company, would have been in a good position to obtain these items when the factory closed in 1899.

6. It is curious that the Phonoharp Company would have registered the trademark in California and not in the U.S. Patent Office. The California secretary of state's office says that it is unusual for a Massachusetts firm to register its trademark in California. There must have been a reason for such out-of-the-ordinary behavior, and it seems more than coincidental that California was the new home of Alfred Dolge.

7. Company records owned by Glen Peterson, Jr., state that in 1925 the Phonoharp Company made 41,175 instruments, of which only 1,838 were Autoharps.

8. The eight-bar-model Autoharp last appeared in the Sears catalog in 1922 and in the Ward catalog in 1920. From 1921 through 1938 the Autoharp appeared sporadically in the Ward catalogs. They did not appear at all in the Sears catalogs from 1925 to 1955.

9. Moore, "The Autoharp: Its Origin and Development from a Popular to a Folk Instrument"

10. Ibid.

11. The corporate record book of the International Musical Corporation was made available to the author courtesy of Oscar Schmidt-International, Inc., Northbrook, Ill. Most of the information about International Musical Corporation comes from that book.

12. The corporate records for the Phonoharp Company after 1909 have unfortunately been burned. Harold Finney, however, signed the transfer documents to International Musical Corporation as the president of Phonoharp Company. Finney's widow says her husband worked for William Copeland, so Copeland must have held a board position higher than president, presumably chairman of the board. Whatever his position with Phonoharp, however, Copeland was the man in control of the board of the new International Musical Corporation.

13. Interviews with Glen Peterson, Jr. (grandson of Oscar Schmidt), March 19 and 20, 1982, and February 2 and 3, 1983.

14. At a very late stage in this research, a Model #73 (twelve-bar) Autoharp made by the International Musical Corporation was located. Its condition was too poor to warrant inclusion in the photograph section, but it does confirm that this model also was made by International Musical Corporation. The soundboard decal is the same as that on the Phonoharp Model #73.

15. Interview with Glen Peterson, Jr., March 19 and 20, 1982, and February 2 and 3, 1983.

16. Ibid.

17. Advertisement for Oscar Schmidt in *Musical Merchandise Review*, June 1977, p. 121.

FOOTNOTES, Chapter 9

1. Interview with Mrs. Harold G. Finney and Barbara Finney, February 5, 1983.

2. For an eight-month period *three* separate corporations had borne the name of Oscar Schmidt: 1) Oscar Schmidt, Inc. (1911–1937), 2) Oscar Schmidt-International Corporation (1931–October 1936), and 3) Oscar Schmidt-International, Inc. (February 1936–present). The following chart may help clarify the transition from the Phonoharp Company to the present-day company:

PHONOHARP COMPANY 1892 to		1928		
OSCAR SCHMIDT, INC.*	1911		to	1937
INTERNATIONAL MUSICAL CORP. 1926 to 1931				
OSCAR SCHMIDT-INTERNATIONAL CORP.		1932 to 1936		
OSCAR SCHMIDT-INTERNATIONAL, INC.		1936 ——		

*Did not make Autoharps but did the mill work for International Musical Corporation.

3. Interviews with Glen Peterson, Jr., March 19 and 20, 1982, and February 2 and 3, 1983.

4. Very late in this research a "07" series Model #73 (#0757) was located. It also has a fancy soundboard decal.

5. Interview with Mrs. H.G. and Barbara Finney, February 5, 1983.

6. The article is a clipping from the collection of Barbara Finney. The name and date of the newspaper are missing, but the article describes Finney as "about sixty years of age," which puts the publication date around 1950.

7. Letter from Sally Paul to A. Doyle Moore, December 11, 1962; interview with Sally Paul, February 1, 1983.

8. Interviews with Glen Peterson, Jr., March 19 and 20, 1982.

FOOTNOTES, Chapter 11

1. Interviews with Glen Peterson, Jr., March 19 and 20, 1982, and February 2 and 3, 1983.

2. Ibid.

3. Interview with Glen Peterson, Jr., March 19 and 20, 1982.

4. Interview with Meg Peterson, March 19 and 20, 1982.

5. Peterson credits many of the changes made in the Autoharp to three men. Robert McKay designed the new trapezoid logo and the plastic "keyboard" music scale. He is listed as the co-inventor on the design patent for the B-model Autoharps, and later helped design the Attaché model. Joseph DiPisa replaced the extruded plastic end-pin covers with the new molded styrene covers and was responsible for setting up the machinery at the new Union, New Jersey, factory. Tom Kole helped design the new aluminum string anchor on the B-model harps.

6. Interview with Glen Peterson, Jr., March 19 and 20, 1982.

7. Ibid.

8. Chris Peterson, manager of advertising and promotion, quoted in *Musical Merchandise Review*, June 1978.

FOOTNOTES, Chapter 13

1. Background information on Fretted Industries came from interviews with Rudolf Schlacher and Richard Johnstone, July 14 and 15, 1982.

2. The Oscar Schmidt Company was founded in 1879, but not incorporated until 1911.

3. For more information on the Festival-series Autoharps, see the closeup look at them in "The Development of the Diatonic Autoharp."

4. Information on the Phoenix harp was provided by Yvonne Dickerson.

FOOTNOTES, Chapter 16

1. Interview with Pop Stoneman by A. Doyle Moore, January 1962.

2. Letter from Patsy Stoneman dated February 6, 1983.

3. Mike Seeger, Liner notes from *Mountain Music Played on the Autoharp* (Folkways Records, 1965).

4. Archie Green, "The Carter Family's 'Coal Miner's Blues' " *University of Illinois Bulletin*, Vol. 59, No. 92 (1962), pp. 228–229.

5. Interview with Maybelle Carter by A. Doyle Moore, September 1962.

6. Earl Scruggs, *The Autoharpoholic*, Vol. 4, No. 2 (1983), p. 4. Special thanks to Roger Siminoff, editor-in-chief of *Frets* magazine, for obtaining Scruggs' comments on the Autoharp for *The Autoharpoholic*.

7. Mike Seeger, Liner notes from *Mountain Music Played on the Autoharp* (Folkways Records, 1965).

8. Ibid.

9. Becky Blackley, "View from the Top: Mike Seeger," *The Autoharpoholic*, Vol. 2, No. 3 (1981), p. 17.

10. A. Doyle Moore, "The Autoharp: Its Origin and Development from a Popular to a Folk Instrument," *New York Folklore Quarterly*, Vol. 19, No. 4 (1963).

11. Blackley, p. 17.

12. Evo Bluestein, "View from the Top: Jean Ritchie," *The Autoharpoholic*, Vol. 2, No. 4 (1980), p. 6 and p. 8.

13. Jim Steptoe and Dick Kimmel, Liner notes from *Mountain State Music* (June Appal Records, 1978).

14. Bill Clifton, album jacket for *Autoharp Centennial Celebration!* (Elf Records, 1982).

15. Lindsay Haisley, album jacket for *Lindsay Haisley Live at the Kerrville Folk Festival* (Gazebo Records, 1980).

16. Becky Blackley, "View from the Top: Lindsay Haisley," *The Autoharpoholic*, Vol. 4, No. 2 (1983), pp. 10–11.

17. Interview with John McCutcheon, February 1982.

18. Cathy Barton, album jacket *Reflections on the Carter Family* (Take Two Productions, 1981).

19. Becky Blackley, "View from the Top: Bryan Bowers," *The Autoharpoholic*, Vol. 2, No. 1 (1981), p. 10.

20. Bonnie Phipps, "FYI: Bonnie Phipps," *The Autoharpoholic*, Vol. 3, No. 2 (1982), p. 9.

21. Becky Blackley, "View from the Top: Stevie Beck," *The Autoharpoholic*, Vol. 4, No. 1 (1983), p. 21.

22. Kilby Snow, "John Kilby Snow, 1905–1980," *The Autoharpoholic*, Vol. 1, No. 3 (1980), p. 9.

CREDITS

Photos by Gordon or Becky Blackley of their own materials: 1, 6, 15, 16, 20, 21, 23-25, 30, 42, 49, 66, 68-70, 74, 75, 78, 79, 81, 105, 107, 108, 112-116, 123, 128, 135, 153, 175, 179, 180, 185, 189, 193, 198, 204, 239, 263, 271, 274, 276, 277, 280, 286, 290, 291, 293, 294, 296-298, 300, 305, 306, 308, 317, 319, 325, 328-330, 333, 336, 340, 363, 369, 378, 379, back cover.

Photos by Gordon Blackley of materials in the John Edwards Memorial Foundation: 3, 7-9, 13, 34, 35, 37, 39, 41, 43, 44, 47, 50, 51, 53-55, 57, 58, 374, 375.

Photos by Becky Blackley of materials of Oscar Schmidt-International, Inc.: 32, 64, 67, 84, 94, 119, 120, 141, 144, 146, 149, 196, 205-207, 210-212, 214, 219, 220, 224, 225, 233, 236, 242, 255, 350, 354-356.

Photos and materials courtesy of Oscar Schmidt-International, Inc.: 134 & 136 (Larry Fitzgerald), 137, 190 (Adams & Frank Co.), 194 (Bob T. Shearwood), 213, 215, 232, 238, 240, 241, 246, 249, 250, 252, 257, 258, 267, 273, 281-285, 287, 289, 292, 295, 299, 301, 312, 315, 341, 376.

Other materials courtesy of the following (parenthetical names are the photographers): [**GB** = Gordon Blackley, **BB** = Becky Blackley, **JEMF** = John Edwards Memorial Foundation]

2. Mike Seeger (Margo Rosenbaum), 4. Ivan Stiles, 5. Philadelphia Historical Commission, 10. Florence Galloway (Ron Galloway), 11. James Kimball, 12. Ivan Stiles, 14. Sally Senior (GB), 17. Rick Whitaker (Art Palmer), 18. Beverly Cox (James Cox), 19. Florence Galloway (Ron Galloway), 22, 26. Ivan Stiles, 27. Mike Seeger, 28. Rick Whitaker (Art Palmer), 29. Willard Smith, 31. Audrey Podl, 33. Glen Peterson, Jr. (William Childs), 36. John Evans, 38. Marilyn Hartzog, 40, 45. JEMF, 46. James Kimball (S. R. Lewis), 48. San Francisco Public Library (GB), 52. Library of Congress (GB), 56. Reproduced from a poster by A. Doyle Moore, 59. Gryphon Stringed Instruments (BB), 60, 62. Merle Zimmerman, (BB) 61. Merle Zimmerman, 63. Ardath Lehmer (Al Kreek), 65. Ivan Stiles, 71. Woody Padgett 72, 73. Mike Seeger, 76. Woody Padgett, 77. Lory Schluenz (Ron Rich), 80, 82. Woody Padgett, 83. Smithsonian Institution Photo #73,942, 85. Ivan Stiles, 86, 87. Washington State Historical Society Museum (Mabel Honeycutt), 88. Music Museum (Art Sanders), 89. Esther Kreek (Al Kreek), 90. Keith Young (GB), 91-92. Paul Keller (Judy Shafer), 93, 95. David Martin, 96. Woody Padgett, 97. Stevie Beck (Charles Hoffman), 98. Woody Padgett, 99-100. Mike Seeger, 101. Glen Peterson, Jr. (Erich Sellin & Co.), 102. Suzanne Mrozak, 103. Montgomery Ward Co., California Historical Society (BB), 104. Sears, Roebuck and Co., 106. JEMF, 109-111. Joe Weed (BB), 117. Country Music Hall of Fame and Museum, 118. Merle Zimmerman (BB), 121. Meryle Korn, 122, 124-127. Woody Padgett, 129. Merle Zimmerman (BB), 130. Woody Padgett, 131. Glen Peterson, Jr., 132. William Foshag 133. Montgomery Ward Co. and California Historical Society (BB) 138. Loyce Chaffin (Evo Bluestein), 139, 140. David Illar, 142. Merle Zimmerman (BB), 143, 147, 148. Tennessee Ernie Ford and Jim Loakes (GB), 145. Michael Hobbs, 150, 151. Ivan Stiles, 152. Woody Padgett 154. Rita Libby, 155. Ivan Stiles (George Gellernt), 156. Stevie Beck (BB), 157. Gryphon Stringed Instruments (BB), 158. Sally Senior (GB), 159. Merle Zimmerman (BB), 160. Michael Hobbs 161, 162. Merle Zimmerman (BB), 163. Michael Hobbs, 164. Stevie Beck (BB), 165. Meg Peterson (GB), 166. Bryan Bradfield, 167. Meryle Korn, 168. Bryan Bradfield, 169. Bill MacKenzie, 170-174. Kyle Wyatt, 176. Bill MacKenzie, 177. Country Music Hall of Fame and Museum, 178. David Fullerton, 181. Evo Bluestein, 182. House of Cash Museum (Peggy Marsheck), 183. David Fullerton, 184. Glen Peterson, Jr. 186. David Moliis, 187. Peggy Marsheck, 188. San Francisco Public Library (Ted Goodman), 191. David Moliis, 192. San Francisco Public Library (GB), 195, 197. Kathryn Nichols (Karen Rodgers), 199. David Fullerton, 200. Brenda Bury (BB), 201. Dawn Such (David Such), 202-203. Brenda Bury (BB), 208, 209. Dawn Such (David Such), 216. Sears, Roebuck and Co., 217-218. Tina Louise Barr (Debbie Cotton-Goff), 221, 222. Rita Libby (BB), 223, 226. David Fullerton, 227. Bill MacKenzie, 228, 229. Brenda Bury (BB), 230. Jane Bennett (Harold Bennett), 231. Bill MacKenzie, 234. Roger Siminoff (BB), 235. Rita Libby, 237. Margaret Worrell (Ray Worrell), 243, 244. Merle Zimmerman (BB), 245. Jane Bennett (Harold Bennett), 247. David Moliis (GB), 248. Bob Larson, 251. Brenda Bury (BB), 253. Sherry Fox (BB), 254. B-model pamphlet, 256. Brenda Bury (BB), 259. Suzanne Mrozak, 260. Mary Lou Colgin, 261. David Fullerton, 262. Joe Weed (GB), 264. Dawn Such (David Such), 265. Michael Stokes, 266. Karen Mueller (Diane Wahto), 268. Ron Rich (Lou Rich), 269. Bonnie Phipps 270. Ivan Stiles (Photographic Illustrations), 272. Paul Keller, 275. Bryan Bowers (Jeri Jacobson), 278. Ivan Stiles (Samuel Paleschic), 279. Onetamae Britton and Garrison Keillor. Used by Permission., 288. Ivan Stiles, 302. JEMF (Sam Causey), 303. Ellen Hudak (Richard C. Carter), 304. Mike Seeger, 307. Jean Ritchie (George Pickow), 309. Bill Clifton, 310, 311. Patsy Stoneman, 313. Peggy Seeger, 314. A. Doyle Moore, 316. Lindsay Haisley, 318, 320. John Evans, 321, 322. JEMF, 323. Peggy Marsheck, 324. JEMF, 326, 327. Peggy Marsheck, 331. Stevie Beck, 332. Woody Padgett, 334. Nathalie Forrest, 335. Mike Seeger (Deloss Shertz), 337. Mike Seeger (Margo Rosenbaum), 338. Tom and Mary Morgan (John Rawlston), 339. Keith Young, 342. Mike Seeger, 343. Neptune Rising, 344. Mike McClellan (Joe Stephenson), 345. Rhythm Band, Inc., 346. Keith Young (Gary Putnam), 347. Carl Dudash, 348. Tom Morgan (John A. McGuire), 349. Meryle Korn, 351. Smithsonian Institution Photo #73,956, 352. Sally Senior, (GB), 353. Patrick Couton (GB), 357. Montgomery Ward Co. and California Historical Society (BB), 358. Musical Museum (Art Sanders), 359. Ron Wall (BB), 360. James Nikl, 361. Ivan Stiles, 362. Woody Padgett, 364. David Martin (GB), 365. Paul Keller (Judy Shafer), 366, 367. Woody Padgett, 368. Ivan Stiles (George Gellernt) 370. Ron Penix (Bob Sonn), 371. Rick Johnstone (Bill Kurth), 372. Keith Young (GB), 373. Smithsonian Catalog (David Sharpe), 377. G. Willikers Catalog (Photographers, Inc.), 380. Florence Galloway (Ron Galloway), 381. Meryle Korn.

Special thanks to James Kimball for the loan of the 1893 catalog. **All Autoharp advertisements, brochures, catalogs, and other materials used by permission of Oscar Schmidt-International, Inc.**

SUBJECT INDEX

AUTOHARP INDEX

C. F. Zimmermann

# Strings	# Bars	# Shifters	Page(s)
21	3	0	25-26
23	4	0	27
23	5	0	28-30
28	4	5	31
28	5	6	32
28	5	8	33
32	6	10	34
44	13	27	35

C. F. Zimmermann Company (The Zimmermann Autoharp Company)

# Strings	# Bars	# Shifters	Page(s)
18	3	0	73
21	3	0	74
23	4	0	75
23	5	0	76-80
28	7	0	81
28	4	5	82
28	5	6	83
28	5	8	84
32	6	10	85-86, 90
39	10	13	87
49	6	10/12	88
20	3	0	89
32	8	0	91-92
37	12	0	93
41	13	3 positions	94

Phonoharp Company

# Strings	# Bars	# Shifters	Page(s)
20	3	0	107
23	5	0	108-109
32	8	0	110-111
37	12	0	112-113
32	6	10	114
39	10	13	114

International Musical Corporation

# Strings	# Bars	Page(s)
23	5	115
37	12	115

Oscar Schmidt-International: A-model harps (A-model harps have an exterior wooden bridge with metal rod inset, and the strings go around the end of the harp to hook over the hitch pins.)

# Strings	# Bars	Page(s)
23	5	127-129, 151
37	12	130-137, 139
36	12	138, 139, 152-153, 159, 160
36	15	139, 154-155, 156, 158, 159, 160
36	17	139
24	15	157-158, 207

Oscar Schmidt-International: B- and C-model harps (B- and C-model harps have individual guide posts for the strings at the pin end, and the strings hook into a string anchor.)

# Strings	# Bars	Page(s)
36	12	161-163, 197, 203
36	15	164-165, 166, 171, 198, 199 203, 207
36	21	167, 168-169, 170, 171, 200-201, 202, 203, 204-205, 207
36	10 (3 levers)	206
18	6	208